A CONCISE DICTIONARY OF

COMICS

A CONCISE
DICTIONARY OF
COMICS

Nancy Pedri

Illustrated by Chuck Howitt

University Press of Mississippi / Jackson

The University Press of Mississippi is the scholarly publishing agency of the Mississippi Institutions of Higher Learning: Alcorn State University, Delta State University, Jackson State University, Mississippi State University, Mississippi University for Women, Mississippi Valley State University, University of Mississippi, and University of Southern Mississippi.

www.upress.state.ms.us

The University Press of Mississippi is a member of the Association of University Presses.

First printing 2022

∞

Library of Congress Cataloging-in-Publication Data

Names: Pedri, Nancy, author. | Howitt, Charles, illustrator.
Title: A concise dictionary of comics / Nancy Pedri ; illustrated by Charles Howitt.
Description: Jackson : University Press of Mississippi, 2022. | Includes bibliographical references and index. |
Identifiers: LCCN 2021051566 (print) | LCCN 2021051567 (ebook) | ISBN 9781496838049 (hardback) | ISBN 9781496838056 (trade paperback) | ISBN 9781496838070 (epub) | ISBN 9781496838063 (epub) | ISBN 9781496838094 (pdf) | ISBN 9781496838087 (pdf)
Subjects: LCSH: Comic books, strips, etc.Dictionaries. | LCGFT: Dictionaries.
Classification: LCC PN6707 .P43 2022 (print) | LCC PN6707 (ebook) | DDC 741.5/03dc23/eng/20211213
LC record available at https://lccn.loc.gov/2021051566
LC ebook record available at https://lccn.loc.gov/2021051567

British Library Cataloging-in-Publication Data available

CONTENTS

INDEX OF THEMATIC GROUPINGS

ACKNOWLEDGMENTS

Several people have contributed to this dictionary, which started with strong words of encouragement from Diana Schutz. For being the strongest of cheerleaders and a careful reader, I thank her again and again.

Marco also thought this project was pretty neat from the moment he learned about it on a warm, sunny day in New Mexico. Thank you to him for continuously asking if it was done and for listening to me repeat that I felt like I'd spent my day reading a phone book. Your enthusiasm for this little dictionary warms my heart!

My brother Denny Pedri witnessed the beginning of this dictionary and, with our brother Rudy Pedri and our father Ezio Pedri, has supported and encouraged me throughout its writing. To these three wonderful men, I extend my heartfelt thanks.

Encouragement also came from several friends, especially Renée Marquis Antle, Robin Sgroi, and my walking buddies Lynne Henley, Fiona Polack, and Kristen Romme. I am grateful for their generous ears and hearts.

My department head, Jennifer Lokash, has been supportive in so many ways that they are impossible to list. From her continual encouragement to her attentive administration of my time, and for so much more, I thank her.

Financial support for this project came in the form of several graduate student assistants. Jared Simmonds, William Ping, and Yining Zhou were instrumental in pushing this project forward. To them, a heartfelt thank you. Funding also came in the form of a Memorial University of Newfoundland Scholarship in the Arts grant.

I would also like to thank Chuck Howitt, who illustrated this dictionary. His patience and attention to detail are greatly appreciated. Thank you to Gene P. Kannenberg Jr. and the anonymous manuscript reviewers who offered important, constructive feedback at different stages in the writing process. Thank you also to the editorial and production team at the University Press of Mississippi; your attention to detail is greatly appreciated. A warm thank you to Lauranne Poharec, who was my go-to person when I was stuck.

Finally, for having made things easier, a very special thank you to Franz Wollenschläger.

INTRODUCTION

Since around 2010, there has been a surge in academic studies and peda-gogical books devoted to comics. Several of these studies conclude with a glossary. A quick comparison of these glossaries brings to light differences in definitions of the same term, concept, or phenomenon and little agreement on what terms, concepts, or phenomena are in need of defining. That this state of confusion about the vocabulary of comics poses serious obstacles to the field of comics studies is old news for any of us who write about comics. Indeed, speaking to a large group of academics, students, and fans of com-ics at the 2018 Michigan State University Comics Forum, keynote speaker Diana Schutz lamented the incoherent and untidy use of established comics terminology. This dictionary found its spark at that conference.

I am by far not the first to compose a comics dictionary. Mort Walker's witty and densely illustrated *The Lexicon of Comicana* ([1980] 2000) is perhaps the one that most readily pops to mind. A cross between comics dictionary and cartoon drawing manual, it adopts a casual tone to present readers with witty definitions of both established and invented comics terminology. Kevin J. Taylor also produced a fun and informative comics vocabulary resource with his specialized dictionary of comics sound effects, *KA-BOOM! A Dictionary of Comic Book Words, Symbols & Onomatopoeia* (2007). Easily accessible online comics dictionary and reference resources include Andrei Molotiu's "List of Terms for Comics Studies" (2013), Trevor Van As's "Glossary of Comic Book Terms" (2013), Heritage Auctions's "Glossary of Comic Terms" (2004), and Stephanie Cooke's "A Glossary of Comic Book Terminology" (2019). These and similar online comics dictionaries are aimed at those who are unfamiliar with basic comics terminology. By contrast, Pascal Lefèvre's table of "More than 100 Comics-Related Words in 8 Languages" (2018) is geared toward an expert audience. Instead of crafting definitions, Lefèvre and contributors translate just over a hundred comics terms and concepts into eight European languages. Visual comics dictionaries, such as the Lego DC Super Heroes series published by DK Children, are at the other end of the spectrum, com-bining fun facts, visuals, and lists that guide young readers through the superhero vocabulary and universe. While recognizing the importance of these and other comics dictionaries and glossaries, *A Concise Dictionary of Comics* works differently: it reaches out to students, researchers, and educators of all ages and at all levels of comics expertise, providing them with a dictionary that doubles as a compendium of comics scholarship.

Writing a dictionary of any sort is not something I imagined ever doing. I thought hard about what sort of dictionary a comics scholar could write if she wanted it to serve as a practical research tool for comics critics and students alike. Choices made were many! First, I decided to introduce brief definitions for each entry so not to restrict the thinking behind how certain terms can function in comics. This decision is based in my conviction that comics are extremely malleable and that any explanation of what a certain term can achieve in comics could be easily expanded upon or even contested. I thus thought it best to let critical readers determine what the narrative application of a certain term—whether a concept, strategy, process, or tool—can achieve in a particular comics storyworld. Second, I included a list of references to (mostly) comics scholarship for the majority of entries. These references are to scholarly articles, monographs, and collections of articles devoted to the entry, but they do not include comics scholarship on a single artist or comic. All references are dated and can be found in the extensive bibliography of comics scholarship at the end of the dictionary. Although (obviously!) not exhaustive, it is my hope that this bibliographical information will aid scholars and students to deepen their understanding of a particular entry, and also assist them with their individual research pursuits. Third, although entries are alphabetically ordered, I have also organized them into an "Index of Thematic Groupings" to make the dictionary more user friendly for both students and teachers, who may wish to adopt it in the classroom, as well as for scholars who may be unfamiliar with a particular term but know what type of term they are looking for.

Any work of this nature poses issues of selectivity, of inclusion and exclusion. Whereas some of these inclusions and exclusions are the result of deliberate choices, others are surely due to oversight. Hopefully, these will be put right in a second edition.

Ultimately, I have tried to make the dictionary as close as possible to a handbook or guide that can be kept close at hand when reading, learning, and writing about comics. It is my hope that *A Concise Dictionary of Comics* will become your comics vade mecum, accompanying you as you delve deeper and deeper into the study of comics.

absolute edition: (noun) a line of DC Comics of large 8 in. x 12 in. (20.3 cm x 30.4 cm) deluxe **hardcover reprint volumes** with a **slipcase.**

abstract comics: (noun) comics that rely on the concepts of abstract visual arts to present **nonnarrative** visual material through nonmimetic representation.
See Baetens 2009; Baetens 2011a; P. F. Davies 2013; P. F. Davies 2019a, 33–61; Molotiu 2009; Molotiu 2011; Rommens et al. 2019; Schwenger 2011; Tabulo 2014; Ziang et al. 2019.

abstraction: (noun) a **style** of representation that portrays a subject through a reductive selection and condensation of its recognizable properties; the rendering of a subject into a simplified, minimally detailed form; the depiction of ideas and thoughts, not concrete events.
See Baetens 2011a; P. F. Davies 2019a, 141–62; Groensteen 2013, 9–19; Marcoci 2007; Newall 2011; Rommens et al. 2019; Worden 2015.

aca-fan [also **acafan**]: (noun) an academic who self-identifies as a member of **fandom.**
See Hills 2002; Jenkins 2011.

action: (noun) the process of doing something; the thing done within the story, usually by **characters.**
See McCloud 1994, 70; Postema 2013, 55–77; Purse 2019.

Action Comics: (noun) a long-running American comic book **series** that began by publishing a variety of action, **superhero,** Western, fantasy, and adventure stories. It debuted in June 1938 with an **issue** that included the first Superman story, and the **character** eventually took over the **title.**
See Gavaler 2015; Potsch and Williams 2012.

action lines: (noun) see **motion lines.**

action-to-action: (noun) a type of **panel transition** whereby the **action** of a **character** in one **panel** is linked to its consequent or subsequent action in the next panel.
See McCloud 1994, 70.

adaptation: (noun) the process by which a narrative is translated from one medium to another.

See Asimakoulas 2019; Baetens 2020; Bartosch and Stuhlmann 2013; R. Becker 2009; Blank 2017; Blin-Rolland, Lecomte, and Ripley 2017; M. Bolton 2011; Burke 2015; Cavallaro 2010a; Davis 2018; Dixon and Graham 2017; Jonathan Evans 2019; Jared Gardner 2014; Gordon, Jancovich, and McAllister 2007; Grant and Henderson 2019; Heimerl 2017; Ioannidou 2013; M. Jones 2009; Kidman 2019; Kukkonen 2013c, 73–98; McAllister and Orme 2018; McEniry, Peaslee, and Weiner 2016; Mitaine, Roche, and Schmitt-Pitiot 2018; Morton 2017; Poore 2017; Pratt 2012; Pratt 2017; Tabachnick and Saltzman 2015; Vanderbeke 2010.

additive combination: (noun) a **word and image combination** in a **panel** in which words add to, magnify, or elaborate on the images or vice versa.

See Duncan and Smith 2009, 146; McCloud 1994, 154.

address [also **breaking the fourth wall**]: (noun) an instance or **event** that disrupts the **narrative** flow to directly address readers.

See Braund 2015; Thoss 2011.

adzine: (noun) a magazine whose primary publishing aim is to advertise comics and collectibles.

affective response: (noun) a reaction to the **narrative** that arises without conscious effort.

See Aldama 2009; El Refaie 2012, 179–219; Fall 2014; Keen 2011; Polak 2017; Sandifer 2008.

affordance: (noun) the possible specific properties and characteristics of a **medium** and their **storytelling** capacities.

See Abbott 1986; David Herman 2004; Kukkonen 2011a; Lefèvre 2011b; Venkatesan and Saji 2016.

album: (noun) a bound **edition** of a collection of previously published serialized comics typically printed with a hard **cover**, thick **paper stock**, a large paper size, and high-quality **color** reproduction; originated in French Belgium.

See R. Cook and Meskin 2015, 63–67; Lefèvre 2013b; P. Williams 2020, 51–57.

allusion: (noun) a verbal or visual reference to a **character**, **event**, person, place, or thing.

See Dittmar 2013; Runacres and Mackenzie 2016.

alter ego: (noun) the (usually) secret identity of a superhero.

See Collver and Weitkamp 2018; Easton and Harrison 2010.

alternative comics: (noun) **long-form comics** produced in North America and elsewhere since the 1980s, following the **underground comix** movement of the 1960s; comics that are distinguished from **Action Comics** or **mainstream comics**. See also **independent comics**.

See Dony, Habrand, and Meesters 2014; Flora 1984; S. García 2015, 117–49; Hatfield 2005; Pearson 2018; Sabin and Triggs 2001; Singsen 2014; Tinker 2007; Vieira and McGurk 2018.

American shot [also **Hollywood shot** or **knee shot**]: (noun) an **angle of framing** that depicts a **character** from the knees up.

Ames guide: (noun) a traditional comics **lettering** tool (today rarely used) that helps the **letterer** trace equally **spaced** guidelines for text.

amplification through simplification: (noun) the highlighting of some visual features while downplaying others; the rendering of the bare essentials of an image and accentuating of the features that are shown to heighten its meaning.

See N. Cohn 2013c, 141–42; McCloud 1994, 30.

amplification through simplification

anaphoric: (adj.) referring to or substituting for something that appeared earlier in the **narrative**.

anchorage: (noun) the dialectic interaction of **captions** and **word balloons** that renders visual meaning less ambiguous.

See Groensteen 2007, 129.

angle of framing: (noun) the implied height of the viewing position in relation to what is shown; common angles of framing include **American shot, straight-on**

angle (eye-level framing), high angle (bird's-eye view), and low angle (worm's-eye view).

animated comics: see motion comics.

animation: (noun) a storytelling method in which a rapid succession of sequential images creates an illusion of movement; common animation forms range from traditional two-dimensional drawn images to stop-motion methods with clay figures or puppets to computer-generated three-dimensional images.
See P. Atkinson 2009; Batkin 2017; Bresler 2009; Bukatman 2006; Cavalier 2011; K. Cohen 1997; M. Cook 2013; Crafton 1993; Crafton 2012; Dobbs 2007; Dowd 2004; Forceville and Jeulink 2011; Furniss 2016; Giesen 2015; Hodge 2019; Leslie 2002; Marx 2006; Sigall 2005; T. Ueno 2002; Weaver 2013; Wells 1998.

anime: (noun) a style of animation developed in Japan; Japanese animated films and television programs.
See Baricordi et al. 2000; Berndt 2018; C. Bolton 2018; Brenner 2007; Bresnahan, Inoue, and Kagawa 2006; Cavallaro 2007; Cavallaro 2009; Cavallaro 2010a; Cavallaro 2010b; Cavallaro 2010c; Cavallaro 2011; Cavallaro 2013; Condry 2013; Denison 2015; Hu 2010; Lamarre 2009; MacWilliams 2008; Napier 2001; Napier 2007; Odell and Le Blanc 2013; Patten 2004; Steiff and Tamplin 2010; T. Ueno 2002.

annual: (noun) a higher page count issue of an ongoing comic book series published once a year and in addition to the regular issues of the series.

antagonist: see villain.

anthropomorphism: (noun) the attribution of human appearance, behaviors, and characteristics to nonhuman entities such as animals, deities, or objects. Cf. personification.
See Alaniz 2020; Lisa Brown 2013; Chaney 2011a; David Herman 2012; David Herman 2018; Keen 2011; Lamarre 2008; Lamarre 2011; Quesenberry 2017; Willmott 2012.

antihero: (noun) a main character who lacks the attributes of a conventionally heroic, idealized figure, such as strong moral or social codes.
See Drennig 2010; Sereni 2020; Spivey and Knowlton 2008.

antinarrative: (noun) a story that does not abide by the traditional conventions of narrative, such as a coherent plot.

apa: (noun) amateur press alliance or association; a group whose members publish their work and distribute it among themselves.

archetype: (noun) a typical, easily recognizable **action, character,** or situation.
See Iaccino 1997; Voelker-Morris and Voelker-Morris 2014; C. Wood 2020.

archive: (noun) a place where comics are kept.
See Jared Gardner 2006; R. Miller 2018; Sammond 2018; C. Thomas 2018; R. Weiner 2010.

argumentation: (noun) an **enunciation** that has a specific communicative intention.
See Adler 2011; Adler 2013.

arrangement: see **panel composition.**

arrival date: (noun) a date a distributor or newsstand dealer puts on a comic book's **cover** indicating when the comic book was placed on the newsstand.

art board: (noun) a **page** of original artwork, usually drawn on a stiff **paper stock** such as bristol board.

art form: (noun) a form of creative expression characterized by its own materials and methods.
See Beaty 2012; Flinn 2013; Peltz 2013; Picone 2013; S. Thomas 2009.

artisan process: (noun) a **production** method whereby the **cartoonist** does most of the creative work and usually publishes the comics with a smaller, **independent publisher.**
See Rogers 2006; Suárez and Uribe-Jongbloed 2016.

artist: (noun) someone who produces or manages the artwork or visuals. See also **cartoon artist, cartoonist,** and **comic book artist.**
See Beaty 2012, 71–100; Quattro 2020; G. Schneider 2011; P. Williams and Lyons 2010.

Artist's Edition: (noun) a line of IDW Comics of comic books printed from and the same size as the original art so as to replicate as closely as possible the experience of viewing the original art.

ashcan comics: (noun) historically, an American comic book, often incomplete, created to establish **trademarks** or secure **copyright** on potential **titles** and not intended for **distribution** or sale; promotional comics in the independent self-publishing market; comic book giveaways usually produced on inexpensive **paper stock.**
See Zurier 2006.

Asian comics: (noun) comics created by or about Asians.
See Berndt 2012b; Bhadury 2018; Bhatia 2006; Chiu 2015; Gravett 2017; Lent 1995; Lent 1999b; Lent 2001; Lent 2008; Lent 2014; Lent 2015.

aspect-to-aspect: (noun) a type of **panel transition** featuring consecutive panels with different views of the same **scene** without any indication of temporal change or **narrative** direction.
See Abel and Madden 2008, 43; McCloud 1994, 72.

assembly-line comics: (noun) comics made using a process of **production** whereby specific tasks in the creation of comics are given to collaborators.

asynchronous depiction: (noun) a situation in which the verbal text in a **panel** exceeds what could reasonably be spoken within the **span of time** depicted in that panel.
See Duncan and Smith 2009, 138–39.

Atomic Age: (noun) an informal name designating the American **superhero** comic book era marked by **plots** related to atomic warfare, roughly extending between 1945 and 1955; a subdivision of the **Golden Age.**
See Kaur 2012; Szasz 2012; York and York 2012.

auteur: (noun) the primary "**author**" of the comic who provides a unifying vision to the whole piece.
See Beaty 2012, 77–85; Schumer 2012.

authenticity: (noun) the **narrative** condition of being genuine, reliable, or trustworthy.
See Bake and Zöhrer 2017; Beaty 2009; El Refaie 2010; El Refaie 2012, 135–78; Hatfield 2005, 108–27; Pedri 2019; C. Smith 2012; Weber and Rall 2017.

author: (noun) the creator, and often legal owner, of concepts, **characters**, stories, and/or a comic.
See P. F. Davies 2019b; Fink 2018; Uidhir 2012.

authorship: (noun) the fact of being the creator or one of several creators of a comic.
See Maaheen Ahmed 2017; Gordon 2013; Uidhir 2012.

autobioBD: (noun) a term for **graphic memoir.**
See A. Miller and Pratt 2004.

autobiographical comics: (noun) a term for **graphic memoir.**
See Chaney 2016; El Refaie 2012; Fall 2014; Hatfield 2005; Køhlert 2019; Kunka 2018; Oppolzer 2020.

autographics: (noun) a term for **graphic memoir.**
See Chaney 2016; Hughes et al. 2011; Whitlock 2006.

avatar: (noun) a comics **character** who represents and embodies a specific real-world person or thing as a **character.**
See Fink 2018; Kirtz 2014; Quesenberry 2017; Sidonie Smith 2011.

B&W: (adj.) black and white; describing a **color palette** that uses only black, white, and **values** of gray.
See Baetens 2011b.

back cover [also **cover 4**]: (noun) the protective **cover** of a comic that follows the very last interior page and is part of the same **sheet** of paper as the **front cover.** See also **cover.**

background: (noun) the **action**, objects, or **setting** farthest from the reader in a given **panel** or panels.

back issue: (noun) a comic book that is older than the currently on-sale **issue** available to consumers.

back light: (noun) light that emanates from the **background** of the **panel** and illuminates something in the **foreground.**

backstory: (noun) the history or background of a **character, plot,** or other **story-world** element.

backup feature [also **back-up feature**]: (noun) a short story or **character** that appears after the **cover story** and often not featured on the **cover.**

backup story: (noun) a short story that appears after the **cover story.**

bad girl art: (noun) a comics **style** used to portray femme fatale **superheroines** who are, stereotypically, highly sexualized, action-oriented female **characters.** Cf. **good girl art.**

See Hayton 2014; Noomin 1991.

balloon: (noun) a visual tool used to communicate **dialogue,** thought, or speech and to mark different types of **voices,** tones, and **emotional** qualities, usually composed of a **border** that frames **lettering** and a **tail** that marks the **enunciation's** point of origin; common balloons include **burst, off-panel balloon, radio FX / electronic balloon, thought balloon, whisper balloon,** and **word balloon;** often mistakenly referred to as **bubble.**

See Carrier 2000, 20–45; H. Earle 2014; Forceville 2013; Forceville, Veale, and Feyaerts 2010; Lefèvre 2006; Wallner 2016.

balloon

bande dessinée / **BD:** (noun) Franco-Belgian comics; comics in the Francophone tradition; from the French for "drawn strip," reflecting the image of a single-**tier** **comic strip.**

See Chavanne 2010; Flinn 2013; Grove 2010; Menu 2011; A. Miller 2007; A. Miller 2008; A. Miller 2011; Morgan 2009; Peeters 1998; Picone 2009.

BD mute: see **wordless comics.**

Ben-Day process: (noun) an outdated graphic technique of applying a **pattern** to a **shape** with the use of a **Ben-Day screen.**

Ben-Day screen: (noun) a semitransparent, self-adhesive sheet of plastic film applied to original art to produce a **pattern;** an outdated reproduction tool.

See Karasik and Newgarden 2017, 146–47, 209.

Big Three: (noun) a reference to the three major American **superhero** comic book **publishers**: Marvel Comics, DC Comics, and whoever is in third place in a given month.

Big Two: (noun) a reference to the largest American **superhero** comic book **publishers**: Marvel Comics and DC Comics.
See Comtois et al. 2011; Friedenthal 2019; Howe 2012a; Khoury 2007; Stan Lee 1974; Levitz 2010.

bimonthly: (adj.) published every two months. Cf. **semimonthly.**

binding: (noun) a comic's covering that holds together its **pages.**

bird's-eye view: (noun) an extreme **high-angle shot** in which the subject is framed from very high above at an almost straight angle.

biweekly: (adj.) published every two weeks. Cf. **semiweekly.**

Black comics: (noun) comics created by or about Blacks.
See J. Brown 1999; J. Brown 2000; Cunningham 2010; Duffy and Jennings 2010; M. Earle 2019; W. Foster 2002; W. Foster 2005; Gateward and Jennings 2015; S. Howard 2017; S. Howard and Jackson 2013; Jackson 2016; Lefèvre 2011a; Lendrum 2005a; Peterson 2010; Pigeon 1996; Santos 2019; John Stevens 1976; Strömberg 2012; Wanzo 2020; Whaley 2015; Whitted 2014; Whitted 2019.

blank panel: (noun) a **panel** that does not contain images or words in **captions** or **balloons** or as **sound effects**; a solid-colored panel. Cf. **silent panel.**
See Pont 2012.

bleed [also **page bleed**]: (noun) a comics **page** in which all the artwork extends to all edges of the printed page. Cf. **splash page.**
See H. Earle 2013b.

bleed panel: (noun) a **panel** whose artwork extends, on all sides, outside the edge of the panel **frame.**

blend: (noun) an image that combines two or more incompatible elements that together produce meaning.
See N. Cohn 2019; Fludernik 2015; Forceville 2016.

blog: (noun) an internet delivery platform.
See Carter 2011; Liming 2012.

blue-line color: (noun) a painted **color** process originating in France and popularized in the United States in the 1980s by Lynn Varley on *Batman: The Dark Knight Returns* in which the **colorist** applies paint to a non-photo blue reproduction of each **page** of the art, which sits under an acetate overlay on which the **line** art is printed separately, allowing for a crisp black line and atmospheric, textured **color** in **color separation** and **printing**.

body language: (noun) the nonverbal visual cues regarding attitude, feelings, and **mood** that are discerned from a **character**'s expression, movement, and posture.

bold italic: (noun) **lettering** that is darker and at a different angle than the surrounding lettering to place emphasis on a word or words.

bondage cover: (noun) a comic book **cover** that depicts a female **character** (or, less frequently, a male character) who is physically restrained against her (or his) will.

bookshelf format: (noun) a **perfect-bound** comic book of forty-eight or more **pages** with typically 10–12 pt. cardstock **covers**.

boom balloon: see **burst**.

border: see **frame**.

borderless caption: (noun) a **caption** that is not enclosed by a **frame**.

borderless panel: (noun) a **panel** that is not enclosed by a **frame**.

braiding [also *tressage*]: (noun) the connections between **panels** across the **multiframe**, a chapter, or the entire comic that result in a nonlinear reading practice.
    See Groensteen 2007, 145–49, 156–58; Groensteen 2016; Horstkotte and Pedri 2011, 343–50; Miodrag 2013, 108–41.

breakdown: (noun) the visual division of story details or **action** into a series of **panels** and **pages**; the rough **drawings** of a page that detail the **succession** of images. See also **thumbnail**.
    See Duncan and Smith 2009, 131–38; Groensteen 2007, 117–21; R. Harvey 1979.

breaking the fourth wall: see **address**.

breath marks: (noun) Todd Klein's term for **whiskers**.

briffits: (noun) the visual depiction of a cloud behind an object or **character**, usually at the end of a series of **lines** to indicate quick movement away from the original position.
See Walker (1980) 2000, 32.

British invasion: (noun) the influx of British comics **writers**, including Warren Ellis, Neil Gaiman, Alan Moore, and Grant Morrison, in the American mainstream publishing sphere from the 1980s onward, largely due to DC editor Karen Berger.
See Ecke 2019; Little 2010; C. Murray 2010.

broadcast balloon: see **radio balloon.**

broadsheet: (noun) an early form of mass communication composed of one **sheet** of print material, larger than a **tabloid**, that could include both words and images.
See Kunzle 1983; Lefèvre 2011a.

broadside: see **broadsheet.**

Bronze Age: (noun) an informal name designating the American **superhero** comic book era marked by dark **plots** related to current social issues, roughly extending between 1970 and 1984.
See Eveleth 2014; Jensen 2017; Levitz 2015.

burst: (noun) a type of word **balloon** used to indicate much louder than normal **dialogue** (shouting, for instance), whose elliptical **frame** is made up of jagged edges with long points but whose **tail** is standard; usually, the **lettering** inside a burst is much larger and bolder than the standard lettering of the comic.
See Walker (1980) 2000, 38.

butting balloon: (noun) a type of **balloon** that is cropped flat and placed against the **panel** border.

calligram: (noun) a word or verbal text whose letters are arranged to form an image that relates to the word's or text's meaning.

cameo: (noun) a short **sketch** or quick appearance of a recognizable **character**, person, or **event** in a **storyworld**.

camera: (noun) in comics, the position of the reader vis-à-vis the **panel**.

camera angle: (noun) a perspective that frames the **scene** as if the reader were looking at it.

camera shot: (noun) a filmic term indicating how an image is framed or isolated; common types of camera shots include **close-up / CU**, **establishing shot**, **extreme close-up / XCU**, **extreme long shot**, **full shot**, **high-angle shot**, **long shot**, **low-angle shot**, **medium shot**, **panning / pan shot**, **tilt**, and **point-of-view shot**. See also **shot**.

Canadian whites [also **WECA comics**]: (noun) black-and-white comic books published in Canada primarily during World War II (from 1941 to 1946, a period known as Canada's **Golden Age** of Comics).
See Bell 2006, 41–56; Kocmarek 2016; Kocmarek 2018.

canon: (noun) a list of comics considered to be the most significant and thus noteworthy works in a particular **genre** or **medium**.
See Carter 2008; R. Cook 2013; Dony 2014; Edidin 2008; Freedman 2015; Hoberek 2019; L. Jones 2005; La Cour 2016; Romagnoli and Pagnucci 2013; Romero-Jódar 2013; E. Thomas 2015.

canted framing: (noun) an alignment in which the horizon of the represented **storyworld** is at an angle to the horizontal of the **page**; a slanted perspective.

capes and tights: (noun) colloquial term for **superhero comics**.

caption: (noun) text that stands outside of the **time** and **space** of the **storyworld** or image it is related to; text appended to or placed beneath a single image, including a magazine-style **cartoon**. See also **floating caption**.
See Gerety 2016; Kirchoff 2012; Mikkonen 2010.

caption box [also **text box**]: (noun) a **framed caption**.

caricature: (noun) an image that exaggerates and distorts specific traits of a human **figure** to facilitate recognition, to mock, or to create a social or ethnic type.
See Carrier 2000, 11–25; Gombrich (1960) 2000, 330–58; Hewitson 2012; Kunzle 1983; Maidment 2013; Morgan 2009; Rossiter 2009; Woodis 2007.

cartoon: (noun) a single-**panel drawing**, often accompanied by a humorous **caption**; a hand-crafted drawn image; a work of **animation**; a **style** of drawing that uses an economy of **line** and **stylization** and tends toward **caricature**.
See Carlin and Wagstaff 1983; L. Edwards 2013; Epskamp 1992; Klausen 2009; Nakas 2004; Packard 2006; Pizzino 2020; Scully and Quartly 2009.

cartoon artist: (noun) someone who draws **cartoons**. See also **artist, cartoonist,** and **comic book artist**.
See Bevan 2016.**cartooning:** (noun) a form of art that usually relies on the simplification of **shapes** to achieve clarity in meaning.
See Brunetti 2006; Brunetti 2011; Garbot and Foster 2016; R. Harvey 2014; Lent 1999b; Lent 2005; Mason 2002; Olaniyan 2004; Shwed 2020.

cartoonist: (noun) a comics creator; generally used to refer to **writer-artists**, as opposed to people who only write (**writers**) or only illustrate (**artists**) comics; a **cartoon artist**. See also **artist** and **comic book artist**.
See Falardeau 2018; Gravett 1998; R. Harvey 2014; Hignite 2006; Jackson 2016; Lent 2002; Liu 2006; Robbins 2013; Shen 1997.

cartoon symbols: (noun) marks or **pictograms** that visualize expressions and feelings, sensory information, or **motion**. See also **emanata**.
See Murrell 1935; K. Taylor 2007.

case wrap: (noun) the hard front and back **covers** of **hardcover** comics.

cataphoric: (adj.) referring to something that will appear later in the **narrative**.

causality, maxim of: (noun) a maxim of comics readership stating that readers will assume that all of the elements in the **narrative** combine in a meaningful way (i.e., are motivated).
See P. F. Davies 2019a, 74–75.

CCA: (noun) abbreviation for **Comics Code Authority**.

CCA seal: (noun) an emblem introduced in the United States in April 1955 that was placed on the **cover** of comic books to indicate the approval of the **Comics Code Authority**.

censorship: (noun) the suppression or prohibition of any material in a comic that is deemed to be culturally, politically, socially, or otherwise unacceptable or not suitable for the targeted audience.
See Allison 2000; K. Cohen 1997; Cornog and Byrne 2009; De Syon 2004; Jaquith 1973; Kannemeyer 2019; Kidman 2015; Kořínek 2020; Lent 1999a; Magnussen 2014; Munson 2014a; Schultz 1949; A. Wood 2013; Yezbick 2015; Zanettin 2018.

centerfold: see **centerspread**.

centerspread [also **centerfold**]: (noun) the single **sheet** that forms the middle two **pages** of a conventionally stapled American-style comic book; sometimes drawn as a **double-page spread**.

certification: (noun) a professional evaluation of a comic book's **grade** and condition.

certified grading: (noun) a process whereby a grading **certification** company or service certifies a **grade** given to a comic and then seals the comic in a protective plastic enclosure or **slab**.

Certified Guaranty Company [also **CGC**]: (noun) a corporation that provides a **comics guaranty**.

character: (noun) a **storyworld** participant.
See Abate, Grice, and Stamper 2018; Fishelov 1990; Gilmore and Stork 2014; Groensteen 2013, 121–32; Mikkonen 2017, 90–108; Pigeon 1996; Tseng, Laubrock, and Pflaeging 2018; Unser-Schutz 2015; Wandtke 2007; Withrow and Danner 2007.

characterization: (noun) the qualities and attributes of a **character**, **event**, or group.
See Mikkonen 2017, 174–200.

chiaroscuro: (noun) Italian for light and dark; an art **technique** that creates a strong contrast between white **space** and solid black, light and dark.

children's comics: (noun) comics for early readers.
See Abate and Tarbox 2017; Eedy 2014; J. Foster 1991; Mel Gibson 2018; Melanie Gibson 2020; Gorman 2007; Hatfield 2006; Knox 2016, 21–43; McGlade 2018; Pigeon 1996; Postema 2014; Saguisag 2016; Saguisag 2017; Tarbox 2020; Tilley 2015.

chroma: see **saturation.**

chromium cover: see **foil cover.**

cinema comics: see **film comics.**

citation: (noun) a reference to another text.

classic cover: (noun) a **cover** that is exemplary for its artwork, subject matter, or other features that collectors deem to be of historical importance.

cleaning: (noun) a process by which dust and dirt are removed from the comic.

clear line style: (noun) a **cartoon** drawing **style** that features iconic cartoony imagery, strong homogeneous (not **inflected**) black **lines**, uniformly solid **colors**, minimal **texture**, and equal line weights both in the image's **foreground** and **background**.
See Pleban 2006; Sanders 2013; Sante 2004; Sante 2009; Screech 2016.

cliffhanger: (noun) an unresolved, highly dramatic ending to a **comics page**, comic, or **comic strip** that leaves readers eager to know what happens next.
See Lambert 2009.

close-up / CU: (noun) an **angle of framing** that presents a subject very closely, offering a detailed view that draws attention to an aspect of the subject depicted; in comics, usually a head **shot.**
See Tsai 2018; Wiese 2006.

closure: (noun) the mental construction of a continuous, unified story through reading; the reading process of connecting two or more structurally separate but **juxtaposed panels** into a meaningful whole; the process performed by readers wherein they fill in **narrative** absences, **ellipses**, or gaps.
See H. Earle 2013c; Gavaler and Beavers 2020; McCloud 1994, 63–69; Saraceni 2016.

close-up

cluster: (noun) a group of images or words that together realize one or several **actions**, **events**, or **processes**.

cluster complex: (noun) a group of related **clusters**.

CMYK: (noun) Cyan, Magenta, Yellow, Black; a subtractive **color** definition method used in the computer **coloring** process for comics that will be published in a print **format**. See also **RGB**.

coded color: (noun) a now obsolete process wherein the **colorist** uses codes for **color separation** to indicate the specific **hues** for reproduction on each **page** of the comic.

cognitive response: (noun) the processing of visual and verbal information in order to construct meaning.

See N. Cohn 2010; N. Cohn 2013c; Jee and Anggoro 2012.

closure

cohesion: (noun) the mutual dependence of a **narrative**'s features that guides meaning.
See P. F. Davies 2019a, 169–202; Saraceni 2003, 36–56; Stainbrook 2016.

collaboration: (noun) the process of working with another person or several other people to create a comic.
See J. Ahmed 2016; Gray and Wilkins 2016; Klaehn 2007, 185–98; Stoll 2016; Uidhir 2012.

collected edition: (noun) a collection of several previously published single **issues**. See also **digest, omnibus,** and **trade paperback**.

color: (noun) the use and combination of **hue, value,** and **saturation**; or **chroma, temperature,** and **intensity,** to give a distinguishing quality to the artwork and, in comics, to identify specific **storyworld** elements; one, or any mixture, of the constituents into which light can be separated in a spectrum or rainbow derived from different sensations on the eye as a result of the way an object reflects or emits light.
See Baetens 2011b; Farmer 2006; A. Fox 2014; McCloud 1994, 185–92; Millidge 2009, 112–29; Talon 2007; Wiese 2016.

coloring: (verb) the process of adding **color** to the artwork.
See Chiarello and Klein 2013.

colorist: (noun) the person who adds **color** to the artwork.

color palette: (noun) a range of **colors** used in a particular **cartoon** or comic.

color separation: (noun) the process of separating full-**color** artwork into the four individual **CMYK** color components for the **printing** process.

color separator: (noun) the company, person, or software that separates artwork into the four individual **CMYK color** components when preparing it for the **printing** process.

color touch [also color touch-up or **impaint**]: (noun) a **restoration** process by which colored ink, paint, or other **coloring** substances are used to restore areas of missing **color**.

column: (noun) the vertical **arrangement** of **panels** on a comics **page**.

comic: (noun) any work in the comics **medium**.

comic art: (noun) visual art created in the comics **form** that is appreciated primarily for its aesthetic qualities.

See Alaniz 2010; Amago and Marr 2019; Berndt 2012a; Flinn 2013; Hatfield 2006; Méon 2019; Munson 2009; Munson 2020; Picone 2013; Sabin 1996.

comic book [also comic magazine]: (noun) a magazine-style work or **volume** in the comics **medium** usually printed on magazine or newspaper paper that emerged in the United States in the 1930s with a standard length of thirty-two pages. See also **floppy**.

See Babic 2014; Beaty 2007; Beaty and Woo 2016; Besel 2011; Costello 2009; Gabilliet 2010; Gordon 2000; Hajdu 2008; R. Harvey 1996; Ito 1994; Ito 1995; G. Jones 2004; Klaehn 2007; Lackmann 2004; Leong 2013; Pustz 1999; Rhoades 2008a; Rhoades 2008b; Sheyahshe 2008; Van Lente and Dunlavey 2012; Waugh (1947) 1991; Wright 2003.

comic book artist: (noun) someone who draws the artwork or visuals of a comic. See also **artist** and **cartoonist**.

See Goulart 1986; Malloy 1993; P. Williams and Lyons 2010; Woo 2016.

comic book dealer: (noun) a buyer and seller of comics.

comic book store: see **comics specialty shop**.

Comic-Con [also Con]: (noun) a convention that focuses on comics culture and brings together comics aficionados, creators, **fans**, and scholars.

See Beaty et al. 2020; Bolling and Smith 2014; Salkowitz 2012.

comics: (noun) a **narrative medium** in which stories are told by combining images in a deliberate, meaningful way.

See Abbott 1986; Alaniz 2010; M. Barker 1989; Chute 2008; N. Cohn 2005; Deman 2015; H. Earle 2020; Jared Gardner 2012; Gravett 2013; Groensteen 2007; Groensteen 2009; Hajdu 2008; R. Harvey 2009; Høigilt 2018; Holbo 2012; Inge 1990; Mainardi 2007; Mazur and Danner 2014; McCloud 1994; Meskin 2007; Meskin 2012; Meskin and Cook 2012; Pizzino 2016; Pratt 2009a; Pratt 2009b; Sabin 1993; Sabin 1996; Saraceni 2003; Uchmanowicz 2009; Versaci 2007.

comics album: (noun) a European term for **graphic novel**.

comics anthology: (noun) a comic that collects short stories by different **cartoonists**, usually selected because of a shared characteristic, such as **theme**.

comics code: (noun) a self-imposed set of rules drafted by the **Comics Code Authority** in 1954, acting on behalf of a coalition of American **publishers**, governing what could and could not appear in American **mainstream comics**, which became defunct in 2011.

See Adkinson 2008; Beaty 2001; Beaty 2005, 104–66; Lopes 2009, 29–60; Nyberg 1998.

Comics Code Authority: (noun) a formerly industry-sponsored board that assessed and potentially censored the contents of comic books before **distribution**.

See Nyberg 1998; Oxoby 2013; Tilley 2012; Tilley 2018.

comics collective: (noun) a group of people who are motivated by a common comics-related issue and work together to achieve a shared goal vis-à-vis that issue.

See Salmi 2019.

comics dictionary: (noun) a reference book or lexical resource that provides information on words, concepts, or phenomena related to comics, usually arranged alphabetically.

See Cooke 2019; Heritage Auctions 2004; Lefèvre 2018; Molotiu 2013; K. Taylor 2007; Van As 2013; Walker (1980) 2000.

comics guaranty: (noun) a third-party authentication and evaluation of a comic book's **grade** for buyers, collectors, and sellers.

comics journalism: see **graphic journalism**.

comics literature [also comics lit]: (noun) a designation used to assert the status of comics as literature.

comics page: a single **page** of a comic; the page of a daily newspaper largely devoted to comics.
See Li et al. 2014.

comics pedagogy: (noun) an area of **comics studies** that examines the use of comics within the teaching profession and education.
See Abel and Madden 2008; Abel and Madden 2012; Bakis 2014; Bowkett and Hitchman 2012; Brozo, Moorman, and Meyer 2013; Carter and Evensen 2011; Cary 2004; Dong 2012; Harbi 2016; M. Hart 2010; Jacobs 2007b; Kirtley, Garcia, and Carlson 2020; Kukkonen 2013c; M. Miller 2015; Monnin 2010; Novak 2014; Ripley 2012; Syma and Weiner 2013; Tabachnick 2009; X. Tan 2019; Wallner 2019.

comics poetry [also **graphic poetry** or **lyrical comics**]: (noun) a **nonnarrative** comics **genre** that experiments with poetic devices and word-image combinations. See also **abstract comics**.
See T. Bennett 2014; T. Bennett and Batiz 2014; D. Robertson 2015; Rothman 2015; Surdiacourt 2012b.

comics production: (noun) the process of creating comics.
See Abdel-Raheem 2021; Altehenger 2013; Beaty 2008; Denison 2011; Duin and Richardson 1998; Junid and Yamato 2019; Lackaff and Sales 2013; Lamerichs 2016; Orbaugh 2003; Pellitteri 2018; Rabanal 2005; Rogers 2006; Saduov 2019; Salmi 2019; G. Schneider 2011; Stein and Etter 2018; Tilleuil 2001.

comics specialty shop [also **comic book store**]: (noun) a shop that sells comics and comics-related paraphernalia.
See Gearino 2017; Herrmann 2018; Schiller 1997; Swafford 2012; Woo 2011.

comics studies: (noun) an academic field devoted to the study of comics.
See Aldama 2018a; Aldama 2020b; Brienza 2010; Buhle 2003; Cañero and Claudio 2015; G. Chase 2012; N. Cohn 2014; Duffy 2020; Duncan and Smith 2020; Dunst, Laubrock, and Wildfeuer 2018; Gordon 2020; Hatfield 2010; Heer and Worcester 2009; Jacobs 2020; Labio 2011; Magnussen and Christiansen 2000; Ndalianis 2011; B. Schwartz 2010; Singer 2019; G. Smith 2011; G. Smith et al. 2011; M. Smith and Duncan 2011; M. Smith and Duncan 2017; Woo 2020.

comic strip: (noun) a comic of one horizontal **panel** and/or a single **row** (often composed of three or five panels) usually published serially in newspapers, magazines, or other periodicals.

See Baetens 2003; Black 2009; Couperie and Horn 1968; Dierick and Lefèvre 1998; Jared Gardner 2013; Gordon 1993; Gordon 2016; R. Harvey 1979; R. Harvey 2009; M. Horn 2000; Jacobs 2007a; Kunzle 1973; Kunzle 1990; Lacassin 1972; Lackmann 2004; Lafky and Brennan 1995; Natoli 2009; Pieper, Nordin, and Ursitti 1997; Roeder 2011; Stein and Etter 2018.

comix: (noun) a commonly used spelling for comics published as part of the 1960s **underground comics** movement.

See G. Chase 2012; Daniels 1971; Hatfield 2005, 3–31; Skinn 2004.

commix: Art Spiegelman's preferred term for comics.

See Spiegelman 1988.

complete run: (noun) all **issues** of a comic book **title**.

composition: (noun) the arrangement of text, visual elements (**color, lines, shapes, texture**), and/or **storyworld** details (**characters**, objects) within a **panel** or across a **page**; the **arrangement** of **panels** on a **page**; the overall arrangement of the story and how it unfolds. See also **page composition** vs. **panel composition**.

See Bateman, Veloso, and Lau 2021; Chavanne 2010; Chavanne 2015; Gavaler 2017; Larsen 2015; Pérez Laraudogoitia 2009.

compressed storytelling: (noun) in comics, the short, concise, and controlled telling of a story; a story in which the **plot** is broken down into fewer **panels** than needed or anticipated so as to tell a story in as few **pages** as possible.

Con: see **Comic-Con**.

concrete: (adj.) the state of being material or physical, and not imagined, within a particular **storyworld**.

condition: see **grade**.

connector: (noun) a **symbol** that often resembles an arch used to join two or more separate **balloons**, usually by creating a "bridge" extending from the **frame** of one balloon to the frame of the other balloon.

content: (noun) that which is presented in the story.

continuity: (noun) the continuous **action** and/or consistent references to past **characters** and **events** maintained throughout a comic, **series**, or **narrative**

universe; a situation in which a comic book's past narrative features in other comic books.

See Méon 2018.

Continuity Comics: (noun) an independent comic book company formed by Neal Adams, renowned **artist** of both **Marvel** and **DC Comics**, which published comics from 1984 to 1994.

continuity of space, maxim of: (noun) a maxim of comics readership stating that readers will assume that **space** or place remains the same from rendering to rendering unless a change is indicated.

See P. F. Davies 2019a, 74.

continuity of time, maxim of: (noun) a maxim of comics readership stating that readers will assume that **storyworld event**s are temporally adjacent unless otherwise indicated.

See P. F. Davies 2019a, 74.

continuous narration [also **multiphase narration**]: (noun) the repetition of a **character** moving across the same **setting**.

conventional *mise-en-page*: (noun) a **page layout** where the **panels** on a **page** are arranged in a regular **grid**-like **pattern**. See also **grid**.

See Peeters 2007.

copy editing: (noun) the process of checking for inconsistencies, mistakes, and repetition at the final stage before **publication**.

copyright: (noun) the legal right of ownership of an artistic work.

See Andersen 2021; Gordon 2013; H.-K. Lee 2009; Schroff 2019.

costumed hero: (noun) a **superhero** who wears a characteristic outfit.

See Brownie and Graydon 2016; Coughlan 2009; Nevins 2017; Shepherd 2011; Voelker-Morris and Voelker-Morris 2014.

coupon clipped: see **coupon cut**.

coupon cut [also **coupon clipped**]: (noun) a comic from which a coupon has been cut out.

cover: (noun) the outer wrapper of a comic; the **front cover** (**cover 1**) and **back cover** (**cover 4**) on one side of the paper, along with an inside front cover (**cover 2**) and inside back cover (**cover 3**) on the other side of the paper, binding the **pages** of the comic together. See also **self-cover comic.**
See Brandl 2007; R. Cook 2015; Juricevic and Horvath 2016.

cover detached: (noun) a condition whereby the comic's **cover** has separated from the **spine.**

cover gloss: (noun) the shiny, reflective appearance of a **cover.**

cover story: (noun) the main or featured story of a comic book.

cover trimmed: (noun) a comic that has had the edges of its **cover** cut in order to eliminate damage or roughness.

cover 1: see **front cover.**

cover 2: see **inside front cover.**

cover 3: see **inside back cover.**

cover 4: see **back cover.**

creator-owned: (adj.) indicating an individual, rather than corporate, owner of the **copyright** to the artwork, **characters**, text, or other aspects of the comic.

credits: (noun) the acknowledgment of those who were part of the creative team that produced a comic.

crossbar "I": (noun) the letter "I" drawn with a horizontal **line** across the top and bottom, usually used in comics for the singular first-person personal pronoun, "I."

crosscutting: (noun) a situation in which a **sequence** alternates between different **settings.**

cross-discursivity: see **ironic combination.**

cross-gutter links: see **split panels.**

cross-hatching: (noun) a popular **style** of **shading** achieved by drawing two or more sets of parallel **lines** that intersect or cross each other, usually used to define light and shadow.

crossover: (noun) a scenario in which one or more preexisting **characters**, **settings**, or **storyworld**s feature in another character's story.

cutout: (noun) a feature of comics that instructs readers to cut something out of the comics **page** and engage with it outside of the text.

dailies: (noun) in comics, a newspaper **comic strip** running either six days per week (Monday–Saturday) or seven days per week (Monday–Sunday). See F. King and Moores 2012.

Dark Age: see **Modern Age**.

deacidification: (noun) the process of reducing acid levels in paper.

debut: (noun) the first appearance of a **character**.

decompressed storytelling: (noun) in comics, a long, visually and verbally detailed telling of expansive, drawn-out stories; a scenario in which the **plot** is broken down into more **panels** than needed or anticipated to narrate the **event**.

decorative caps [also **drop caps**]: (noun) an enlarged and/or embellished first letter in a **caption**.

deep focus: (noun) a **depth of field** in which the visual elements within a **panel** are at varied distances from the reader and yet can all be seen clearly.

defamiliarization: (noun) the rendering of a **storyworld** element in an unfamiliar or unusual way that prompts readers to consider it in a new light.

defect: (noun) any flaw in the appearance or structure of a comic.

degree of abstraction: (noun) a measurement of how abstract or realistic a **drawing** is. See also **levels of abstraction**.
See McCloud 1994, 28–52.

deluxe edition: (noun) a **hardcover reprint volume** with a **slipcase**, usually a limited edition with bigger and higher-quality **pages**, sketchbook material, manuscripts, and other additional material not available in other editions.

democratic grid: see **grid**. Cf. **undemocratic grid**.

depiction: (noun) the visual representation and the subject visually represented.
See Miers 2015.

depth of field: (noun) the span of distances covered by visual elements within a **panel**. See also **deep focus** and **shallow focus**.

description: (noun) a traditional **mode** of discourse that tells about a thing by drawing on the five senses.

design: (noun) the organization of formal elements of a comic combined together to present and communicate **storyworld** information; (verb) in comics publishing, to craft all the nonstory elements of a book, such as ad pages, **covers 1–4**, letters, and the **logo**.
See Gunawan 2014; Millidge 2009.

diagrammatic text: (noun) **nonnarrative** text that provides directives or clarifications for reading, such as labels, legends, lists, and **titles**.

dialogue: (noun) a verbal exchange between two or more **characters**; in comics, dialogue is often presented in **word balloons**.
See Mikkonen 2017, 220–42; W. Robertson 2019.

diary comics: (noun) a comics **genre** characterized by thematically contained daily or quasi-daily entries that portray the minutiae of daily life.
See Cates 2011; A. Chase 2013.

die-cut: (noun) a **cover** or interior **page** that has been printed with a special **shape** cut into part of the **design**.

diegesis [also **storyworld**]: (noun) the represented world of the story; the **space** of the **storyworld action**.

diegetic: (adj.) belonging to the represented world of the story or to its **action**. Cf. **extradiegetic**.

diegetic images: (noun) images or pictured words that can be seen by **characters** within the comics **storyworld**.
See Szawerna 2017.

digest: (noun) a smaller than normal, resized **format** (usually 5 in. x 7 in. / 12.7 cm x 7.8 cm) of trade **paperback** comic books, most notably used for **manga** or **reprint collected editions**.

digital color: (noun) a combined **color** and **color separation** process for comics using a computer and, typically, a raster graphics software program. Cf. **coded color** and **painted color**.
See B. Miller and Miller 2008.

digital comics [also **e-comics**]: (noun) comics that are available on digital platforms, such as **blogs** or other websites, and accessed on computers, e-readers, mobile phones, tablets, and other IT devices.
See Aggleton 2019; Baudry 2018; Crucifix and Dozo 2018; Dittmar 2012; Gilmore and Stork 2014; Goodbrey 2013a; Kashtan 2018; Kirchoff 2013; Kirchoff and Cook 2019; Kirtz 2014; C. Martin 2017; N.-V. Nguyen, Rigaud, and Burie 2018; Nichols 2013; Rageul 2018; P. Smith 2014; Wershler 2011; Wilde 2015; F. Williams 2013.

digital first: (noun) a comics that is initially exclusive to a digital platform and then later published in print **format**.

diptych: see **split panel**. See also **polyptich**.

direction of reading: (noun) the way in which readers move through a story in response to **page layout**, **panel composition**, and other reading directives.
See N. Cohn 2013b; Del Rey Cabero 2019; Gunning 2014; Hassoun 2013.

direct market: (noun) the system of comic book **distribution** to **specialty comics shops**; the primary distribution and retail network for North American comic books whereby retailers make direct purchases from **publishers** without the possibility of returning unsold merchandise.

dirty comics: see **Tijuana Bible.**

disjointed panel: (noun) a **panel** in which the words and images are not contiguous.

display lettering: (noun) any text not contained in **captions** or **word balloons,** such as signs, **sound effects,** and story **titles.**

dissonance: (noun) a literary device in which inharmonious story elements are used to create a nonlinear, plural, or otherwise disconnected presentation of **storyworld** details.

distance of framing: (noun) the implied distance of that which is represented from the reader. See also **close-up, extreme close-up, extreme long shot, long shot,** and **medium shot.**

distribution: (noun) a stage in which comics are moved from the producer to the exhibitor or retailer.

distributor stripes [also distro ink]: (noun) **color** on the edges of comic book stacks that distributors use to code them.

dites: diagonal **lines** that indicate that a surface, such as a mirror or a window, is reflective.
See Walker (1980) 2000, 30.

documentary comics: (noun) comics that claim to truthfully represent historical people, sociohistorical issues, and events in specific, actual contexts.
See J. Adams 2008; D. Davies and Rifkind 2020; Lefèvre 2013a; Mickwitz 2016; A. Miller 2008; Muanis 2011; Schmid 2019.

Dollar Comics: (noun) a DC Comics comic book **series** launched in 1976 and running until 1983 that published special **issues** with an eighty-page count (roughly four times the length of a comic book story) and a slightly larger **page format** than DC's standard issues.

double cover: (noun) two or more **covers** bound to the same comic book that, although resulting from a mistake in the production process, adds value to the **issue.**

double-outline balloon: (noun) a balloon with two frames, usually to add emphasis to the words.

double-page spread: (noun) an image that extends across facing pages with no central margin or gutter to divide it, usually intended to be read as a single unit; an image that spans across the left-hand and right-hand pages.

double-sized issue: (noun) a comic book issue that has roughly twice as many pages as a standard issue.

double time: (noun) a scenario in which figures or things appear to be moving twice as fast as they should.

downshot: see high-angle shot.

draw: (verb) to make a graphic representation with pencil or pen as opposed to paint.

drawing: (noun) a graphic representation that uses lines to delineate the form of what it depicts.
See Grennan 2017; Lefèvre and Meesters 2018; Massironi 2001; Miers 2015; Muanis 2011.

drawn novel: (noun) a serialized comic book introduced in 1946 that mimics a film story, narrating the story through the drawing of cinematic images and the adoption of cinematic techniques.
See Baetens 2018b.

drop caps: see decorative caps.

duo-specific combination: (noun) a word and image combination in a panel in which words and images communicate the same message; a doubling of narrative information in a panel through words and images.
See McCloud 1994, 153.

duotone: (noun) a printing process by which black and one other color are used, common in the 1930s.

duration [also temporality]: (noun) the temporal relationship between successive panels and sequences in a comic.
See Lyndsay Brown 2013; Conard and Lambeens 2012; G. Schneider 2010.

dust jacket: (noun) the detachable outer **cover** of a comic.

dust shadow: (noun) a darkened area (usually an edge) of a comic caused by prolonged exposure to dust particles. Cf. **oxidation shadow** and **sun shadow**.

Dutch angle: see **canted framing**.

E

echo [also **visual rhyme**]: (noun) a **narrative** strategy—question / answer, agreement / disagreement, repetition—that links and accentuates **actions**, **storytelling** elements, and **themes** across a **page** or comic.

ecocomics [also eco-comics]: (noun) comics that address environmental issues.
See Blum 2018; Buhle 2009; Curto 2020; Dobrin 2020; Dunaway 2008; C. Jones 2020; Laplante 2005; Lioi 2016; M. McLaughlin 2013; Pike 2012; Staats 2016; Vold 2015.

e-comics: see **digital comics**.

editor: (noun) the person who coordinates, revises, and provides a comprehensive assessment of the material for **publication** and often also coordinates different stages of a book's development and publication.

editorial cartoon: see **political cartoon**.

educational comics: (noun) comics that have a pedagogical purpose.
See Craig 1991; Davidson 2008; Gomez 2014; Jüngst 2000; Rifas 1988; Van Hook 2008; Witek 2008.

eight-pagers: see **Tijuana Bible**.

80-Page Giant: (noun) a DC Comics series that ran from 1964 to 1971 and published comic book special **issues** with roughly eighty-page counts, often containing reprinted material.

electronic balloon: see **radio balloon**.

elision: see **ellipsis**.

ellipsis [also **elision**]: (noun) a **narrative** strategy that omits visual or verbal information from the story; in text, a punctuation mark of three dots used to communicate the omission of verbal information.
See N.-H. Nguyen 2006.

emanata: (noun) graphic **lines** and **symbols** (dots, spirals, straight lines) and all
the conventional comics visual signs (flying stars, hearts, light bulbs) and marks
(sweat beads) that emanate from **characters** and function as **visual metaphors**
to communicate psychological or **emotional** states, smells, sounds, and other
sensory or mental functions. See also **cartoon symbols**.
See McCloud 1994, 128–31; Walker (1980) 2000, 28–29.

emanata

embedded narrative: see **nested story**.

embedding: (noun) an arrangement in which a **panel** or part of an image's content
is contained within another **panel**. See also **inset panel**.

embodiment: (noun) a **character**'s **cartoon**ed body, including both its physical
and **emotional** implications.
See Avery-Natale 2013; C. Donovan 2014; Eisner 2008b; El Refaie 2019; Haslem, MacFarlane, and
Richardson 2019; Horstkotte and Pedri 2016; Szép 2020.

embossed cover: (noun) a **cover** that has a **design**, image, **pattern**, or **shape** pressed into it to create a raised area.

emotion: (noun) an affective state of consciousness; feelings.
See Humphrey 2018; Kendall et al. 2016; Shinohara and Matsunaka 2009.

encapsulation [also **slabbing**]: the process of sealing certified comics in a plastic protective covering or **slab**.

enclosure: (noun) **lines**, **spaces**, or other comics elements that function to emphasize, frame, or isolate verbal, visual, or verbal-visual text.
See P. F. Davies 2018.

encrustation: (noun) an arrangement in which **panels** appear layered over each other.

end flap: (noun) a common feature of **paperback** comics, **cover** foldouts that are smaller than the cover often providing information about the **author**, a summary of the **story**, or reviews.

endpapers [also **endsheets**]: (noun) the **nonnarrative pages** at the beginning and end of a **hardcover** book, each consisting of a double-sized **sheet**, with one half pasted against the inside board of the **cover**.

endsheets: see **endpapers**.

engagement: (noun) the process by which readers actively partake in the creation of **narrative** meaning.

engraver: (noun) an **artist** who etches **designs**, images, or words into different types of material such as those used in relief-printing comics techniques.

entrenchment: (noun) the ongoing reorganization and reworking of **narrative** information.

enunciation: (noun) the act of putting language into use.

Essentials: (noun) a line of Marvel Comics trade **paperbacks** reprinting **color** comics in black-and-white and on a lower-quality paper.

establishing shot: (noun) an **angle of framing**, usually a **long shot** or an **extreme long shot**, that provides the visual context and/or **setting** of the subsequent **panels** in the scene.

euromanga: (noun) comics produced in Europe that reproduce **manga form** and **style**.
See Lamerichs 2016; Nijdam 2020; Pellitteri 2018.

event: (noun) a constitutive feature of narrativity; a segment of information that is central to the **narrative**.

event comics: (noun) a company-wide **story arc** typically involving multiple **characters** and **titles** as well as multiple creative teams.

exhibition: (noun) a comics industry event during which entities display and sell products to consumers.

expressionism: (noun) a **style** that rejects **realism** for an overt subjective filtering of reality.

exterior shot: (noun) a perspective of an outdoor **space**. Cf. **interior shot**.

extradiegetic: (adj.) not belonging to the represented **storyworld** or to its **action**, but superimposed on it. Cf. **diegetic**.

extreme close-up / XCU: (noun) a **shot** in which a minutely detailed view of an object or **figure** fills the **frame**; if a figure, the XCU usually includes only a part of the face.

extreme long shot: (noun) a **shot** taken from a great distance, usually an **exterior shot** showing much of the **setting**.

eye appeal: (noun) the overall appearance of a comic considering its **condition**.

eye-level framing [also **straight-on angle**]: (noun) a perspective in which the **angle of framing** is straight in relation to what is shown.

F

facing pages: (noun) in comics, two contiguous pages that abut each other at the spine.

facture: (noun) a term for when the surface quality of an image, comics page, or work provides evidence of its making.

fan: (noun) a committed audience member who is engaged in the discourse and events about comics.
See J. Brown 2000; Gabilliet 2016; Groene and Hettinger 2016; Norris 2005; Pustz 2007; J. Richard Stevens and Bell 2013; Tankel and Murphy 1998.

fanboy: (noun) a term for a male comics fan, at times used as an insult.
See Oberman 2015; Pustz 1999; Whitt 2013.

fandom: (noun) the community of fans.
See Berenstein 2012; Booth 2015; Brienza 2013; Brooker 2013; J. Brown 1997; J. Brown 2012; Bryan 2018; Chen 2007; Click and Scott 2018; Coogan 2010; Costello 2013; Healey 2009; Helvie 2014; Lamerichs 2018; H.-K. Lee 2009; Levi, McHarry, and Pagliassotti 2010; L. Lewis 1992; Lopes 2009, 91–120; Orme 2016; Schelly 1999; Schelly 2018; Tankel and Murphy 1998; Winge 2018; A. Wood 2013.

fangirl: (noun) a term for a female comics fan, at times used as an insult.
See Cicci 2016; Healey 2009; S. Scott 2013; S. Scott 2019; L. Thomas and Ellis 2014.

fantasy comics [also phantasy comics]: (noun) comics that are works of speculative fiction, with elements of the fantastic, marvelous, and uncanny coming together in the narrative universe.
See K. A. Adams and Hill 1991; Fawaz 2011; C. Harvey 2015; Ito 2002b; G. Jones 2002; Sung-Ae Lee and Stephen 2016; Mulligan 2014; Napier 1996; Palumbo 1983; Palumbo 1999; Penney 2007; Peppard 2020; Purse 2019; Saguisag 2013; Sasaki 2013; Saunders 2011; Shigematsu 1999; Skidmore and Skidmore 1983; Teampău 2014; Torres Pastor 2019; Varis 2016; Wasko 2001.

fanzine: (noun) a fan-produced magazine, generally devoted to a specific title, topic, or property, that often contains comics, illustrations, and text. Cf. zine.
See Krantz 2018; Roy and Schelly 2008; Sabin and Triggs 2001; Wertham 1973.

feathering: (noun) the use of parallel inflected strokes to form a comb-like pattern that functions to soften a hard edge, graduate values from light to dark, and give form and volume to characters and objects.

feathering

figure: (noun) the graphic representation of a person.

figures: see shape and form.

file copy: (noun) a high-grade comic from the publisher's file.

film comics [also cinema comics]: (noun) comics in which film stills, and not drawings, are the principal visual component.
See Chun et al. 2006; Masahiro, Kunihiro, and Mao 2012.

final order cutoff (FOC): (noun) the amount of time a comics specialty shop has before a comics' release date to place an order with the distributor.

finish: (verb) to engage in inking penciled artwork, especially when provided with only pencil layouts rather than full pencils.

finishes: (noun) the detailed penciled or inked artwork. See also ink art.

first-person narration: (noun) the narration of a story from the point of view of a character, as recognized by the use of "I" or "we."
See Nodelman 1991.

flashback: (noun) a situation in which the narrative jumps backward in time; in comics, an interruption of the storyworld's current temporal frame by a panel or sequence of panels representing the past.

flashforward: (noun) a situation in which the narrative jumps forward in time; in comics, an interruption of the storyworld's current temporal frame by a panel or sequence of panels representing the future.

flat color [also flats]: (noun) solid uniform blocks of color, without variation or nuance.

flat-color comics: (noun) comics colored in flats.

flats: see flat color.

flatting: (noun) a modern computer coloring process of filling in the line work of a comic in solid blocks of color resulting in a two-dimensional visual aesthetic, usually the preliminary step in full digital coloring, often later embellished with color choices and aesthetics for the final publication. See also rendering.

flayed look: (noun) an artistic style that highlights detailed musculature. See Avery-Natale 2013.

flick book: see flipbook.

flipbook [also flick book]: (noun) a book with a series of pictures that vary slightly from one page to the next so to appear animated when the pages are turned quickly. See Hurtado 2016; Palpanadan et al. 2019.

flip take [also plop take]: (noun) a comedic device whereby a character gets knocked off his or her feet, sometimes completely out of the panel, by some development, remark, or punch line that does not warrant such a strong reaction.

floating caption: (noun) a borderless caption often positioned in a blank area of the artwork.

floating panel: see inset panel.

floppy: (noun) slang for comic book.

flyleaf: (noun) the endpaper that is not attached to the board.

focalization: (noun) the filtering of **storyworld** information through the conscious-ness of a **character** or a **narrator**; the epistemic stance adopted toward what is represented in the **narrative**. See also **modality**.

See Badman 2010; Horstkotte and Pedri 2011; Kunert-Graf 2018a; Mikkonen 2011a; Mikkonen 2017, 150–73; Round 2007.

focus panel: (noun) a **panel** that commands maximum attention on a **comics page**, but that is not a necessary condition of a comics page.

foil cover [also **chromium cover**]: (noun) a **cover** or part of a cover that has a thin metallic foil hot stamped on it.

fold-in: (noun) a **narrative** feature that asks readers to fold a comics **page** or **cover** in a way that reveals an unexpected message, invented by Al Jaffee in 1964 for *Mad* magazine and included on its **back cover** in almost every **issue** since then.

foldout: (noun) a folded **leaf** of paper that when unfolded is larger in some dimen-sion than the **page**, allowing for triple- or even quadruple-**spread** pages.

following pan sequence: (noun) a **pan sequence** in which the same **character** recurs in every **panel**, as if moving across a continuous **space**.

following tilt sequence: (noun) a **following pan sequence** that is vertical rather than horizontal.

font: (noun) the **style**, weight, and width of a **typeface**.

See Kannenberg 2001.

fore edge: (noun) the book's vertical edge opposite the **spine**, where the **pages** are unconnected.

foreground: (noun) the **action**, object, or **setting** closest to the reader in a given **panel** or panels.

form: (noun) the way in which comics **storytelling** elements are combined and presented to tell a **story**.

See Maaheen Ahmed 2016; Chaney 2013; Chute 2011; Duncan and Smith 2009; Gavaler 2017; Hatfield 2009b; Køhlert 2017; Lefèvre 2016; Miodrag 2013.

format: (noun) the **shape**, size, and general configuration of a comic; the transmission **medium** of information (e.g., digital vs. physical).
See Alexio and Sumner 2017; Ashwal and Thomas 2018; Couch 2000; Jüngst 2000; Jüngst 2010; Lefèvre 2000b; Rota 2008; Vergueiro and Ribeiro Mutarelli 2002; Żaglewski 2020.

fotonovela: (noun) a short story narrated using photography, usually in combination with **dialogue** and/or **captions**.
See Flora 1980a; Flora 1980b; Flora 1984; Flora 1989; Flora and Flora 1978; Hill and Browner 1982.

four-color printing [also **full-color**]: (noun) a **printing** process that combines black, cyan, magenta, and yellow ink to create different **hues**.
See Edidin 2008.

foxing: (noun) an age-related process that causes light brown to rust-colored spots or browning to appear on the **pages** of a comic.

fracture: (noun) a literary device in which two parts are at once distinguishable from one another and intrinsically linked.

fragmentation: (noun) the presentation of **narrative** material in a nonlinear order and/or across an inconsistent or heterogeneous **layout**.
See Mitchell 2010; Postema 2013.

frame: (noun) a visual device that contains and limits what is shown; a **border** that demarcates a **balloon**, **caption**, or **panel**.
See Denson 2012; Gray 2016; Groensteen 2007, 39–57; Kwa 2020a; Kwa 2020b; Postema 2013, 37–45; Rosen 2009; Sabhaney 2014; G. Smith 2013.

frame narrative: see **frame story**.

frame story [also **frame narrative**]: (noun) the main **narrative** in a story that introduces **nested stories**; a literary device used to support the introduction of nested stories. Cf. **nested stories**.

framing: (noun) the set of choices made by the **cartoonist** to emphasize, exclude, or isolate visual elements in a **panel** or across a **page**; these include but are not limited to **angle of framing**, **canted framing**, **depth of field**, **distance of framing**, and **point-of-view framing**, all of which are commonly grouped under **camera shot** or **shot**.
See Rowe 2016.

freelancer: (noun) an independent contractor hired to work on particular comics assignments.

See P. R. Murray 2013.

front cover [also **cover 1** or **front panel**]: (noun) the protective **cover** of a comic that is on the facing side of its **back cover**.

full: (noun) the popular name for a **full-page comic strip**.

full-bleed image: (noun) an **image** that extends to all edges of the **page** and thus does not show a **frame** or white **space** around the edges.

full-color: see **four-color printing**.

full-page comic strip: (noun) a **newspaper comic strip format** popular in North America until the mid- to late 1930s in which the comic strip filled a full newspaper **page**, usually 20 in. x 14 in. (50.8 cm x 101.6 cm) (although newspaper sizes vary).

full-page panel: (noun) a framed **panel** that extends over the whole **page**.

full script: (noun) the written story specifications, broken down **page** by page and **panel** by panel, including complete visual descriptions of each panel and all the text that will appear in each panel, including **captions**, **display lettering**, and **word balloons**.

full shot: (noun) a **shot** of an entire body, from head to toe.

full-width panel: (noun) a comics **panel** that extends horizontally across the **page** so that it is the same size as a full **row** of panels.

fumetti [also **photocomics**]: (noun) a form of comics particularly popular in Latin America and Italy in which photographs, and not drawings, are the principal visual component; Italian comics.

See Baetens 2010; Baetens and Gonzalez 1996; Baetens and Mélois 2018; Calafat and Deschamps. 2017; Castaldi 2004; Flora 1980a; Flora 1980b; Flora 1984; McKean 1995; Quaresima, Sangalli, and Zecca 2009; Saint 2010.

funnies: see **comic strips**.

G

---

gag cartoon [also **panel cartoon** or **gag panel**]: (noun) a single-**panel cartoon**, usually with a **caption** below the image, intended to provoke laughter.
See R. Harvey 2001; R. Harvey 2009; Lent 1994.

gag cartoon

gag panel: (noun) see **gag cartoon**.

gag strip: (noun) a humorous **comic strip** intended to provoke laughter, often including a closing **punch line**.

game comics: (noun) comics based on a video game.
See Goodbrey 2015a; Hemovich 2018; Ng 2010; Rauscher, Stein, and Thon 2020; L. Taylor 2004; Weaver 2013.

gatefold cover: (noun) a **cover** that folds out to a size larger in dimension than the comic.

gatekeeper: (noun) a deprecating term for a person who believes in preserving the stereotypical status quo of comic book readership, specifically that comic books are only meant for a cisgender, heterosexual, male, white audience.
See Deluliis 2013; Lefèvre 2015.

gem mint: (noun) a comic book in virtually perfect **condition** and thus **graded** as Mint 10.0.

genre: (noun) a category, class, kind, or type of comics **narrative** that can be distinguished from other kinds of comics narratives because it is marked by certain **character** types, conflicts or situations, and **storyworld** possibilities and realities that it shares with other narratives of the same category, class, kind, or type.

See Abate 2020; Abell 2012; Baudinette 2017; Bramlett, Cook, and Meskin 2017, 117–218; Hescher 2016; Labarre 2020; Llorence 2011; Singsen 2014; Sommers 2014; P. L. Thomas 2010; P. L. Thomas 2011.

gesture: (noun) the representation of the kinetic energy in a **figure**'s pose at a specific moment in **time**.

See D. Cohen, Beattie, and Shovelton 2010; Fein and Kasher 1996; E. Tan 2001.

ghetto librettos:(noun) Mexican comics that accentuate crime, melodrama, and sexuality.

See Hinds and Tatum 1992; Rubenstein 1998.

giant size: (noun) a special comic book **issue** of new, reprinted, or a combination of new and reprinted material that has an extended **page** count and/or is published in a larger print **format** or **tabloid size**, especially popular in the **Bronze Age**.

giveaway: (noun) a comic book not intended for sale but to be distributed free of charge as a promotional strategy or a premium.

glasses attached: (noun) a 3-D comic book with cardboard, blue-and-red cellophane lens glasses attached. Cf. **glasses detached**.

glasses detached: (noun) a 3-D comic book with cardboard, blue-and-red cellophane lens glasses not still attached. Cf. **glasses attached**.

Golden Age: (noun) an informal name designating the American **superhero** comic book era that marks the beginning of mass popularity, roughly extending between 1938 and 1956.

See Benton 1992a; Darowski 2014; Kaplan 2003a; Levitz 2013a; Madrid 2013; Madrid 2014; O'Brien 1977; Quattro 2020; Savage 1998; Streb 2016; Wasielewski 2009; Zupan 2000.

good girl art: (noun) a comics art **style** in which stereotypically sexualized attractive female **characters** are provocatively posed for the pleasure of the male gaze. Cf. **bad girl art**.
See Goulart 2008; Hayton 2014.

grade [also **condition**]: (noun) the state of preservation of a comic book; (verb) to determine the state of preservation of a comic book.

grader: (noun) a person who determines the state of preservation or who **grades** comic books for a **certification** company.

Grand Comics Database (GCD): an internet open database devoted to comics from around the world.

graphiation: (noun) the graphic, drawn quality of comics, including the **design** and **lines** of the visuals and **lettering**; the individual graphic **style** of a comics **artist** that marks the **visual track** as their own utterance; the **artist's** graphic signature.
See Baetens 2001; Crucifix 2020; Marion 1993, 33–36.

graphiator: (noun) a term coined by Philippe Marion to designate the **narrative** agent responsible for visual **enunciation**. See also **monstrator**.
See Marion 1993; Surdiacourt 2012a.

graphic biography: (noun) a comics **genre** that narrates the story of a real person who is not the **author** of the comic. See also **nonfiction comics**.
See Boykin 2019; Rifkind 2015; Rifkind 2019.

graphic enunciation: (noun) the discursive function or **narrative voice** of images and their composition.
See Baetens 2001; Surdiacourt 2012a.

graphic essay: (noun) in comics, a nonfiction article in comics **form**.

graphic journalism [also **comics journalism** and **graphic reportage**]: (noun) a type of journalism that uses comics to depict the news and other noteworthy nonfiction **events**. See also **nonfiction comics**.
See J. Adams 2008; Banita 2013; Borggreen 2015; Castaldi 2012; Chapman and Ellin 2012; Chute 2016; D. Davies and Rifkind 2020; Duncan, Taylor, and Stoddard 2016; C. Fox 1988; Han 2006; Iadonisi 2012; Ludewig 2019; Mendonça 2016; A. Miller 2008; Nyberg 2006; Schlichting 2016; Weber and Rall 2017.

graphic justice: (noun) an area of **comics studies** that examines the intersection of comics, justice, and legal discourse.

See Giddens 2012; Giddens 2015; Giddens 2016; Giddens 2018; Gomez Romero and Dahlman 2012; Phillips and Strobl 2013; Pitkäsalo and Kalliomaa-Puha 2019.

graphic medicine: (noun) an area of **comics studies** in the field of medical humanities that examines the intersection of comics and illness, health care, medicine, medical education, and other issues of medical discourse.

See Alaniz 2014; Cioffi 2009; Czerwiec and Huang 2017; Czerwiec et al. 2015; De Rothewelle 2019; C. Donovan 2014; Drew 2016; El Refaie 2019; Foss, Gray, and Whalen 2016; Glazer 2015; Green and Myers 2010; Kasthuri and Venkatesan 2015; Mohring 2018; Nayar 2015; Pedri and Staveley 2018; Squier 2007; Squier 2008; Squier and Krüger-Fürhoff 2020; Tensuan 2011; Vaccarella 2012; Venkatesan and Peter 2019; Venkatesan and Saji 2016; Venkatesan and Saji 2018a; Venkatesan and Saji 2018b; I. Williams 2011; I. Williams 2012.

graphic memoir: (noun) a frequently used designation for autobiographical writing in comics form; a life-writing **genre** that has also been referred to as **autobiocomics** or **autobioBD** (A. Miller and Pratt 2004), **autobiographical comics** (El Refaie 2012; Fall 2014; Hatfield 2005; Kunka 2018), **autographics** (Chaney 2011b; Chaney 2016; Hughes et al. 2011; Whitlock 2006), and other less popular designations. See also **nonfiction comics**.

See Beaty 2009; Chaney 2011b; Chaney 2016; Chute 2010; El Refaie 2012; Jared Gardner 2008; Hatfield 2005; Hughes et al. 2011; Køhlert 2019; Kunka 2018; A. Miller and Pratt 2004; Pedri 2013; Pedri 2015b; Pedri 2018; Rifkind 2008; Rifkind and Warley 2016; Schell 2020; Scherr 2013; Whitlock 2006.

graphic narrative: (noun) a term used by narratologists and several literary and comics scholars as a synonym for comics.

See Chiu 2015; Chute 2008; Chute and DeKoven 2006; D. Davies 2019; Jared Gardner and Herman 2011; Petersen 2010; Round 2013.

graphic novel [also **long-form comics**]: (noun) a highly contested term used to designate a stand-alone, self-contained comic-book-length story or set of stories sold as a trade **volume**; a marketing term to sell **long-form comics** that distinguishes them from serialized **floppies** and marks their status as a respectable literary **form**; also misused as a synonym for comics or comic books.

See Baetens and Frey 2015; Baetens, Frey, and Tabachnick 2018; Beaty and Weiner 2012a; Cutter and Schlund-Vials 2018; Drucker 2008; S. García 2015; Goldsmith 2005; Herald 2011; Nabizadeh 2019; Pizzino 2016; S. Weiner 2003; P. Williams 2020; Wolk 2007.

graphic pathography: (noun) illness **narratives** about the patient experience in comics **form**.

Green and Myers 2010; Myers and Goldenberg 2018; Squier and Krüger-Fürhoff 2020; Vaccarella 2013; M. Yu 2018.

graphic poetry: see **comics poetry**.

graphic reportage: see **graphic journalism**.

grassroots comics: (noun) comics created by socially and politically active **artists** about social and political issues.

See Dicks 2015; Packalen and Sharma 2007; Surbhi and Anand 2017; Surbhi and Anand 2019.

gravure: (noun) an image produced from an etched plate; an **illustration** method that is used in comics.

gray-tone cover: (noun) a **cover design** using charcoal or pencil in the original **drawing**, enhancing the effect of light and shadow once **color** is applied to the toned **inks**.

gray wash: (verb) a brush-**inking** technique using ink diluted with water to form gray **tones**.

grid [also **democratic grid**]: (noun) an arrangement in which **panels** on a **page** share the same horizontal and vertical size and meet at right angles; a **page layout** with equally sized and uniformly **spaced** panels; often misused to designate the placing of panels in regularly spaced **tiers**.

See Witek 2009.

ground [also **negative space**]: (noun) the surrounding **space** around **shapes** and **forms** against which shapes and forms become visible.

groundlevel comics: (noun) small, independently published comics that draw from the **genres** of **fantasy**, **horror**, **science fiction**, and **superhero comics**; a term that originated to describe Mike Friedrich's Star*Reach line of comics in the mid-1970s. Cf. **underground comics**.

See Singsen 2017.

gutter: (noun) the **space** between and around **panels** that separates and connects panels in a meaningful relation, usually blank (white or black) and at times demarcated by a **frame**.

See Bearden-White 2009; Berlatsky 2009; Boykin 2019; G. Chase 2012; Dittmer and Latham 2015; Goggin 2010; Gray 2016; McCloud 1994, 60–93; McHale 2010; Moszkowicz 2013; Postema 2013; Saraceni 2003, 35–56.

---

half: (noun) a popular term for a half-page **comic strip**; a newspaper comic strip **format** introduced in the 1920s and popularized by the 1940s in which the comic strip fills half of a full newspaper **page**.

½ hatching: (noun) fine parallel lines used to achieve the impression of a greater **shading** or **texture** than ¼ hatching.

half-page panel: (noun) a **panel** that occupies roughly half a **comics page**.

½ shot: (noun) see **medium shot**.

half tabloid [also half tab]: (noun) a **comic strip format** in which a newspaper comic strip fills half a **page** of a tabloid newspaper that measures roughly 10 in. x 14 in. (25.4 cm x 35.6 cm), as opposed to the larger 14 in. x 20 in. (35.6 cm x 50.8 cm) format of some newspapers.

halftone: (noun) a photographic and/or **printing** process wherein the continuous **tones** of an image are broken up into minute, finely **spaced** dots.

See Kopf and Lischinski 2012.

hardback: see **hardcover**.

hardcover [also hard cover or **hardback**]: (noun) a **squarebound volume** bound in a stiff board **cover** that is denser than a **paperback**'s cover.

hatching: (noun) the close, repetitive placement of fine parallel **lines** used to achieve the impression of **shading** or to add **texture** to an image.

headlights: (noun) a euphemism for a comic book **cover** featuring female breasts in a sexually provocative way.

held-framing sequence: (noun) a **sequence** with the same or closely similar framings of the **background** depicting different **characters** from **panel** to panel.

hero: (noun) a male **character** celebrated for his courage, skill, strength, and other positive attributes. See also **protagonist**.
See Eury 2017; Feiffer (1965) 2003; Hopkins 2002; Huxley 2018; G. Jones and Jacobs 1996; Riches 2009.

heroine: (noun) a female **character** celebrated for her courage, skill, strength, and other positive attributes. See also **protagonist**.
See Abate, Grice, and Stamper 2018; Bajac-Carter, Jones, and Batchelor 2014; J. Brown 2011a; J. Brown 2015; Hopkins 2002; Knight 2010; Madrid 2009; Madrid 2013.

high-angle shot: (noun) an **angle of framing** that shows the **scene** or subject from overhead; also referred to as a **downshot**, since the "**camera**" is looking down on the scene or subject.

historical comics: (noun) a comics **genre** that narrates real historical **events**. See also **nonfiction comics**.
See Boykin 2019; Chute 2016; D. Davies and Rifkind 2020; Dolle-Weinkauff 2018; J. Howell 2015; Iadonisi 2012; Perna 2008; Robbins 2002; Santos 2019; Witek 1989.

historietas: (noun) "little stories" or Mexican comic books.
See Alary 2002; B. Campbell 2009; De Valdés 1972.

hites: (noun) straight **lines** drawn behind an object, meant to indicate a fast speed.
See Walker (1980) 2000, 30.

hollow sound effects: (noun) **sound effects** that are outlined but not colored in so that the focal art can be viewed.

Hollywood shot: see **American shot**.

hologram cover: see **holographic cover**.

holographic cover [also **hologram cover**]: see **3-D cover.**

horror comics: (noun) a comics **genre** that aims to disgust, frighten, or startle readers by inducing feelings of terror.
See Arndt 2013; M. Barker (1984) 1992; Schoell 2014; Sennitt 1999; P. Smith and Goodrum 2017; Walton 2019.

hot stamping: (noun) the process of pressing foil, prism paper, or **inks** onto a comics **cover.**

hourly comics: (noun) a comics journal in which the **artist draws** an entry for every hour they are awake.
See Berry 2013.

hue: (noun) the discernible **color** or color group.

hybrid: (noun) a **narrative** that combines qualities from two or more **genres** or **modes** of representation.
See Bainbridge and Norris 2010; Batinić 2016; Lamerichs 2016; Miodrag 2013, 83–107; C. Smith 2015.

hybrid comics: (noun) comics that use several **modes** of representation in different combinations with comics to tell a story.
See Goodbrey 2015a; Pedri 2017.

hybridity: (noun) the quality of being **hybrid.**
See Hatfield 2005, 36–41; Kuechenmeister 2009; McCracken 2001; Miodrag 2013, 83–107; Schell 2020; Smolderen 2014b.

hypercadre: (noun) French for **hyperframe.**

hypercomic: (noun) a **webcomics genre** that has a multicursal **narrative** structure and asks readers to engage text commands to make choices about **characters** and **setting** that contribute to the story's development and influence the narrative.
See Duffy 2015; Goodbrey 2013b; Goodbrey and Nichols 2015.

hyperframe: (noun) a translation of the French *hypercadre* to designate the **space** of the **comics page** that frames all the **panels** located on it; the explicit or implicit outline of the page.
See Groensteen 2007, 30–31.

I

icon: (noun) per Scott McCloud, any image used to represent an idea, person, place, or thing; per Charles Sanders Peirce, a visual sign that exists in a relationship of resemblance to the thing to which it refers; a famous comics **character** who represents a set of morals and beliefs.
See Babic 2018; Booker 2014; Duncan and Smith 2013; McCloud 1994, 26–28; Misiroglu 2012; Pigeon 1996.

I-con: (noun) an **author's** self-representation as a **character** in **graphic memoir** and other **nonfiction comics genres.**

iconic abstraction: (noun) a visual **style** that represents without visual resemblance to real-world details; how "cartoony" a particular comics **style** is.
See McCloud 1994, 46–57.

iconic redundancy: (noun) the superfluous use or application of pictorial representations.

iconic representation: (noun) abstract visuals that stand as a general representation of an idea, person, place, or thing.

iconic solidarity: (noun) the notion that **panels** in comics are always read in the context of all other panels that make up the **story**; the correlation and interrelationship between **panels** that are separated from each other and, at the same time, coexist, both physically and semantically.
See Groensteen 2007, 18.

iconography [also **graphic shorthand**]: (noun) visual **symbols** that **cartoonists** tend to use, especially those that represent qualities and sensations—**emotions, motion,** senses—that are difficult to render in realistic **drawings.**
See Müller and Özcan 2007.

iconostasis: (noun) the perception of the **layout** of a **comics page** as a unified whole to be read not linearly, but as one would read a painting. See also **iconic solidarity.**
See Molotiu 2011.

identification: (noun) the understanding of or caring for a **character**.
See M. Barker 1989, 109; Frome 1999; McCloud 1994, 30–36.

identity, maxim of: (noun) a maxim of comics readership stating that readers will assume that a **figure** similarly rendered designates the same **character** unless otherwise indicated.
See P. F. Davies 2019a, 74.

illuminated book: (noun) a book that includes images that embellish, enhance, and/or explain the story.
See M. Brown 1994; Whitlark 1988.

illustration: (noun) the visual component of comics; in verbal texts, an image that functions as **description** and exposition, completing, elucidating, nuancing, or supporting the text.
See Gregov 2008; Moszkowicz 2012; Sousanis 2017; Zbaracki and Geringer 2014.

illustrator: (noun) an **artist** who creates **drawings** and other visual art for a comic or other publication **format**.
See Kaenel 2005; Lefèvre and Di Salvia 2011; Liu 2006; Schwarcz 1982.

image panel: see **silent panel**.

image/text interplay: see **interplay of words and images**.

impaint: see **color touch**.

incentive cover: (noun) a type of **variant cover** that retailers redeem after ordering above a certain number of a comic book **issue**.

incrustation: see **inset panel**.

independent comics: (noun) originally, comics published by an **independent publisher**; today, the term is often replaced by **alternative comics**.
See Beaty and Weiner 2012c; Chu 2018; Groth 2001; Hatfield 2014; Lavin 1999; Lavin and Hahn 1999; Munson 2014a; Munson 2014b Vandenburg 2012.

independent publisher [also independent]: (noun) a **publisher** that is not part of a large publishing house conglomerate or multinational corporation, but that may publish corporately owned comics.

index: (noun) per Charles Sanders Peirce, a visual sign that exists in a relationship of physical connection or contiguity to the thing it represents.

indicia: (noun) legal and publishing information containing the full **title** of the publication and **issue number**, and indicating ownership, including **copyright** and **trademark** information, usually found at the beginning or end of a comic, often in small print.

indie comics: (noun) comics published by **independent** ("indie") **publishers** or small presses; comics not published by a large corporate **publisher**. See also **independent comics.**
See Spector 2016; A. Wood 2015.

indotherm: (noun) **emanata** that indicate heat rising from an object.
See Walker (1980) 2000, 29.

industrial process: (noun) a process of **production** whereby specific tasks in the creation of comics are given to collaborators. See also **assembly-line comics.**

inference: (noun) the conclusions readers draw from visual and/or verbal clues on the **comics page** that can lead to **closure.**
See N. Cohn and Wittenberg 2015; Saraceni 2003, 51–55.

infinite canvas: (noun) the potential for limitless **space** afforded to **webcomics;** the feature whereby comics can be made using a variety of **formats.**
See McCloud 2000, 220–29; Shivener 2019.

infinity cover: (noun) a **cover** containing a *mise-en-abyme.*

inflected line: (noun) a **line** that changes in thickness.

information comics: (noun) comics that transfer real-world information to readers with the aim to educate them about a particular issue.
See Bahl, Figueiredo, and Shivener 2020; Bucher and Boy 2018; Jüngst 2010; H. Yu 2015.

ink art [also **inks**]: (noun) a **drawing** that has been finished using ink; the stage of **drawing** when an **artist** reinforces the pencil art with ink, often finishing light sources, **shading**, **texture**, and areas of solid black. See also **finishes.**

inker: (noun) the person who reinforces the line art of the comic by adding ink to the **penciller**'s artwork and, occasionally, additional details.

inking: (noun) the process of reinforcing the **pencil art** with ink, often finishing light sources, **shading**, **texture**, and areas of solid black.
See Janson 2013a; Martin, Rude, and Vitalis 2019; Whaley 2015.

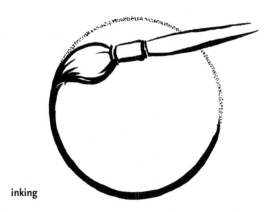

inking

inks: see **ink art**.

inner states: (noun) a **character**'s **emotion**al and mental experiences that are not a tangible part of the **diegesis**.

inset panel [also **incrustation** or **floating panel**]: (noun) a **panel** contained or embedded within a larger panel.

inside back cover [also **cover 3**]: (noun) the part of a **cover** on the other side of the back cover's (**cover 4**) paper.

inside front cover [also **cover 2**]: (noun) the part of a **cover** on the other side of the **front cover**'s (**cover 1**) paper.

intellectual property [also **IP**]: (noun) original **character**s, images, or words that are the result of creative activity and for which one may apply for **copyright**, **trademark**, or a patent.
See Gordon 2013; J. Richard Stevens and Bell 2013.

intensity: (noun) a characteristic of **color** as either bright or dull.

interactive comics: (noun) a **webcomics genre** that encourages readers to navigate somewhat freely through a 3-D **storyworld** environment and make choices about **events**, **settings**, and other **storyworld** elements.
See Gomez 2014; Mamolo 2019; Orlov and Gorshkova 2016.

interdependent combination: (noun) a **word and image combination** in a **panel** in which words and images partake equally in narrating something that neither could narrate alone.
See McCloud 1994, 155.

interior monologue [also **internal monologue**]: (noun) a method of **narration** that grants readers access to a **character**'s personal thoughts and perspective. Cf. **stream of consciousness**.

interior shot: (noun) a perspective of an indoor **space**. Cf. **exterior shot**.

intermediality: (noun) the transgression of boundaries between media.
See T. Becker 2011; Berninger, Ecke, and Haberkorn 2010; Boschenhoff 2014; Chute and Jagoda 2014; Lamerichs 2018; Perron 2016; Rippl and Etter 2013.

internal monologue: see **interior monologue**.

interplay of words and images [also **image/text interplay**]: (noun) an arrangement in which meaning is reached through words and images, placed either beside, inside of, or on top of each other; the blending or synergy of word and image to convey meaning.
See Abel and Madden 2008; Abel and Madden 2012; Maaheen Ahmed 2014; Cuccolini 2010; Geyh 2017; R. Harvey 1994; R. Harvey 2001; R. Harvey 2009; Hatfield 2009a; David Herman 2010; Mandaville and Avila 2009; Sundberg 2017; Varnum and Gibbons 2001; Wartenberg 2012; Wolk 2007, 118–34.

intertextual image: (noun) an image that triggers associations with something encountered in other media.

intertextuality: (noun) the influence of other texts on a comic or their referencing or evocation within the comic.
See Kukkonen 2009; Kukkonen 2013a, 51–86.

investment grade copy: (noun) a comic book of high **grade** and in high demand that can be sold for a profit.

ironic combination [also **cross-discursivity**]: (noun) a **word and image combination** in a **panel** in which the words and images are narrating opposite things. See Varnum and Gibbons 2001, xiv.

issue: (noun) a short serialized comic book of thirty-two **pages**, whose stories run between twenty and twenty-six pages long, issued as part of a **series**.

issue number: (noun) a **title**'s edition number.

juxtapose: (verb) in comics, to place words and images as well as other **narrative** elements side-by-side.

K

kern: (verb) to adjust the **negative space** between two characters in a **typeface**.

kerning: (noun) the spacing between letters.

key: see **key issue**.

key book: see **key issue**.

kerning

key issue [also **key** or **key book**]: (noun) a comic book **issue** that is a desired collectible because it is a **debut**, an **origin**, or important for another of its features.

kids' comics: see **children's comics**.

king-size special: (noun) an **annual** published by Marvel between 1966 and 1982 with a higher **page** count than a standard comic book and often featuring more than one story.

knee shot: see **American shot**.

L

Latino comics [also Latinx comics]: (noun) comics created by or about Latinos. See Aldama 2009; Aldama 2017; Aldama 2018b; Aldama 2020a; Aldama and González 2016; Carrasco, Drinot, and Scorer 2017; D. W. Foster 2016; E. King and Page 2017; Lent 2005; L'Hoeste 2013; L'Hoeste and Poblete 2009; Nama 2013; Risner 2010.

layout: see **page layout**.

LCS: an abbreviation for "local comic store/shop." See also **comics specialty shop.**
See Herrmann 2018; Loubert 1997; Woo 2011.

leaf: (noun) a single **sheet** of paper bound in a book that makes up the **recto page** and the **verso page.**

lenticular cover: see **3-D cover.**

leporello: (noun) a comic that is folded in the accordion-style pleat of a concertina **format** to present an uninterrupted scroll of visual **narrative.**

letter column [also letter col, **letter pages,** or **letters to the editor**]: (noun) a feature, often at the end of a comic book, that reproduces letters from readers about the comic they have read and, at times, responses to those letters from the **editor** or assistant **editor** of the comic book **series.**
See Franklin 2001; T. Hanley 2018.

letterer: (noun) the person who fills in the verbal text in **word balloons** and **captions** as well as any other text on the **comics page,** paying particular attention to the **shape,** size, and weight of the letters and words.
See De Assis 2015.

lettering: (noun) any verbal text on a **comics page;** the process of adding verbal text to a comic.
See Abel and Madden 2008; Chiarello and Klein 2013; Kannenberg 2001; Millidge 2009, 90–101; Pellitteri 2019a, 517–20; Pellitteri 2019b; Starkings and Roshell 2003.

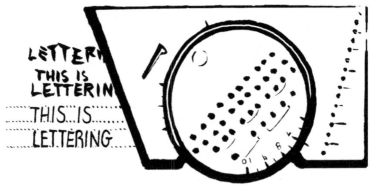

lettering

letter pages: see **letter column.**

letters to the editor: see **letter column.**

levels of abstraction: (noun) the degree to which visual art strays from and is free from traditional realist representational qualities. See also **degree of abstraction.**
See Kendall et al. 2016.

licensing: (noun) the assigning of rights by a **trademark** holder to a licensee to use a **character** for marketing purposes.
See Pillai 2013; Proctor 2018.

life-writing comics: (noun) a **genre** of comics that relates the **author**'s personal experiences or the experiences of another person. See also **autobiographical comics.**
See Rifkind and Warley 2016.

ligne claire: (noun) French for **clear line style.**

limited liability corporation [also LLC]: (noun) a corporation that provides **comics guaranty.**

limited series: (noun) a comic book **series** that has a planned, finite number of issues. Cf. **ongoing series.**

line: (noun) a mark that is greater in length than width; in comics, the most basic visual unit of meaning.
See P. Atkinson 2009; McCloud 1994, 118–26.

linear progression: (noun) a sequence in which the **events** of the story are presented chronologically (i.e., in the temporal order in which they have occurred).

line-drawn cover: (noun) a traditional comic book **cover** where **sketches** in pencil are drawn over with **ink** and **color**ed.

line of vision: (noun) the imagined **line** that traces the **character**'s eye to the point on which the character's eye focuses.

line quality: (noun) the thickness or thinness of a drawn **line**; the line's weight and dynamism; the characteristic **style** of **line work** used by an **artist.**

line work: (noun) drawings with a distinct mixture of straight or curved **lines** made with a pencil or pen.

logo: (noun) the distinctive graphic **symbol** that brands a comic's **title** or a publishing company and promotes easy identification and recognition of that particular title.

long-form comics: see **graphic novel**.

long shot: (noun) a wide **angle of framing** depicting a greater distance than a **full shot** in which the **character** does not fill the **frame**.

low-angle shot: (noun) an **angle of framing** in which the **scene** or subject depicted in the **panel** is shown from below; also referred to as an **upshot**, since the "**camera**" is looking up into the **scene**.

lowercase: (noun) a **form** of letter that is a different form and often smaller than **uppercase**; a miniscule or small letter; *a* instead of *A*. Cf. **uppercase**.

lucaflect: (noun) an illustrative technique used to indicate that an object is round, shiny, or wet, signified by a small square containing four smaller squares.
See Walker (1980) 2000, 36.

mainstream comics: (noun) an American comics **form** associated with the **horror, fantasy, science fiction**, and **superhero genres** and published by corporate publishing houses such as DC Comics and Marvel; comic books produced by corporate **publishers**; widely popular or broadly accepted comics **genres**. See also **Action Comics**.
See Aldama 2017; Burke 2012; Cocca 2014; Cools 2011; Cunningham 2010; Dar 2018; Dobbs 2007; J. Katz 2008; Krantz 2015; Kvaran 2014; Lendrum 2005a; Murphy 2014; C. Murray 2010; Risner 2010; Singsen 2014; Singsen 2017; Soper 2001; Talon 2004; Tju 2014; Vacchelli 2020; Voelker-Morris and Voelker-Morris 2014.

manga: (noun) Japanese comics; comics in the Japanese tradition.
See Beaty and Weiner 2013; Berndt 2013; Berndt and Kümmerling-Meibauer 2014; Berndt and Richter 2006; Brienza 2016; Gravett 2004; Grennan 2018; Hirohito 2002; Ito 2002a; Ito 2005; Johnson-Woods 2010; Kern 2006; Kinsella 2000; MacWilliams 2008; Natsume 1997; Nijdam 2020; Ōgi et al. 2019; Pasfield-Neofitou, Sell, and Chan 2016; Patten 2004; Rommens 2000; Saitō 2011; Schodt 1986; Schodt 1996; A. Schwartz and Rubinstein-Ávila 2006; J. Thompson 2007.

mangaka: (noun) professional **manga cartoonists.**

manga magazine: (noun) an anthology that collects multiple **manga** stories from different **series** usually printed on newsprint. Cf. **tankōbon.**
See Ledden and Fejes 1987; Okamoto 2001.

manhua: (noun) Chinese comics; comics made, for the most part, in China.
See De Masi and Chen 2010; Lent and Xu 2017; Wong 2002.

manhwa: (noun) Korean comics; comics made, for the most part, in Korea.
See Berndt 2012b; Chie 2013; C. Hart 2001.

margin: (noun) the **space,** usually a solid border, that separates artwork from the edges of the **page.**

marketing: (noun) the promotion and selling of comics.

Marvel chipping: (noun) a **defect** characterized by a series of chips and tears at the edges of a comic book due to a dull paper trimmer, common in 1950s and 1960s Marvel comics.

Marvel Masterworks: (noun) a line of Marvel Comics **hardcover** comic books that reprints **issues** on superior-quality paper.

Marvel method [also **plot style**]: (noun) a collaborative **production** process whereby, working from a brief description provided by the **writer,** the **artist** breaks down the story into **panels** and **pages,** controlling emphasis and pacing, and only then does the writer produce a **script** to fit the **artwork.**
See Stan Lee and Buscema 1984.

masking effect: (noun) a pronounced artistic split between the **character** in a **panel** and the **background** art of the same panel, in which the character is drawn in a simplified, cartoony fashion and the **background** is unusually realistic or naturalistic in comparison.

See McCloud 1994, 43.

masking effect

masthead: (noun) the brand logotype or **title** of a comic book usually appearing on the top of the **cover** or editorial **page** that identifies the particular comic book.
See Millidge 2009, 142–45.

match-cut: (noun) a linking of two distinct moments in **time** via the continuation of an **action**, **character**, image, or other visual element across two separate **panels** that represent different spatio-temporal contexts.

materiality: (noun) the comic's physical **format**, **shape**, size, weight, and general configuration, and the cultural connotations attached to its physical presentation.
See K. M. Brown 2018; Kashtan 2018; Thon and Wilde 2016; Schell 2020; Tinker 2007.

maxiseries [also maxi-series]: (noun) a **limited series** of twelve **issues** or more. Cf. **miniseries**.

mediality: (noun) the cultural, technical, textual, and other characteristics that define a particular **medium.**

See Thon and Wilde 2016; Wilde 2015.

medium: (noun) the material and technological parameters used for communication; a **mode** of or channel for communication.

See Abbott 1986; Denson 2012; Heer and Worcester 2004; J. Williams 2000.

medium close-up (MCU): (noun) an **angle of framing** in which the **character** is depicted from the chest up.

medium shot (MS) [also a ½ shot]: (noun) a relatively close **angle of framing** in which the **character** is emphasized and some **setting** is pictured.

meganarrator: (noun) in comics, an implicit and fundamental narrating instance responsible for the book's comprehensive verbal-visual **narrative** process; first introduced in film narratology by André Gaudreault.

See Gaudreault 2009, 88–89; Groensteen 2013, 95–97; Marion 1993, 131–33; Mikkonen 2017, 131–34; A. Miller 2007, 108, 120–24.

metacomic: (noun) a comic that is about comics; a comic that self-consciously recognizes and highlights the art of making comics.

See R. Cook 2012; Inge 1991; Kidder 2008.

metacomics

metafiction: (noun) fiction that self-consciously recognizes and highlights its status as fiction.

See P. Atkinson 2010; González 2014; Mellier 2017; Moula and Christodoulidou 2018; Thoss 2011.

metalepsis: (noun) the transgression of a narrative element across narrative levels or narrative worlds.

See Kukkonen 2011b; Mellier 2017; Thoss 2015, 125–75.

metonymy: (noun) the use of a part or detail to represent the whole; in comics, the representation of a whole character, event, setting, or story by depicting parts or fragments of the character, event, setting, or story.

See P. F. Davies 2019a, 244–46; Kukkonen 2008; Whitted 2014.

middle distance: see middle ground.

middle ground [also middle distance]: (noun) the area in a panel situated between the foreground and background.

mimetic: (adj.) meaningful through resemblance; per Charles Sanders Peirce, characteristic of iconic signs rather than symbolic or indexical signs.

See Inose 2012; Kaur 2012.

minicomic [also mini-comix]: (noun) a short, creator-owned published homemade comic that is usually self-produced and made from one 8.5 in. x 11 in. (21.6 cm x 27.9 cm) sheet of paper folded twice.

See Spurgeon 2005; Todd and Watson 2006.

mini-comix: see minicomic.

miniseries [also mini-series]: (noun) a limited series of two to eleven issues. Cf. maxiseries.

mise-en-abyme: (noun) French for "placed into the abyss"; the artistic technique of suggesting an infinitely recurring image by placing a copy of an image within the original image, thus evoking an abyss. See also infinity cover.

See Chaney 2011c; Chaney 2016, 19–55.

mise-en-page: (noun) French for page layout.

mise-en-scène: French for "placing on stage"; in comics, how the elements on display contribute to the presentation and meaning of the **narrative**'s **action**, **character**(s), and **setting**.

See D'Arcy 2020; Dolle-Weinkauff 2013; Groensteen 2007, 117–21; Jenkins 2020.

modality: (noun) the slant or point of view given to the **storyworld**'s reality.

See El Refaie 2010.

mode: (noun) the set of semiotic resources, such as **gestures**, images, **sounds**, or words, through which a story is told; the material substance, such as **drawing**, speech, or writing, through which a story is narrated.

See Fagence 2011; Lefèvre 2013a.

model sheet: (noun) see **style guide**.

Modern Age [also **Dark Age**]: (noun) an informal name designating the American **superhero** comic book era marked by an increase in serious **content**, the rise of **antiheroes**, new artistic standards, and the rise of **independent publishers**, roughly from the mid-1980s to the present.

See Reyns and Henson 2010; Voger 2006.

moment-to-moment: (noun) a type of **panel transition** whereby an **action** or **character** in one **panel** is repeated in the next panel with a very slight temporal or visual variation.

See Abel and Madden 2008, 39; McCloud 1994, 70.

monochromatic: (adj.) the use of one **color** in varying shades of brightness.

monologue: (noun) a long speech by a **character**.

monomyth [also the hero's journey]: (noun) an archetypical story that is a template for any story wherein the **hero** goes on an adventure, emerges victorious, and subsequently is transformed by the experience.

See J. Campbell (1949) 2009, 1–41; Francis 2016; Lang and Trimble 1988; Sadri 2018.

monstration: (noun) visual **narration**.

See Marion 1993, 33–36; Mikkonen 2017, 82–85.

monstrator: (noun) the **narrative** agent responsible for graphic **enunciation**.

See Groensteen 2010; Groensteen 2013, 84–86.

montage: (noun) a sequence of panels that is meant to be read almost simultaneously to give the impression of a unified action, idea, or setting or to compress time. See Dittmer 2010; Rickman 2009.

montage panel: (noun) a single panel or a single-panel page in which several different scenes or settings appear, usually as a borderless sequence of images, within the one large overriding panel, thus collapsing multiple times and/or locations into one space.

mood: (noun) the atmosphere of the action, narrative, or scene.

motif: (noun) a recurring visual element such as a decorative design, pattern, or symbol.

motion: (noun) movement through space or time. See P. Atkinson 2009; P. Atkinson 2018; Juricevic and Horvath 2016; Lamarre 2002; Pedler 2009.

motion blur: (noun) a series of parallel lines, or digital blurring, that indicate the quick movement of an object or figure through space.

motion comics [also animated comics]: (noun) a webcomics genre that combines elements of print comics and animation. See Morton 2015; C. Smith 2012; C. Smith 2015; Tsao and Yu 2016.

motion lines [also action lines]: (noun) lines drawn to represent the path of a moving object or figure through space. See N. Cohn and Maher 2015; Worisch 2015.

movement: (noun) a united group of artists who share common artistic goals and ideas. See Di Ricco 2015; Kinsella 1998; Lim 2018.

multiframe [also multicadre]: (noun) the sum of all of the hyperframes; the relation of all panels and frames that constitute a comic; the different structural systems that regulate the meaning of panels, such as the tier, the page, and the book. See Groensteen 2007, 22–23.

multimodality: (noun) a characteristic of a text that communicates or narrates using more than one mode, such as comics that commonly use words and images. See Abdel-Raheem 2021; Bateman 2008; Bateman and Wildfeuer 2014b; Borkent 2017; Borodo 2015; N. Cohn 2016; N. Cohn, Taylor, and Pederson 2017; Dickinson and Werner 2015; Grant and Henderson 2019;

David Herman 2010; Jacobs 2007a; Jacobs 2014; Kaindl 2004; Leber-Cook and Cook 2013; Matthiessen 2007; Pedri 2015a; Pedri 2017; Ryerson 2019.

multimodal literacy: (noun) the ability to read a text that combines more than one **symbol** system.

See Del Rey Cabero 2019; Grunzke 2017; Hammond 2009; Jacobs 2007a; Jacobs 2013; Wierszewski 2014.

multiperspectivity: (noun) the telling of the story from the **emotions**, perspectives, and views of multiple **characters**.

multiphase narration: see **continuous narration**.

multiple images [also **photographic streaking**]: (noun) the layering or placing in close succession of a **figure**'s temporally short movement such that each consecutive presentation of the figure is more detailed than the previous one.

See McCloud 1994, 112.

multiverse: (noun) a set of alternative, multiple **storyworlds** in which alternative versions of **characters** and **events** are located.

See R. Hanley 2005; Kukkonen 2010; Proctor 2017b.

narration: (noun) the process of telling a story.

See Lefèvre 2000a; Lefèvre 2013b; Mikkonen 2017, 73–89; Postema 2007.

narrative: (noun) a chain of **events**, often involving a conflict and/or the development of **characters**, told by a **narrator**, who could but doesn't have to be a **character**; a story.

See Danziger-Russell 2013; Jared Gardner and Herman 2011; Mikkonen 2017; Miodrag 2012; Pratt 2009b.

narrative box: see **caption**.

narrative breakdown: see **breakdown**.

narrative thread [also **plot thread**]: (noun) a partial view of the **plot** from the point of view of a **character** or a set of characters.

narrator: (noun) in comics, a commentator whose **"voice"** often appears in **captions**, and who interprets, remarks on, or tells the story and can but does not have to be a **storyworld** participant.

See Gavaler 2019; Groensteen 2010; Groensteen 2013, 79–120; Kukkonen 2013c, 31–44; Mikkonen 2011b; Mikkonen 2017, 129–49; Surdiacourt 2012a; Thon 2013; Thon 2014b; Thon 2016, 125–220.

negative space: (noun) the area surrounding **shapes** and **forms** that defines those shapes and forms, while sharing linear edges with them; the opposite of **positive space**. See also **ground**.

negative
space

nested story: (noun) the presentation of a story within another story.

nested structure: (noun) the presentation of worlds within worlds and the shifting between one **narrative** level and other narrative levels.

See P. F. Davies 2019a, 2003–238.

newave: (noun) a **movement** of **minicomics artists** in the 1980s following on the heels of the **underground comics** movement who produced and published their comics independently of a **publisher**.

newave comics [or newave comix]: (noun) **minicomics** produced and published by **cartoonists** independently of a **publisher**.

See Dowers 2010.

new comics: (noun) a short-lived designation for comics published mostly in the 1980s, created with an eye toward renewing the experimental attitude of **underground comics** and gaining respect for the **comics medium**.

See Wiater and Bissette 1993.

newspaper cartoon: (noun) a **single-panel drawing**, usually humorous in intent, published in a newspaper. See also **political cartoon**.
See Diamond 2002; El Refaie 2011; Groensteen 1997; Speckman 2004.

newspaper comic strip: (noun) a short-form comic, usually not longer than three or four **rows**, that is published regularly in a newspaper.
See K. Barker 1997; Blackbeard 2003; R. Donovan et al. 2009; Gifford 1971; Glascock and Preston-Schreck 2004; R. Harvey 2009; Jacobs 2007a; Kunzle 1983; Kunzle 1998; Meyer 2012; Pieper, Nordin, and Ursitti 1997; Robb 1995; John Stevens 1976; Vold 2015.

newsstand copy: (noun) a comic book sold on a returnable basis at convenience stores, grocery stores, and periodical vendors.

ninth art: (noun) English translation of the French *neuvième art*, a term introduced in 1964 by Claude Beylie for the comics **art form** to accentuate its place among the other arts.
See Di Ricco 2015; Grove 1999; Screech 2005.

no date: (adj.) indicating the absence of a date on a comic book **cover** or **indicia page**.

noir comics: (noun) a **genre** of black-and-white comics characterized by highly stylized artwork, dramatic lighting, and intense **emotional** moments.
See H. Allen 2011; Goulart 1998; Lyons 2013; Martinbrough 2007; Royal 2010.

nonfiction comics: (noun) an umbrella term for comics **genres** that relate real-world events or experiences. See also **autoBD, autobiographical comics, auto-graphics, diary comics, documentary comics, graphic biography, graphic jour-nalism, graphic reportage, historical comics, information comics, life-writing comics**, and **true comics**.
See Clark 2013; Duncan, Taylor, and Stoddard 2016; Fink 2018; Lawson 2014; Mitchell 2012; Wierszewski 2014.

non-grid layout: (noun) a **page** that is not organized in a **grid layout**.

nonnarrative: (adj.) in reference to the presentation of visual and verbal material that does not tell a story, as with **abstract** or **educational** comics.

non sequitur: (noun) a type of **panel transition** whereby the **action** or **scene** in one **panel** would appear to be not logically connected to the action and scene in the following panel.
See McCloud 1994, 72.

no number: (adj.) indicating the absence of an **issue number** on a comic book **cover** or **indicia page**, often indicating a first **issue** or a **one-shot**.

nouvelle manga: (noun) a **movement** of French-Belgian and Japanese comics **artists** who combine French and Japanese comics **styles** to tell realist **narratives** of everyday life.
See Trifonova 2012.

observer: (noun) a **character** or **narrator** who experiences **storyworld events** and/ or characters through their point of view, and often relays their own thoughts and feelings, but not those of other characters.

off-panel: (adj.) occurring outside of the **panel border**.

off-panel balloon: (noun) a **word balloon** whose **tail** points out of the **panel** to the speaking **character**, who is within the **scene** but not within the **frame** of what the panel shows.

omnibus: (noun) a **collected edition** of **series**, sometimes in a large **hardcover format**, that contains the entirety or a significant part of a **run**.

omniscient narration: (noun) **narration** in **caption** form, written from an "all-knowing," anonymous, objective third-person point of view.

100-Page Super Spectacular: (noun) a DC comic book **series** that ran from 1971 to 1975 and published **reprint**-themed **annuals** or new **reprint**ed collections with roughly one-hundred-**page** counts.

one-shot [also 1-shot]: (noun) a comic with a self-contained story published in a single **issue**.

ongoing series: (noun) a comic book **series** with an unfixed number of future **issues**. Cf. **limited series**.

onomatopoeia: (noun) a word or phrase that imitates, reflects, resembles, or visualizes a **sound**; the mimicking of sound by invented words.

See Amaral 2016; Busch 2017; C. V. García 2008; Guynes 2014; Inose 2012; Salgueiro 2008; K. Taylor 2007.

original graphic novel [also OGN]: (noun) a perfect-bound **softcover** or **hardcover** comic with a higher **page** count than the traditional **floppy**, created specifically as a one-story unit.

origin story: (noun) a **narrative** that explains how a **superhero** obtained his or her powers and heroic identity; the story of a **character**'s creation.

See J. Duggan 2016; Gavaler 2015; Méon 2018; Pagello 2017.

over guide: (adj.) describing a situation in which a comic book's price exceeds the Guide list price. Cf. **under guide.**

over-the-shoulder shot: (noun) an **angle of framing** in which the **scene** is presented slightly above the shoulder of a **character**, thus depicting a point of view that mostly corresponds to that of the character whose shoulder is in the **shot.**

oxidation shadow: (noun) damage to a comic caused by prolonged exposure to air. Cf. **dust shadow** and **sun shadow.**

pacing: (noun) the meter, or measured **rhythm**, of the **narrative** information in either the story as a whole or in a specific **sequence**; the speed at which a **story** or **sequence** evolves. See also **timing.**

See Bares 2008; Palmer 2014; Talon 2002.

page: (noun) the printed **content** or total **design** unit of one side of a **leaf** of paper; *planche* in French comics studies.

See Ecke 2010; Ghosal 2018; Labarre, Barnard, and Northfield 2012; Li et al. 2014; Peeters 2007; Verano 2006.

page bleed: see **bleed.**

page composition: see **page layout**.

page density: (noun) the number of **panels** per **page**.

page layout [also **layout** and *mise-en-page*]: (noun) the **arrangement**, number, and shape of the **panels** on a **page**; the structure of a page; the particular **design**, **composition**, or organization of the page; the formal **arrangement** of panels within the **space** of the page; rough page **sketches** of a comics.

See Bares 2008; Bateman et al. 2017; Caldwell 2012; J. Cohn 2009; N. Cohn 2013b; N. Cohn and Campbell 2015; N. Cohn et al. 2017; Gavaler 2018b; Kelp-Stebbins 2020; Labio 2015; Lefèvre 2009a; Millidge 2009, 60–89; Pederson and Cohn 2016.

page turn: (noun) the turning over of one **leaf** in a comic, often used to heighten suspense before a **reveal**.

pagination: (noun) the **arrangement**, number, and/or numbering of **pages** within a comic.

See Astor 2002.

painted color: (noun) in comics, any **color** process involving the use of hand-painting materials, such as gouache or watercolors, on physical **art board** to render the color for **color separation**.

See Groensteen 1993.

painted comics: (noun) comics that are colored in paint.

See Lawrence et al. 2016.

painted cover: (noun) a comic **cover** that uses a painting instead of a **line drawing**.

See Lawrence et al. 2016, 69–102.

palindrome: (noun) a word, phrase, or **sequence** that has the same meaning when read forward or backward.

pamphlet: a nonpremium short-form comics **format** whereby the **pages** are stitched or **stapled** together with a paper **cover**.

panel: (noun) a discrete unit of static imagery depicting a single segment of **action**, **space**, and/or **time**, often bounded on all sides by a **frame**, though not necessarily; considered by many to be the basic unit of a comics **page** or the basic sequential element of comics **storytelling**.

See Bares 2008; Berlatsky 2009; Brandl 2007; N. Cohn 2011; N. Cohn, Taylor-Weiner, and Grossman 2012; Horstkotte 2013; Kilgore 2015; Millidge 2009, 32–59; Natsume 2010; Packard 2018; Pantaleo 2013; Pedri 2018; Perret 2001; Rosen 2009; Sabhaney 2014; Sealy-Morris 2015; G. Smith 2013; Steiling 2012; Szawerna 2014; Talon 2002; Talon and Thompson 2010; Wucher 2019.

panel border: (noun) the **frame** that demarcates a **panel**, distinguishing it from other panels on the **page**.

See Berlatsky 2009; Denson 2012; Horstkotte 2013; Kwa 2020b; Rosen 2009.

panel
border

panel cartoon: see **gag cartoon**.

panel composition: (noun) the placement of all the artistic elements in a **panel** to form a unified whole, guide the reader's eye, highlight important features, and impact readers **emotionally**.

See Caldwell 2012; N. Cohn 2011; Harkham and Nadel 2010; Horstkotte 2013; Kilgore 2015; Natsume 2010; Sabhaney 2014; G. Smith 2013; Spandler 2020; Steiling 2012; Szawerna 2014.

panel duration: (noun) the implied amount of **time** represented in an individual **panel**.

See Abusch 2014; Bares 2008; Conard and Lambeens 2012.

panel shape: (noun) the configuration or look of a **panel** as delineated by its **frame**, traditionally and most often a square, although it carries the potential to be any conceivable **shape**.

panel transition: (noun) a change in visual information from one **panel** to the next, which allows the reader to logically connect the two, to perform **closure**.
See Bateman and Wildfeuer 2014a; N. Cohn 2010; H. Earle 2013c; Hammontree 2017; McCloud 1994, 70–72; Mikkonen 2017, 38–43.

panning [also **pan shot**]: (noun) in comics, a wide, continuous image divided into multiple **panels**, so that the entire image is gradually revealed, panel by panel, to the reader.

panoramic breakdown: see **pan sequence**.

pan sequence [also **panoramic breakdown**]: (noun) a **sequence** that divides an otherwise unified **diegetic space**.

pan shot: see **panning**.

pantomime cartoon: (noun) a wordless **gag cartoon**.

pantomime comics: see **wordless comics**.

paperback [also **softcover** or soft cover]: (noun) a book bound in flexible cardboard or a stiff paper **cover**.

paper stock: (noun) the finish and weight of paper; the material from which paper is made.

parallel combination: (noun) a **word and image combination** in a **panel** in which words and images narrate parallel but unrelated **storyworld** information.
See McCloud 1994, 154.

parody [also **send-up**]: (noun) the imitation of an author's **style** or work for comic effect or in ridicule.
See Croissant 2008; J. Donovan 2012; Frahm 2000; Grail 2007.

pastedown: (noun) the half of the **endsheet** that is attached to the **cover board**.

pattern: (noun) a repetitive **design** intended to be decorative; a recurring sequence of **events**.
See K. Allen and Ingulsrud 2005; Berenstein 2012; Bourdaa 2013; Brent 1991; Ingulsrud and Allen 2009; Ledden and Fejes 1987; Wertham 1954.

pause panel: (noun) a **silent panel** that breaks the story's flow and, therefore, slows the reader for a "pause" or beat.

pedigree: (noun) a comic book that was owned by a widely known comic book collector.

pencil art [also **pencils**]: (noun) the stage of **drawing** in which the **artist** uses a pencil to fully delineate, in much greater detail than at the **layout** stage, the **composition** (or **contents**) of each **panel**, while finalizing the layout of the entire **page**. See Janson 2013b.

penciler:(noun) the person who draws the basic **pencil art**, including the distribution and placement of visuals in the **panels** and panel **arrangement**; the person who translates the **script** into active **sequences** of static images on a page-by-page, panel-by-panel basis, indicates light sources and **shading**, and makes all essential **drawing** decisions, except when explicitly indicated in the script.

penciling: (verb) the act of sketching of **thumbnails** and illustrating the comic using pencil. See Janson 2013b.

pencil layouts: (noun) a preliminary **drawing** process, executed in pencil on a full-size **art board** (in current US **mainstream comics**, typically with an image area of 10 in. x 15 in.), wherein the main **shapes** in each **panel** are loosely blocked in for every **page**. See also **breakdowns**. See Janson 2013b, 61–81.

pencil layouts

pencils: see **pencil art.**

perfect bound: (noun) a **softcover** book **binding** method whereby the **pages** and **cover** are glued together along the **spine** with a strong, flexible thermal glue, and the other three sides of the cover are trimmed to give them clean, "perfect" edges.

personification: (noun) the attribution of human characteristics to something nonhuman. See also **anthropomorphism.**

phantasy comics: see **fantasy comics.**

photocomics: see *fumetti.*

photo cover: (noun) a comic **cover** that uses a photograph instead of or in combination with a **line drawing.**
See R. Cook 2015.

photo essay (noun) a short piece or article on a particular subject that relies heavily or exclusively on photographs to communicate.

photographic streaking: see **multiple images.**

photo novel: (noun) a book-length story narrated using a combination of photography, **dialogue**, and/or **narrative captions.**
See Baetens 2010; Baetens 2013a; Baetens 2013b; Baetens 2015; Baetens 2017; Baetens 2018a; Baetens and Bleyen 2010; Bonifazio 2017; Bonifazio 2020; Flora 1984; McBride 2012; Peeters and Plissart 1995.

photo panel: (noun) a **panel** that uses a photograph instead of or in combination with a **line drawing.**

photorealistic style: (noun) a **style** of art that engages a meticulously detailed realism.

photo story: (noun) a story narrated using a sequence of photographs, **dialogue**, and/or **narrative captions.**

physiognomy: (noun) a pseudo-science that proposes to analyze a person's character based on their outer appearance, especially their facial features.
See Gombrich 1972; Töpffer 1965.

pictogram: see **pictograph.**

pictograph [also **pictogram**]: (noun) a pictorial **symbol** for a word.
See Cornilliat 2011.

pictorial embodiment: (noun) the physical appearance of a **character**; the engagement with one's own identity through multiple **self-portraits**; a graphic memoirist's way to represent themself, which visually recurs through their work or works. Cf. **self-portrait**.
See Avery-Natale 2013; Couser 2018; N. Edwards, Hubbell, and Miller 2011; El Refaie 2012, 49–92.

pictorial metaphor: see **visual metaphor**.

picture book: (noun) a short book, usually intended for children, that is heavily illustrated with **drawings** that relay the story.
See Arizpe 2013; J. Bennett 1982; Janet Evans 2013; J. Foster 2011; Mel Gibson 2010a; Mel Gibson, Nabizadeh, and Sambell 2014; Gutierrez 2014; Horsman 2014; Kümmerling-Meibauer 2015; Kümmerling-Meibauer 2018; Lent 2001; Nel 2012; Nikolajeva and Scott 2001; Nodelman 1988; ob de Beeck 2012; Palmer 2014; Sanders 2013; Shen 1997; Spaulding 1984; Spaulding 1995; Spitz 2000; Trabado 2015.

picture plane: (noun) an imaginary plane that corresponds to the image's surface, located between what is being viewed and the viewer's eye.
See P. Atkinson 2018.

picture-specific combination: (noun) a **word and image combination** in which images provide the primary **narrative** function and words fulfill a minor narrative function. Cf. **word-specific combination**.
See McCloud 1994, 153.

picture story: (noun) a story narrated in a single image, across two images, or in a series of images, often coupled with **captions** and/or **dialogue**.
See Andrews 1997; Beringer 2015; Grünewald 2012; Kunzle 1973; Mikkonen 2017, 245–76.

pinup [also pin-up]: (noun) a one- or two-**page nonnarrative** image included in some comics, usually following the story, often featuring the lead **character** and drawn by **artists** other than the **penciler**.

planche: (noun) in comics, French for **page**.

Platinum Age: (noun) an informal name designating the first age of comics with the introduction of newspaper **comic strips**, roughly extending between 1897 and 1938.

plewds: (noun) beads of sweat depicted as jumping off a **character** to indicate heightened **emotion**.
See Walker (1980) 2000, 28.

plop take: see **flip take**.

plot [also **storyline**]: (noun) the string of **events** that form the story, including setup, conflict, and resolution.

plot style: see **Marvel method**.

plotter: (noun) the person who creates the comic's **plot** or basic **storyline**.

plot thread: see **narrative thread**.

pointer: see **tail**.

point-of-view shot [also point-of-view framing]: (noun) the **angle of framing** used to approximate that of a particular **character** in the story, allowing the reader to see exactly and only what the character sees. Cf. **over-the-shoulder shot**.
See Mikkonen 2017, 139–44.

political cartoon [also **editorial cartoon**]: (noun) usually a single-**panel cartoon** that contains political or social commentary.
See Abdel-Raheem 2020; Meena Ahmed 2010; Bounegru and Forceville 2011; Chaney and Chaney 2020; Conners 2005; Conners 2007; Diamond 2002; J. Edwards and Ware 2005; El Refaie 2009a; El Refaie 2009b; Fischer 1996; Gökçen 2015; Hou and Hou 1998; M. B. Katz 2013; Lamb 1996; Schilperoord 2013; Serrano 2020; Sheppard 1994; Spencer 2007; Stoll 2010.

polygraphy: (noun) the combination of different graphic **forms**, **registers**, **styles**, and/or traditions.
See Smolderen 2014a, 58–60.

polyphony: (noun) the juxtaposition of two or more simultaneous **narrative threads** in one **panel** or from panel to panel.

polyptych [also **superpanel**]: (noun) a **comic strip**, a set of adjacent **panels**, or a comics page in which a particular **figure** or figures are imposed over a continuous **background** that is broken up over individual panels, as a means of indicating **motion**. Cf. **split panel**.
See Poharec 2018.

popup: (noun) a feature whereby a **storyworld** element physically juts out of the **comics page** to create a three-dimensional **page**.
See Trebbi 2017.

positive space: (noun) the area in an image that is painted, filled with **lines**, or otherwise covered; the opposite of **negative space**.

post-code: (adj.) in reference to comic books published after the **Comics Code Authority** came into effect in 1955.

poster layout: (noun) a **page layout** composed of one image that does not use **panel frames**.

pre-code: (adj.) in reference to comic books published before the **Comics Code Authority** came into effect in 1955.

pregnant moment: (noun) an art history term coined by German philosopher Gotthold Ephraim Lessing to designate the most suggestive moment of **action** in a story that in graphic art is then visually depicted.

prepress: (noun) the processes and procedures that prepare the printed manuscript for **production**.

prestige comic book: see **bookshelf format**.

price variant: (noun) a **cover** price that is different from that on the covers of other copies of the same comic book intended for sale in the same country.

primary movement: (noun) the principal implied movement of **characters** or objects in the **panel**.

printer: (noun) the businesspeople or other people who take the prepared manuscript from the **publisher** and manufacture multiple copies (of comic books, for example) according to the **publisher's** instructions.

printing: (noun) the process of impressing or reproducing text and images on paper with a printing press.

prism cover: (noun) a **cover** that is made from a reflective material that creates a repeated three-dimensional **design**.

production: (noun) the process of **printing** numerous impressions of a comic for **distribution**.
See Norcliffe and Rendace 2003; Rogers 2006.

production value: (noun) in comics publishing, the technical qualities of a **production**, including **paper stocks**, **binding** techniques, and **color** and **printing** processes.

proofreading: (noun) the examination of the manuscript for inconsistencies, mistakes, or omissions before it goes into **production**.

protagonist [also **hero**]: (noun) the central **character** in the story with whom the reader is most likely to identify.
See Mel Gibson 2010b; Hemovich 2018.

proto-comics: (noun) a term coined by M. Thomas Inge to designate early forms of art that could be considered comics in our contemporary understanding of them, including cave drawings, European tapestries, hieroglyphics, and **pulps**.
See Chapman et al. 2015, 56–76; Inge 2016.

provenance: (noun) information about the comic book owner, often used to authenticate and document the comic book's history.

prozine: (noun) a **fanzine** with higher than ordinary **production values** and produced by a person or people who have higher than amateur standing.

psychological image: (noun) an image that communicates some mental aspect of a **character**.

publisher: (noun) the businesspeople or other persons who order, prepare, and oversee creative material for **printing** and then for public sale or **distribution**.
See Lavin 1998; Lavin 1999.

pull list: (noun) a list of comics **titles** someone has on file at their local **comics specialty shop** that allows the shop to place comics aside for them until they can pick them up on a **weekly**, **biweekly**, monthly, or **bimonthly** basis and thus not miss a subscription.

pulps: (noun) cheaply produced magazines popular in the 1930s printed on inexpensive wood-pulp **paper** and featuring sensational fictional stories.
See DeForest 2004; Gifford 2003; Madison 2013; Maglio 2017; Scolari, Bertetti, and Freeman 2014.

punch line: (noun) the final, crucial component of a joke or story needed to provoke laughter.
See Kunzle 1983.

¼ hatching: (noun) fine parallel lines used to achieve the impression of light shading or texture.

queer comics: (noun): comics created by or about people who identify as LGBTQIA+.
See Abate, Grice, and Stamper 2018; Aldama 2021; Alexander 2018; Baudinette 2017; Bhadury 2018; B. Bolton 2012; M. Earle 2019; Faris 2019; Franklin 2001; Greyson 2007; Hall 2012; Kvaran 2014; Lendrum 2005b; Levi, McHarry, and Pagliassotti 2010; Manchester 2017; Mangels 1988a; Mangels 1988b; McAllister 1992; Padva 2005; Pfalzgraf 2012; Risner 2010; Ryerson 2019; Sewell 2001; Shyminsky 2011; Stein 2018; A. Wood 2006; A. Wood 2013.

radio balloon [also radio FX, **electronic balloon**, or **broadcast balloon**]: (noun) a **word balloon** usually made up of a jagged edge with short points and jagged **tail** used to indicate speech that is projected electronically.

rage comics: (noun) comics that cast **characters** with premade **cartoon** faces or rage faces, usually to tell a story based on real-life experience.

rare: (adj.) in reference to a comic of which a very small number of copies (fewer than twenty) are believed to be extant.

rat or mouse chew: (noun) damage to a comic caused by a rodent.

reader's crease: (noun) damage to a comic's **spine** caused by readers folding back **pages**.

realism: (noun) an art **style** that strives to represent reality in an accurate and detailed depiction. Cf. **photorealistic style**.
See Clayton 2010; Newall 2011; Pizzino 2018.

realistic representation: (noun) visual images that tend to resemble a real-life issue, **event**, person, place, or thing.
See Carmack 1997; Newall 2011.

reboot: (noun) a **series** that has been restarted with revisions to the mythos of previous versions of the series.
See Elmslie 2008; Proctor 2012a; Proctor 2012b; Proctor 2013; Proctor 2017a.

recap: (noun) a short summary of **storyworld** details that readers may have missed or forgotten, often used in **superhero comics**.

recolored comic [also **remastered comic**]: (noun) a comic that has been **color**ed again, usually when reissued, reprinted in a new edition, or collected in a **comics anthology**.
See R. Cook and Meskin 2015.

recto page: (noun) the first page that one reads on a **leaf**; in Western printing traditions, the right-side **page** in a two-page opening. Cf. **verso page**.

register: (noun) the **tone** or **style** of a **narrator's** or **character's voice**.

remaindered: (adj.) in reference to a comic that has been marked down in price and is usually physically marked (either on its **cover** or across the bottom side of its **pages**).

remastered comic: see **recolored comic**.

remediation: (noun) the inclusion or representation of one **medium** in another medium.
See Kirchoff 2012; Mikkonen 2010.

rendering: (noun) a modern computer **coloring** process of blending solid shadows, highlighting areas of the artwork, adding **texture** to **figures** and objects, and using other effects to further depict **form**. See also **flattening**.

reprint: (noun) a reproduction of a comic that is already in print.

restoration: (noun) a process that returns a comic as close as possible to its original state with the addition of nonoriginal material.

retcon: (noun) short for **retroactive continuity.**

retroactive continuity [also **retcon** or **retroconning**]: (noun) a literary device wherein details and facts of a comics story, book, or **series** are contradicted, omitted, or reworked in a subsequently published comics story, book, or **series**, thus breaking continuity with the former; when the past events in the **continuity** of a comics **series** are actively and purposely changed.
See Denson 2013; Friedenthal 2017; Proctor 2013; Proctor 2017a; Ratto 2017.

retroconning: see **retroactive continuity.**

reveal: (noun) a literal "page-turner" in that a **cliffhanger** is presented at the end of a right-hand **page** and resolved on the following (left-hand) page, keeping the reader in suspense until the page is turned.

reverse angle: (noun) a type of **shot** that shifts the perspective from one viewing position to the perspective of another viewing position that looks back at the first viewing position.

revival: (noun) an **issue** that reintroduces a **character** after a period of dormancy.

RGB: (noun) short for red, green, blue; an additive **color** definition method often used in the computer **coloring** process only for comics published in a digital **format**. See also **CMYK.**

rhythm: (noun) the pace at which the **action** unfolds; the reader's reading pace.
See Palmer 2014; Shores 2016.

rhythm

rogues gallery: (noun) a grouping of a respective **superhero**'s foes.

rolled spine: (noun) a misalignment or shifting of the comic's **spine** due to rolling back pages. See also **spine roll**.

romance comics: (noun) a comics **genre** that narrates stories about desire, relationships, and romantic love.
See Best 2013; Jeanne Emerson Gardner 2012a; Jeanne Emerson Gardner 2012b; Jeanne Emerson Gardner 2013; Heifler 2020; Nolan 2008; Robbins 2002; Shamoon 2008; A. Wood 2015.

rough balloon: (noun) a **word balloon** that has an unsmooth **frame**, usually indicating a distorted or monstrous **voice**.

round bound: standard **saddle-stitched** binding.

row [also **tier**]: (noun) the horizontal **arrangement** of **panels** on a comics **page**.

run: (noun) the consecutive grouping of **serial** comics according to the work a particular creative team did on a particular **character**.

saddle-stitched [also **stapled**]: (adj.) in reference to a **binding** whereby **sheets** of **paper** are folded and then stapled together.

sans paroles: (noun) French for "without words." See **wordless comics**.

saturation [also **chroma**]: (noun) the intensity of the **color**; a characteristic of **color** as either pure or diluted.

scene: (noun) a **sequence** that transpires in one place and in one continuous **time** period; a unit of the **story**.

scene-to-scene: (noun) a type of **panel transition** that links one **scene** in a **panel** to another scene in the next panel that is distant in **time** and/or **space**.
See Abel and Madden 2008, 42; McCloud 1994, 71.

science comics: (noun) comics about science.
See Collver and Weitkamp 2018; Farinella 2018b; Friesen, Van Stan, and Elleuche 2018; Hosler and Boomer 2011; Lin et al. 2015; McDermott, Partridge, and Bromberg 2018; Sousanis 2017; Tatalovic 2009; White 2017.

science fiction comics [also **sci-fi comics**]: (noun) speculative fiction comics that focus on advanced science and technological innovations, outer space, and the future.
See Aragão 2012; Benton 1992b; Blanc-Hoàng 2017; Cappello 2019; Chiba and Chiba 2007; Costello 2015; Creekmur 2014; Kashtan 2019; Kawa 2009; Kling 1977; Kripal 2011; Kukkonen 2018; Nama 2009; Noh 2008; Palumbo 1999; Parkinson 2015; Suzuki 2010; Teampău 2014; Wasielewski 2009.

sci-fi comics: see **science fiction comics**.

screen: (noun) in **webcomics**, the equivalent of the **page**.

screentone: (noun) adhesive plastic film printed with **patterns** of dots, **lines**, or other **shapes** used as an alternative to **hatching** for applying **textures** and shades to **drawings**; also known as **Zip-a-Tone**, which was one commercial brand name.

script: (noun) the written story that serves as a basis for creating comics.
See W. Robertson 2019.

scripting [also **scriptwriting**]: (noun) the act of writing a **script** undertaken by a **writer**.
See Bendis 2014; Kneece 2015; Stan Lee et al. 2011; Moore and Burrows 2003; Peeters 2010; Root and Kardon 2004; Salisbury 2002; Schmidt 2018.

scriptor: (noun) the creator of the **script** responsible for detailing the **dialogue** and **action** of each **panel** and, often, providing instructions for the visuals and **page composition**.

scriptwriting: see **scripting**.

secondary movement: (noun) the implied movement of the **panel**.
See Lefèvre 2011b.

second-person narration: (noun) the narration of a story from the point of view of a narrator who uses the pronoun of the second-person singular or plural, "you."

self-cover comic: (noun) a comic made exclusively from printed signatures of paper, without the use of additional paper stock for the cover; a comic that has covers 1–4 printed on the same paper signature as the story pages.

self-portrait: (noun) an artist's representation of him- or herself. Cf. pictorial embodiment.
See Chaney 2016, 121–44.

semi-autobiographical: (adj.) in reference to a fictional comic strongly influenced by the author's personal life experiences.

semimonthly: (adj.) published two times a month, but not necessarily biweekly. Cf. bimonthly.

semiweekly: (adj.) published twice a week. Cf. biweekly.

send-up: (noun) see parody.

sequence: (noun) in comics, a series of consecutive panels united by a narrative thread; a unit of discourse.
See Abusch 2013; Carrier 2000, 47–59; Denson 2012; Groensteen 2007, 103–43; Horstkotte 2013; Lefèvre 2011b; Legrady 2000; Weng et al. 2019.

sequential art: (noun) any artwork that tells a story through elements arranged in a sequence; an artistic and literary form that narrates a story through the arrangement of images in sequence, such as comics.
See Eisner (1985) 2008a; Johnson 2012; Piepoli 2011; Talon 2004.

sequential dynamism: (noun) the directing of the reader's eye across the comics page by way of a number of formal visual elements.
See Molotiu 2011.

sequentiality: (noun) the depiction or presentation of events in linear, successive sequences.
See N. Cohn 2010; Groensteen 2013, 21–41.

serial: (noun) a recurring series.
See Boillat 2017; Dittmer 2007; Eco 1990, 155–80; Falgas 2020; M. Horn 2000; Pratt 2013; Stein 2013; Stein and Etter 2018; Wüllner 2010.

seriality: (noun) the quality of breaking down a sequence of events into discrete units.
See R. Cook 2013; Dittmer 2014b; Jared Gardner 2017; Gordon 2013; Oltean 1993; Pedler 2007; Proctor 2017b; Reimer et al. 2014; Romaguera 2015; Tilley and Bahnmaier 2018; Uidhir 2013; Uidhir 2017.

series: (noun) a number of comics having the same characters, format, and theme and having a continuing story.
See Clarke 2014; Oltean 1993.

set: (noun) a grouping of comic books made up of a title's complete run.

setting: (noun) the time and place of the storyworld.

setting shot: see establishing shot.

sewn spine: (noun) the spine of a comic that has been bound by folding and stitching its pages together with thread before being glued to the cover.

SFX: see sound effects.

shading: (noun) the lines or other visual marks used to fill in outlines of a drawing to represent gradations of darkness, revealing the various sources of light within an image or a panel and thereby adding dimension to its subject(s); a coloring technique that uses lines or other visual marks to fill in outlines of a drawing to represent gradations of darkness.

shallow focus: (noun) a depth of field in which one picture plane of the panel is in focus and the rest is out of focus, typically used to emphasize one part of the image over the rest.

shape: (noun) a closed space giving form to something or someone.
See A. Fox 2014.

sheet: (noun) a single piece of loose paper.

shōjo manga: (noun) manga aimed at a teenage female demographic.
See Birmingham 2013; Monden 2014; Ōgi 2001; Prough 2011; Sasaki 2013; Toku 2005; Toku 2007; J. Ueno 2006; Unser-Schutz 2015; Welker 2006.

shōnen manga: (noun) **manga** aimed at a teenage male demographic.
See Birken 2014; Chua 2016; Gallacher 2011; Grennan 2018; Unser-Schutz 2015.

shop system: (noun) a **production** method in which independent contractors work together in a shop or studio to produce **content** for major **publishers** in a fashion that resembles an assembly line, with different production steps allocated to different **artists**.
See Gabilliet 2010, 112–14.

short story comics: (noun) comics that are short in length, yet have a fully developed **narrative**.

shot: (noun): in comics, the **angle of framing** or perspective through which an **action**, **character**, or **scene** is presented; common types of shots include **close-up / CU**, **establishing shot**, **extreme close-up / XCU**, **extreme long shot**, **full shot**, **high-angle shot**, **long shot**, **low-angle shot**, **medium shot**, **panning / pan shot**, **tilt**, and **point-of-view shot**. See also **camera shot**.

shot / reverse-shot sequence: (noun) a two-**character scene** in which **panels** alternate by focusing on one **character** and then reversing the **shot** to focus on the other.

sidelining: (noun) an arrangement in which the cropped edge of a **butting balloon** is against the left or right side of a **panel border**.

silent captioned panel: (noun) a **silent panel** that has a **caption**.
See McCloud 1994, 98.

silent comics: (noun) see **wordless comics**.

silent panel [also **image panel**]: (noun) a **panel** that does not contain words in **captions** or **balloons** or as **sound effects**. Cf. **word panel**.
See McCloud 1994, 98.

silhouette: (noun) an image that represents a **figure** as a solid **shape** with its edges matching the outline of the subject.

Silver Age: (noun) an informal name designating the American comic book era that marks the second surge in mass popularity in **superhero comics**, roughly extending between 1956 and 1970, inaugurated with DC's *Showcase* #4 and its **reboot** of the Flash.

See Alaniz 2004; Alaniz 2006; Alaniz 2014; Bamberger 2017; Barbee 2008; Benton 1991; Casey 2009; Darowski 2017; Hatfield 2009c; Daniel Herman 2004; Jenkins 2009; G. Jones and Jacobs 1996; Kaplan 2003b; Kawa 2009; Levitz 2013b; Pizzino 2018; Schoell 2010; Schumer 2014; M. Smith 2014.

silhouette

simple story layout: (noun) a **grid**-shaped **story layout** with same-sized **panels** arranged in **tiers**.

sketch: (noun) an unfinished **drawing**.
See Mendonça 2016; Thorne 2000.

slab: (noun) colloquial term for the plastic enclosure used to seal comics after they have been graded by a grading certification company.

slabbed: (adj.) colloquial term describing the state of a comic book that has been professionally **grade**d for condition and sealed in a plastic sheath.
See Woo 2012.

slabbing: see **encapsulation**.

slapstick humor: (noun) a comic incident characterized by stylized, exaggerated **action**, boisterous violence, horseplay, or physical misfortune.

sleeve: (noun) a covering that protects a book.

slice-of-life story: (noun) a story that presents a **sequence** of **event**s in a **character**'s life, often without apparent concern for character development or **plot** progress.

slipcase: (noun) a close-fitting covering for printed material open at one end.

softcover: see **paperback**.

solicitations: (noun) detailed ordering information for upcoming releases from a **publisher**.

soliloquy (noun): the voicing of a **character**'s internal thoughts by that character who does not have an audience. Cf. **monologue**.

solrad: (noun) a form of **emanata** used to denote brightness, heat, and the emanation of light.
> See Walker (1980) 2000, 29.

sound: (noun) in comics, the use of visual signs such as **lettering, symbols**, and **word balloons** to communicate noise in all its variations of intensity, pitch, and tone.
> See Balzer 2006; K. M. Brown 2013; Carney 2008; Carrier 2000, 27–46; Dey and Bokil 2015; Dey and Bokil 2016; Goodbrey 2015b; Groensteen 2007, 67–85; Hague 2012; Hague 2014; Manfredi, Cohn, and Kutas 2017; Mickwitz 2016, 38–43; Petersen 2007; Schmitz-Emans 2011.

sound effects [also **SFX**]: (noun) the use of stylized **lettering** or other typographic features to represent particular noises; the visual rendering of **onomatopoeias**, such as *pow, bang*, or *swoosh*.
> See Inose 2012; Pollmann 2001; Pratha, Avunjian, and Cohn 2016; K. Taylor 2007; Warner 2008.

space: (noun) the area between and around **shapes** and **forms**; the place where the **storyworld action** is situated. Cf. **setting**.
> See Ahrens and Meteling 2010; D'Arcy 2020; D. Davies 2019; Dittmer 2014a; Dittmer and Latham 2015; P. Johnston 2016; Lefèvre 2009a; Lefèvre (2007) 2009b; Lent 2000; A. Miller 2008; Round 2008; Round 2014b; Tsaousis 1999; Zurier 2006.

span of time: (noun) **time** length; the amount of elapsed time.

spatio-topical system: (noun) a term coined by Thierry Groensteen to designate the spatial extension and relations on a **page layout** that impact **order, time duration**, and **rhythm**.
> See H. Earle 2013a; Groensteen 2007, 24–102.

speculator: (noun) a collector who purchases comics and comics paraphernalia as investments.
See Beaty 2012, 153–82.

speech balloon: (noun) see **word balloon**.

speed lines: (noun) visual streaks or **motion lines** that convey the impression of mobility, usually suggesting rapid movement.

spine: (noun) the vertical edge of a book where its **pages** are connected.

spine roll: (noun) a bowing of the **spine** due to folding back **pages** over the spine while reading. See also **rolled spine**.

splash page [also **splash**]: (noun) a single-**panel page** with a **border**; a full-page **panel**, often the first page of a comic or some other dynamic moment in the **story**; traditionally, the single **illustration** on the first page of a comic book. Cf. **bleed**.

splash panel: (noun) a **panel** that is significantly larger in size than other panels in the comic. Cf. **bleed panel**.
See W. R. Johnston 1989.

split panel: (noun) the extension of an image or **background** across two or more **panels**; an image created in two parts that join together. Cf. **polyptych**.
See Hatfield 2005, 53–58; Poharec 2018.

spoiler: (noun) information about a **plot** that ruins the **story**'s surprise or suspense.
See Hassoun 2013.

spotting blacks: (noun) the graphic technique of adding heavy areas of ink to specific areas of a **page** to balance **composition** or influence the **direction of reading**.

spread: (noun) two facing **pages** that make up a single horizontal image; a two-page image composed of one left-hand and one right-hand **page** side by side; a single **panel** that takes up two pages. See also **recto page** and **verso page**.

square back: see **squarebound**.

squarebound [also **square back**]: (noun) a square **binding** on a comic book, usually for **giant size** or **bookshelf format**.

spread

squeans: (noun) **symbols** similar to asterisks radiating from a **character**'s head meant to depict comic injury, disorientation, or drunkenness.

See Walker (1980) 2000, 29.

stapled: see **saddle-stitched**.

steampunk comics: (noun) a subgenre of **science fiction comics** that incorporates the aesthetic **designs** and technology of nineteenth-century industrial steam-powered machinery.

See B. Baker 2008; Pagliassotti 2017; Sulmicki 2011.

stellar layout: (noun) an arrangement of **panels** that form a star **pattern** with a **focal panel** in its center.

stereotype: (noun) conventionally standardized or generalized physical characteristics associated with members of an ethnic, racial, sexual, occupational, or other group.

See Baetens 2013b; Brabant and Mooney 1997; Bresnahan, Inoue, and Kagawa 2006; Davenport 1997; Eisner (1996) 2008c, 11–14; W. Foster 2002; Glascock and Preston-Schreck 2004; Horton 2007; K. Thompson 2006; S. Wood 1989.

stipple: (noun) a **drawing** technique in which dots are used to delineate areas of light and shadow.

store stamp: (noun) rubber ink–stamped information about a **comics specialty shop** stamped on a comic book.

story arc: (noun) an extended or continuous **storyline** across several **issues** in serialized comic books.

storyboard: (noun) a graphic organizer in the form of images and **panel frames** displayed in **sequence** for the purpose of visualizing a comic book, **comics page**, or **spread** before creating it.
See Doyle 2008; J. P. Hart 2008; Salinas 2015; Spaulding 1984.

story breakdown: see **breakdown.**

story layout: (noun) the manner in which **events** are arranged in a given comic.

storyline: see **plot.**

storytelling: (noun) the conveying of a **narrative.**
See Bladow 2019; Bourdaa 2013; DeForest 2004; Dittmar 2015; Dolle-Weinkauff 2018; Eisner (1996) 2008c; Jared Gardner 2012; Hembrough 2019; David Herman 2010; David Herman 2012; Kukkonen 2008; Kukkonen 2013a; Lowe 2017; McCloud 2006; McKean 1995; Packard 2016; Scolari, Bertetti, and Freeman 2014; Sklar 2012; Talon 2007; Talon and Thompson 2010; Wüllner 2010.

storyworld [also **diegesis**]: (noun) the world represented by a **narrative.**
See C. Harvey 2015; David Herman 2011; David Herman 2018; Horstkotte 2013; Packard 2015; Surdi-acourt 2012c; Thon 2016, 35–70; Thoss 2015; Weaver 2013.

storyworld participant: see **character.**

straight-on angle: see **eye-level framing.**

stream of consciousness: (noun) a method of **narration** that renders the flow of **emotions**, memories, sensory feelings, thoughts, and other happenings as they unfold in a **character**'s mind. Cf. **interior monologue.**
See Harnett 2019.

stress lines: (noun) bends on or along a **spine** that may damage the **color.**

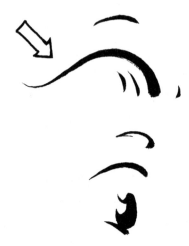

stroke

stroke: (noun) a **line** on the **page**.

style: (noun) in comics, an individual artistic expression that takes into account the **artist's** influences, the quality of **line work**, **page layout** preferences, **shading** and other **inking** techniques, as well as other significant visual characteristics representative of the artist's work; the combination of distinctive features of artistic expression that characterize an **artist's** particular **drawing**s; the artist's or work's graphic "signature"; particular schools of artistic expression, for example, a "Renaissance style."

See Maaheen Ahmed and Crucifix 2018; Bateman, Veloso, and Lau 2021; Ecke 2019; Jonathan Evans 2016; J. Foster 1991; Gomes and Peuckert 2010; R. Harvey 1996; P. Horn 2001; P. Howell 2001; Humphrey 2018; Jeffries 2017; Kacsuk 2018; Karaminas 2007; Kothenschulte 2008; Lamerichs 2016; Lefèvre 2016; Mahamood 2003; Mikkonen 2013; Mikkonen 2017, 110–25; Morton 2017; Nijdam 2020; Pellitteri 2018; Peppard 2019.

style guide [also **model sheet**]: (noun) in comics, **sketch**es, usually on a single **sheet** of paper, of a **character** from multiple angles and in several different poses that define the character's visual **design**.

stylistic signature: (noun) a specific, idiosyncratic aspect of the **style** associated with a specific **artist**.

See Forceville, El Refaie, and Meesters 2014.

stylization: see **degree of abstraction**.

subjective motion: (noun) an image wherein the moving object is drawn in focus, while the **background** is streaked or blurred, as if a "camera" were moving at the same speed as the moving object.

subjectivity: (noun) the quality of being marked by a subject's personal attitudes, emotions, or tastes; the quality of experiencing self and the world one inhabits (the **storyworld** or **diegesis**) across one's mental world.
See Etter 2016; Horstkotte and Pedri 2016; J. Howell 2015; Kokanović and Flore 2017; Mikkonen 2013; Ôgi 2003; Packard 2016; Pedri 2015b; Pedri 2018; Thon 2014a; Tolmie 2013.

subject-to-subject transition: (noun) a type of **panel transition** featuring different **characters** or objects from one panel to the next panel within the same **scene**.
See Abel and Madden 2008, 41; McCloud 1994, 71.

subscription copy: (noun) a comic book mailed out by the **publisher**.

subscription crease [also **subscription fold**]: (noun) a fold and resulting missing ink that runs down the middle of a **subscription copy** that was folded in half.

subscription fold: see **subscription crease**.

subtitle: (noun) a subordinate **title** that provides additional information about the comic's content; a translation of the verbal text that appears alongside the original verbal text.

succession: (noun) the process by which one image in a **sequence** follows or is replaced by another image in the sequence, thus giving the impression that **time** is passing; an organization of multiple images implying that one image logically leads to the next image; a way of representing time by dividing **space** into visual units.
See Abusch 2014; Gunning 2014.

Sunday comics [also Sundays]: (noun) **comic strips** that run in newspapers on Sundays, frequently in full **color**.
See K. Barker 1996; Brabant and Mooney 1997; F. King 2014; Mooney and Brabant 1987; Sofalvi and Drolet 1986; Spiggle 1986.

sun shadow: (noun) damage to areas of comic inks due to prolonged exposure to sunlight or strong light. Cf. **dust shadow** and **oxidation shadow**.

superhero: (noun) a type of **character** who exhibits exceptional or superhuman ability, generally wears a costume, adopts a moniker, and uses their powers for "good," including protecting others from **supervillains**.

See Arnaudo 2013; Austin and Hamilton 2019; Beaty and Weiner 2012b; Benedetti 2019; Bongco 2000; J. Brown 2000; J. Brown 2017; Carney 2005; Chambliss, Svitavsky, and Donaldson 2013; Coogan 2006; Curtis 2016; Curtis and Cardo 2018; Davis 2015; DiPaolo 2011; Eckard 2017; Fawaz 2016; Fingeroth 2007; Garrett 2008; Mel Gibson, Huxley, and Ormrod 2014; Gilmore and Stork 2014; Goodrum, Prescott, and Smith 2018; Gresh and Weinberg 2002; Harris-Fain 2018; Hassler-Forest 2012; Hatfield, Heer, and Worcester 2013; Knowles 2007; A. D. Lewis and Lund 2017; LoCicero 2008; Maslon and Kantor 2013; Morrison 2011; Nama 2011; Ndalianis 2009a; Nevins 2017; Oropeza 2005; Parson and Schatz 2019; Peppard 2020; Reynolds 1994; Romagnoli and Pagnucci 2013; Rosenberg and Canzoneri 2008; Saunders 2011; Schatz and Parson 2018; Schott 2010; Tilley 2017; Wandtke 2007; Weinstein 2006.

superhero comics: (noun) a very popular type or **genre** of comics that focuses on the adventures and exploits of **superheroes**.

See J. Brown 2011b; Chambliss 2012; Chute 2017, 69–102; Cocca 2014; Coogan 2006; Flores 2013; Gavaler 2018a; Guynes and Lund 2020; Hyman 2017; Ioannidou 2013; Klock 2002; J. Scott 2016; Scott Smith and Alaniz 2020; Stein 2013; Stein 2016; Wandtke 2012; S. Wood 1989.

superheroine: (noun) a female **superhero**.

See Abate, Grice, and Stamper 2018; Benedetti 2019; Cocca 2016; Condis 2001; D'Amore 2008; Dowling 2009; E. García 2018; Nelson 2015; Simone 2012.

superpanel: see **polyptych**.

superhero
comics

superteam: (noun) a group of **superheroes** or **supervillains** who work together toward a common goal.

See Alaniz 2014, 116–37; Darowski 2017; Howe 2012b.

supervillain: (noun) a type of **character** who is the "evil" opponent of a **superhero**, using their exceptional or superhuman power for harm, undue profit, or terrorizing others.

See Buchenberger 2011; Cunningham 2010; Dyer 2009; Fennel 2012; Gresh and Weinberg 2004; Maguire 2012; Mayer 2013; Misiroglu and Eury 2006; Morris 2016; Peaslee and Weiner 2020.

surface: (noun) typically, the **storytelling** value or **design** of the overall **comics page**. Cf. **sequence**. See also **tabularity**.

surface quality: (noun) the **texture** of an image that can be seen or felt.

surface
quality

surrealism: (noun) an art **style** that aims to depict the reality of desires, dreams, and the unconscious.

See Parkinson 2015; Rosemont 1979.

suspension points: (noun) a punctuation mark of three dots used to communicate when a **character's dialogue** trails off or thought is suspended.

swipe: (noun) material in a comic—**cover**, **panel**, **sequence**, or **story**—obviously copied from a previously published source.

See Crucifix 2017.

symbol: (noun) per Charles Sanders Peirce, a visual sign that exists in a relationship of convention to the thing it refers; something that represents something else.

See Burke, Gordon, and Ndalianis 2020; Cavallaro 2011; Dey and Bokil 2015; Dey and Bokil 2016.

symbolic transition: (noun) a type of **transition** between **panels** in which a panel depicting something nonliteral is paired with a panel depicting something concrete that is taking place within the **storyworld**.
Abel and Madden 2008, 44.

synchronism (noun) in comics, a **panel** that conflates more than one **event**.

syndicate: (noun) a company that functions as an agent for **cartoonists**, selling **cartoons** and **comic strips** to newspapers on their behalf.

syndicated strip: (noun) a **comic strip** that a **syndicate** has sold to a newspaper or magazine.
See Galewitz 1972; Heintjes 2020; Strickler 1995.

synecdoche: (noun) a figure of speech in which a part of something is made to stand in for the whole or vice versa; in comics, also an image that represents a larger **event**, object, **space**, or **story**.
See Glaser 2014; Harnett 2016.

tab: (noun) short for **tabloid**.

tabloid [also **tab**]: (noun) a **comic strip format** in which a comic strip is published on a full **page** of a tabloid newspaper that measures roughly 10 in. x 14 in. (25.4 cm x 35.6 cm), as opposed to the larger 14 in. x 20 in. (35.6 cm x 50.8 cm) format of some newspapers.

tabloid size: see **treasury edition**.

tabularity: (noun) the translinear function of the **panel**, for example as an element in an overall **page design**; the function of the page as a distinct unit of **storytelling**. See also **surface**.
See Baroni 2016; J. Cohn 2009; Peeters 1998.

tail: (noun) part of a **word balloon** that indicates its point of origin.

takōbon: see *tankōbon.*

tankōbon [also *takōbon*]: (noun) an independent **volume** of multiple installments from a single **manga series** printed on good-quality paper. Cf. **manga magazine.**
See Couch 2000.

technique: (noun) an **artist's** specific **style** of **drawing.**
See Beaty and Weiner 2012a; Cavallaro 2007; Martinbrough 2007; Nielsen and Wichmann 2000; E. Williams 2018.

temperature: (noun) the warm or cool characteristic of **color.**

temporality: see **duration.**
See Christiansen 2000; Round 2014b.

tension: (noun) the balance maintained between opposing elements, such as words and images, in the story and/or art.
See Hatfield 2005, 32–67; Hatfield 2009a; G. Schneider 2016, 123–39.

text box: see **caption box.**

texture: (noun) a quality of **line** that creates a sense of tangibility by appearing, for example, rough or smooth, soft or hard.

theme: (noun) a pervasive and recurring concept in a work, which is not always explicit and sometimes requires reflection on the part of the reader to make it apparent; it can be, but is not always, the intended meaning of a work.
See K. A. Adams and Hill 1991; Beaty and Weiner 2012a; Belk 1987; Bowden 2013; Cavallaro 2007; Cavallaro 2009; Cavallaro 2012; Chaney 2013; Helsel 2018; Huska 2014; Lent 1999b; Pike 2012; C. Scott 2008; Skidmore and Skidmore 1983; Tu 2011.

third-person narration: (noun) the **narration** of a story from the point of view of a **narrator** who uses third-person pronouns such as "he," "she," and "they."

third tabloid [also third tab]: (noun) a newspaper **comic strip format** in which a comic strip takes up one-third of a tabloid newspaper **page.**

thought balloon: (noun) a **bordered**, usually cloud-like **balloon** with a trail of bubbles for a **tail** used to represent a **character**'s unspoken thought; a **word balloon** that conveys private thoughts; often mistakenly referred to as thought bubble.

See Cadieux 2011; Camden 2020; N. Cohn 2013a; Saraceni 2003, 65–68; Sousanis 2012.

3-D cover [also **holographic cover** or **lenticular cover**]: a **cover** or **sleeve** that gives the illusion of depth or **movement** when viewed from different angles or with special 3-D glasses.

¾ hatching: (noun) fine parallel **lines** used to achieve the impression of an intense **shading** or **texture**.

throwaway panels: (noun) **panels** in a **newspaper strip** that often provide a loose introduction or a gag, which are omitted on more compact **pages**.

thumbnails [also thumbnail breakdowns or thumbnail sketches]: (noun) a preliminary **drawing** in which each **page** is broken down into a sequence of quick, tiny, undetailed delineations of the **action** of the **story**, usually sketched out on blank letter-size (or smaller) **sheets** of paper, and not on **art board**; a visual correlate of **narrative breakdown**.

tier: see **row**.

Tijuana Bibles [also **eight-pagers** or **dirty comics**]: (noun) sexually explicit comics that first appeared in the United States in the 1920s, often featuring well-known cartoon **characters** in contravention of **copyright** laws.

See Adelman 1997; T. Atkinson 1971; Barry 2017; Pilcher and Kannenberg 2008; Wadsworth 2019.

Tijuana Bible

tilt

tilt: (noun) an **angle of framing** whereby the subject or subjects of the **panel** appear to be tilted on a diagonal, whether or not the **border** of the panel **frame** is tilted.

tilt sequence: (noun) a vertical **pan sequence**.

time: (noun) the phenomenon of **duration** and its experience as influenced by the order of the **story's events** (story-time) and the order of their presentation (discourse-time); in comics, the sense of time or duration is primarily achieved through a succession of **panels** (time = **space**) so that, usually, more time = more panels.

See Baetens and Pylyser 2017; Lyndsay Brown 2013; Chute 2016, 69–110; N. Cohn 2010; Dittmer and Latham 2015; H. Earle 2013a; P. Johnston 2016; Kukkonen 2013b; Lent 2000; Maynard 2001; Mikkonen 2010; Mikkonen 2017, 33–70; Moszkowicz 2012; Ndalianis 2009b; Packard 2018; Peñalba García 2014; Rabkin 2009; Rommens 2019; Singer 1999.

timing: (noun) the **artist's** manipulation or control of **story** information within a specific **sequence** of **panels** to slow down or speed up the **story**. See also **pacing**.

See Bares 2008; Rabkin 2009.

title: (noun) the name of the story or of the comic.

title page: (noun) the page that gives the title and sometimes also the credits and indicia, usually the first page of a comic.

tone: (noun) the particular attitude imparted by the narrative; the tint, shade, or quality of a color.

top-lining: (adj.) in reference to the cropped edge of a butting balloon directly bordering the upper side of a panel frame.

topper strip: (noun) a small newspaper comic strip added to the top or bottom of the main strip, popular from the 1920s to the 1930s and very rare by the mid-1950s.

TP: see trade paperback.

TPB: see trade paperback.

tracing paper: (noun) a thin, semitransparent paper.

tracking [also traveling]: (noun) a comics technique that simulates the motion of a camera eye moving continuously through space across a sequence of panels.

trade: see trade paperback.

trademark: (noun) a proprietary mark indicating usage on a specific type of product. For example, a publisher might trademark a logo or a costume design for use in or on comics as a means of ensuring that publisher's exclusive usage of a designated character.

trade paperback [also TP, TPB, or trade]: (noun) a squarebound volume in softcover format of reprinted comic book issues, usually linked either by theme or by story; a squarebound, softcover format collected edition of a comic book series.

transition: (noun) the bridge from one moment or one scene to another; the change in visual information created by the artist from one panel to the next, which allows the reader to logically connect the two and to perform closure. See also panel transition.
See Abel and Madden 2008, 38–48; N. Cohn 2010; H. Earle 2013c; McCloud 1994, 70–81.

transmedial comics: (noun) comics whose story is narrated across different media.
See D. A. Jones 2014; Proctor 2018; Yezbick and Alexandratos 2020.

transmediality: (noun) the condition whereby stories can be realized across different **media.**

See Bourdaa 2013; Freeman 2014; Kukkonen 2011a; Mikkonen 2011a; Packard 2015; Perron 2017; Pillai 2013; Rippl and Etter 2013; Thon 2014a; Thon 2014b; Thon 2016; Thon 2017.

traveling: see **tracking.**

treasury edition [also **tabloid size**]: (noun) originally, a newspaper-size (11 in. x 17 in. / 28 cm x 43 cm) comic book with a card **cover** or **hardcover** published in a much larger **page format** than standard comic book **issues**; today, treasury editions measure 8.5 in. x 13 in. (21.6 cm x 33 cm).

tressage: (noun) French for **braiding.**

true comics: (noun) a popular term used to designate comics that present stories that are fact based or based in reality. See also **nonfiction comics.**

24-hour comics: (noun) a twenty-four-**page** comic created in twenty-four hours, initially developed by Scott McCloud.

two-page spread: (noun) see **double-page spread.**

two-shot: (noun) a **shot** that frames two main **characters.**

type: (noun) the **font**, printed **characters**, and letters of a comic.

See Jüngst 2000; Unser-Schutz 2010; Unser-Schutz 2011.

typeface: (noun) a family of related **fonts.**

typography: (noun) the **style** or quality of **lettering**; the art and technique of arranging **type** through **line** and letter spacing, line lengths, point sizes, and the selection of **typefaces** to make written language legible and appealing when displayed.

See Abate 2018; Calvert 2011; De Assis 2015; Lannon 2013; Unser-Schutz 2011.

undemocratic grid: (noun) an arrangement in which **panels** on a **page** do not share the same horizontal and vertical size and do not meet at right angles; a **page lay-out** with unequally sized and nonuniformly **spaced** panels. Cf. **democratic grid**.
See Gavaler 2018b.

underground comics [also underground **comix**]: (noun) adult comics that emerged in the United States in the 1960s that were published independently of and in reaction to the mainstream **publishing** sphere and encouraged a loosening of formal and thematic restrictions of the dominant **mainstream comics** publishing industry; such comics were exempt from the **comics code** and other forms of traditional industry **censorship**. Cf. **groundlevel comics**.
See Arffman 2019; Ault 2005; Bae 2017; Bailey 2002; Beaty and Weiner 2012c; Bradley 2015; Chute 2017; Danky and Kitchen 2009; Estren (1974) 1993; W. Foster 2002; Gabilliet 2018; S. García 2015, 96–116; Groth 1988; Y. Howard 2018; Huxley 2002; Kirtley 2018; Magnussen 2004; Merino 2008; Misemer and Galvan 2019; Noys 2018; Pilcher and Kannenberg 2008; Raeburn 2004; Rifas 2018; Rosenkranz 2008; Skinn 2004; Spiggle 1986; Vandenburg 2012; Vieira and McGurk 2018; Wadsworth 2019.

under guide: (adj.) describing a situation in which a comic book's price is below the Guide list price. Cf. **over guide**.

uppercase: (noun) a form of letter that is different in form and often larger than **lowercase**; a majuscule or capital letter; *A* instead of *a*. Cf. **lowercase**.

upshot [also **low-angle shot**]: (noun) an **angle of framing** that presents what is pictured from an upward angle.

V

value: (noun) the distribution of light and dark areas in an image.

variant cover: an alternative **cover** of a single comic book **issue**, often including art by a different **artist**, that is often regarded as a collectible. See also **incentive cover**.

verbal track: (noun) in comics, one of the primary two **narrative** tracks, consisting of **dialogue, narration**, and other verbal text, and most often excluding visual representations. Cf. **visual track**.

See Fein and Kasher 1996; Lannon 2013; Miodrag 2010; Unser-Schutz 2010; Unser-Schutz 2011.

verso page: (noun) the **page** one reads when one turns over the **recto page**; in Western printing traditions, the left-side **leaf** in any two **facing pages**.

Victorian Age: (noun) an informal name designating early European comics that developed out of the established traditions of **caricature** and **illustration**, roughly extending from the late 1830s to the turn of the century.

See Gifford 1975.

viewpoint: (noun) the point of view that is established in a **panel**.

See Badman 2010; Borkent 2017; Gunning 2014; C. Schneider 2013.

vignette: (noun) a **cartoon** or short comics included in a larger work that captures a defining detail about a **character**, an idea, or another **story** element.

villain [also **antagonist**]: (noun) a character who opposes the **protagonist**. See also **supervillain**.

See Alsford 2006; Drennig 2010; Easton 2013; Madrid 2014; Oehlert 2000; Sereni 2020.

visual iconography: (noun) the vocabulary of comics.

See N. Cohn 2007; Crafton 1979; Kunert-Graf 2018b; Müller and Özcan 2007.

visual literacy: (noun) the ability to read images.

See Frey and Fisher 2008; Nakazawa 2016; Sousanis 2015.

visual
metaphor

visual metaphor [also **pictorial metaphor**]: (noun) an image of one thing that evokes the idea or experience of something else.

See P. F. Davies 2019a, 248–61; El Refaie 2003; El Refaie 2009a; El Refaie 2015; Farinella 2018a; Forceville 2016; Juricevic 2018; Juricevic and Horvath 2016; Kennedy 1982; Pedri and Staveley 2018; Potsch and Williams 2012; Schilperoord and Maes 2009; Shinohara and Matsunaka 2009; Szawerna 2017; Yus 2009.

visual pun: (noun) an image that has a double meaning, at once communicating literally and metaphorically.

visual quotation: (noun) the repetition or close imitation of the **style** or work of another **artist**.

visual rhyme: see **echo**.

visual storytelling: (noun) the conveying of a **narrative** solely by means of images.

See Dooley and Heller 2005; Eisner (1996) 2008c; Martinbrough 2007; Talon and Thompson 2010.

visual track: (noun) in **comics**, one of the primary two tracks, consisting of **drawing**s, images, and other visuals and often excluding text. Cf. **verbal track**.

See Gavaler 2017.

vites: (noun) vertical **lines** used to indicate a shiny surface.

See Walker (1980) 2000, 30.

voice: (noun) the **style** in which a particular author writes; the expression of a **character**'s, a collective's, or a **narrator**'s attitudes, **emotions**, point of view, or **tone** through a combination of rhetorical devices.

See Black 2009; Danziger-Russell 2013; McGlade 2018; Merino 2001; Mickwitz 2020; Munson 2014b; Ōgi 2011; Robertson 2019; Round 2007; Surdiacourt 2012a.

voice-over narration: (noun) **dialogue** set within quotation marks or indicated through other graphic means within a **caption** to denote a speaker who is absent from the **scene** being depicted. Cf. **off-panel balloon.**

volume: (noun) a portion of a **series** that has been restarted with a "Number 1" **issue**; a book.

waffle-iron grid: see **grid.**

waftarom: (noun) a form of **emanata** used to indicate smell.
See Walker (1980) 2000, 29.

want list: (noun) a list of **titles** that a collector or purchaser is interested in acquiring.

warehouse copy: (noun) a comic from a large stock stored in a **publisher's** warehouse.

webcomics [also **web comics**]: (noun) comics published via the internet on the World Wide Web.
See T. Allen 2007; Bae 2017; Batinić 2016; Bramlett 2018; T. Campbell 2006; Carter 2011; Close 2015; M. Duggan 2008; Fenty, Houp, and Taylor 2004; Garrity 2011; Hicks 2009; Jacobs 2014; Kleefeld 2020; Kukkonen 2014; McCloud 2000; Misemer 2018; Slipp 2017; Thoss 2011; Zanfei 2008.

webtoon: (noun) an **infinite canvas format** popular in South Korean **webcomics.**
See Bae 2017.

WECA comics [also **Canadian whites**]: (noun) Canadian War Exchange Conservation Act comics.

weekly: (adj.) published once a week.
See Ito 1994; Ito 1995; Kunzle 1998; Soper 2001.

web comics

whiskers [also **breath marks**]: (noun) diacritical-type marks, usually three-pronged, on either side of a word within a **word balloon** to indicate the non-onomatopoeic **sound** described by that word, especially sounds that cannot easily be turned into **onomatopoeia**, such as choke or sob; popularized by Todd Klein and Tom Orzechowski, longtime hand-**letterer**s for DC and Marvel, respectively.

whisper balloon: (noun) a **word balloon** whose **frame** is broken in short, regular intervals to indicate a low **sound** level; a standard-bordered **word balloon** whose **lettering** is in cursive and/or a much lighter gray **tone** than the other letters to indicate a low sound level.

wide shot: see **long shot**.

woodcut: (noun) a relief **printing** technique wherein the **engraver** carves a relief image into a block of wood, which is then covered in ink and stamped onto the **page**.

woodcut novels: (noun) a type of **wordless comics** usually composed of a single **panel** per **page** printed from a **woodcut**.
    See Beronä 2001; Beronä 2008; Beronä 2013; M. Cohen 1977; Xiao 2013.

word and image combination: (noun) the coupling of words and images within a **panel** or across a **comics page** to create meaning. See also **additive combination**, **interdependent combination**, and **parallel combination**.

See Bateman 2014; K. M. Brown 2018; N. Cohn 2013a; Cuccolini 2010; Gedin 2019; Grove 2005; Lambeens and Pint 2015; Lefèvre 2017; McCloud 1994, 152–61; Sundberg 2017.

word balloon [also **speech balloon**]: (noun) a graphic device, containing letters or other **symbols**, used to represent a **voiced** utterance and to indicate its point of origin; often mistakenly referred to as word bubble.

See Brialey 2013; Carrier 2000, 27–45; N. Cohn 2013a; Dufner and Kim 2014; Lefèvre 2006; Mikkonen 2017, 220–42; Millidge 2009, 102–11; Pellitteri 2019a, 520–26.

wordless comics [also *BD mute, sans paroles,* **silent comics**, and **pantomime comics**]: (noun) a **form** or **genre** of comics that relies entirely on visual images to narrate the story.

See Beronä 2001; Beronä 2008; Groß 2013; P. Johnston 2016; Postema 2014; Postema 2016; Postema 2018.

word panel: (noun) a **panel** that does not contain images. Cf. **silent panel**.

word-specific combination: (noun) a **word and image combination** in which words narrate and images function to illustrate, but not significantly add to, the verbal narrative. Cf. **picture-specific combination**.

See McCloud 1994, 153.

work-for-hire: (noun) a type of contract for creative work in which the contractor legally agrees to renounce any claim to ownership of the work.

worm's-eye view: (noun) an **angle of framing** where the **scene** is presented from a view very close to the ground; an extreme **low angle**.

wraparound cover: (noun) **cover** artwork that extends from the **front cover** to the **back cover**.

writer: (noun) the person who conceptualizes and creates the **story** and **dialogue** for a comic; also referred to as the **author** and, at times, the **scriptor** or **plotter**.

See Bendis 2014; Marx 2006; J. McLaughlin 2009.

writer-artist: see **cartoonist**.

Y

Yellow Kid Thesis: (noun) the belief that the **comics medium** began in 1895 with Richard Felton Outcault's *Hogan's Alley*, featuring the **character** of the Yellow Kid.
See Blackbeard 1995; S. García 2015, 38–49; R. Harvey, West, and Walker 1998; Olson 1993.

Z

---

zero issue: (noun) an **issue** set before the first issue of a comics **series** that acts as a prelude to the rest of the series.

zine: (noun) originating from the word "magazine," an independently published or self-published **minicomic** with a very small circulation. See also **fanzine**.
See Buchanan 2012; Duncombe 1997; Farrelly 2001; Garvey 2002; Hays 2017; Kempson 2014; Kempson 2018; Klanten, Mollard, and Hubner 2011; Licona 2012; R. Miller 2018; Piepmeier 2009; Poletti 2008a; Poletti 2008b; Poletti 2008c; Radway 2011; S. Thomas 2009; Todd and Watson 2006.

Zip-a-Tone: see **screentone**.

zombie comics: (noun) comics that portray zombies or dead **characters** who are brought back to life but who lack human qualities.
See Gries 2015; Perron 2016; Perron 2017; Round 2014a; Servitje and Vint 2016; Sheikh 2014.

zoom: (noun) a visual change between two **panels** toward (zoom in) or away from (zoom out) the same subject.
See Horstkotte 2013.

zoomorphism: (noun) the attribution of animal features or characteristics to **events**, human **figures**, objects, or any other nonanimal thing.
See S. Baker 2001, 121–62; Lamarre 2008.

BIBLIOGRAPHY

Abate, Michelle Ann. 2018. "Reading Capital: Graphic Novels, Typography, and Literacy." *English Journal* 108, no. 1 (September): 66–72.

Abate, Michelle Ann. 2020. "All by Myself: Single-Panel Comics and the Question of Genre." In *The Oxford Handbook of Comic Book Studies*, edited by Frederick Luis Aldama, 132–47. Oxford: Oxford University Press.

Abate, Michelle Ann, Karly Marie Grice, and Christine N. Stamper, eds. 2018. "Lesbian Content and Queer Female Characters in Comics." Special issue, *Journal of Lesbian Studies* 22, no. 4.

Abate, Michelle Ann, Karly Gwen Athene Tarbox, eds. 2017. *Graphic Novels for Children and Young Adults*. Jackson: University Press of Mississippi.

Abbott, Lawrence L. 1986. "Comic Art: Characteristics and Potentialities of a Narrative Medium." *Journal of Popular Culture* 19, no. 4 (Spring): 155–76.

Abdel-Raheem, Ahmed. 2020. "Identity Chains in Newspaper Cartoon Narratives: An Integrative Model." *Journal of Visual Literacy* 39, no. 1: 1–26.

Abdel-Raheem, Ahmed. 2021. "The Multimodal Recycling Machine: Toward a Cognitive-Pragmatic Theory of Text/Image Production." *Journal of Graphic Novels and Comics* 12, no. 3 (June): 207–39.

Abel, Jessica, and Matt Madden. 2008. *Drawing Words and Writing Pictures: Making Comics; Manga, Graphic Novels, and Beyond*. New York: First Second.

Abel, Jessica, and Matt Madden. 2012. *Mastering Comics: Drawing Words and Writing Pictures Continued*. New York: First Second.

Abell, Catharine. 2012. "Comics and Genre." In *The Art of Comics: A Philosophical Approach*, edited by Aaron Meskin and Roy T. Cook, 68–84. Chichester, W. Susx., England: Wiley-Blackwell.

Abusch, Dorit. 2013. "Applying Discourse Semantics and Pragmatics to Co-Reference in Picture Sequences." In *Proceedings of Sinn und Bedeutung 17*, edited by Emmanuel Chemla, Vincent Homer, and Grégoire Winterstein, 9–25. Paris: École Normale Supérieure.

Abusch, Dorit. 2014. "Temporal Succession and Aspectual Type in Visual Narrative." In *The Art and Craft of Semantics: A Festschrift for Irene Heim*, edited by Luka Crnič and Uli Sauerland, 9–29. Cambridge, MA: MIT Working Papers in Linguistics, vols. 70–71.

Adams, Jeff. 2008. *Documentary Graphic Novels and Social Realism*. Bern: Peter Lang.

Adams, Kenneth Alan, and Lester Hill Jr. 1991. "Protest and Rebellion: Fantasy Themes in Japanese Comics." *Journal of Popular Culture* 25, no. 1 (Summer): 99–127.

Adelman, Bob. 1997. *Tijuana Bibles: Art and Wit in America's Forbidden Funnies, 1930s–1950s.* New York: Simon and Schuster Editions.

Adkinson, Cary D. 2008. "*The Amazing Spider-Man* and the Evolution of the Comics Code: A Case Study in Cultural Criminology." *Journal of Criminal Justice and Popular Culture* 15, no. 3: 241–61.

Adler, Silvia. 2011. "Silence in the Graphic Novel: Silence as a Pragmatic Phenomenon." *Journal of Pragmatics: An Interdisciplinary Journal of Language Studies* 43, no. 9 (July): 2278–85.

Adler, Silvia. 2013. "Silent and Semi-Silent Arguments in the Graphic Novel." *Pragmatics* 23, no. 3 (September): 389–402.

Aggleton, Jen. 2019. "Defining Digital Comics: A British Library Perspective." *Journal of Graphic Novels and Comics* 10, no. 4 (August): 393–409.

Ahmed, Jameel. 2016. "Negotiating Artistic Identity in Comics Collaboration." In *Cultures of Comics Work*, edited by Casey Brienza and Paddy Johnston, 175–88. New York: Palgrave Macmillan.

Ahmed, Maaheen. 2014. "The Art of Splicing: Autofiction in Words and Images." *International Journal of Comic Art* 16, no. 1 (Spring): 322–38.

Ahmed, Maaheen. 2016. *Openness of Comics: Generating Meaning within Flexible Structures.* Jackson: University Press of Mississippi.

Ahmed, Maaheen. 2017. "Comics and Authorship: An Introduction." *Authorship* 6, no. 2: 1–13.

Ahmed, Maaheen, and Benoît Crucifix, eds. 2018. *Comics Memory: Archives and Styles.* Cham, Switzerland: Palgrave Macmillan.

Ahmed, Meena. 2010. "Exploring the Dimensions of Political Cartoons: A Case Study of Pakistan." *International Journal of Comic Art* 12, nos. 2–3 (Fall): 525–42.

Ahrens, Jörn, and Arno Meteling, eds. 2010. *Comics and the City: Urban Space in Print, Picture and Sequence.* New York: Continuum.

Alaniz, José. 2004. "Supercrip: Disability and the Marvel Silver Age Superhero." *International Journal of Comic Art* 6, no. 2 (Fall): 304–24.

Alaniz, José. 2006. "Death and the Superhero: The Silver Age and Beyond." *International Journal of Comic Art* 8, no. 1 (Spring): 234–48.

Alaniz, José. 2010. *Komiks: Comic Art in Russia.* Jackson: University Press of Mississippi.

Alaniz, José. 2014. *Death, Disability, and the Superhero: The Silver Age and Beyond.* Jackson: University Press of Mississippi.

Alaniz, José. 2020. "Animals in Graphic Narrative." In *The Oxford Handbook of Comic Book Studies*, edited by Frederick Luis Aldama, 326–34. Oxford: Oxford University Press.

Alary, Viviane. 2002. *Historietas, comics y tebeos españoles.* Toulouse: Presses Universitaires du Mirail.

Aldama, Frederick Luis. 2009. *Your Brain on Latino Comics: From Gus Arriola to Los Bros Hernandez.* Austin: University of Texas Press.

Aldama, Frederick Luis. 2017. *Latinx Superheroes in Mainstream Comics.* Tucson: University of Arizona Press.

Aldama, Frederick Luis, ed. 2018a. *Comics Studies Here and Now*. New York: Routledge.

Aldama, Frederick Luis. 2018b. *Tales from La Vida: A Latinx Comics Anthology*. Columbus, OH: Mad Creek Books.

Aldama, Frederick Luis, ed. 2020a. *Graphic Indigeneity: Comics in the Americas and Australasia*. Jackson: University Press of Mississippi.

Aldama, Frederick Luis, ed. 2020b. *The Oxford Handbook of Comic Book Studies*. Oxford: Oxford University Press.

Aldama, Frederick Luis, ed. 2021. *The Routledge Companion to Gender and Sexuality in Comic Book Studies*. Abingdon, Oxon., England: Routledge.

Aldama, Frederick Luis, and Christopher González, eds. 2016. *Graphic Borders: Latino Comic Books Past, Present, and Future*. Austin: University of Texas Press.

Alexander, Dorian. 2018. "Faces of Abjectivity: The Uncanny Mystique and Transsexuality." In *Gender and the Superhero Narrative*, edited by Michael Goodrum, Tara Prescott, and Philip Smith, 180–204. Jackson: University Press of Mississippi.

Alexio, Paul A., and Krystina Sumner. 2017. "Memory for Biopsychology Material Presented in Comic Book Format." *Journal of Graphic Novels and Comics* 8, no. 1 (February): 79–88.

Allen, Harriet. 2011. "Anime-Noir; or, How Three Key Anime Participate in the Lasting Legacy of Noir." *Crimeculture*, Summer. http://www.crimeculture.com/?page_id=1641.

Allen, Kate, and John E. Ingulsrud. 2005. "Reading Manga: Patterns of Personal Literacies among Adolescents." *Language and Education* 19, no. 4: 265–80.

Allen, Todd W. 2007. *The Economics of Web Comics: A Study in Converting Content into Revenue*. Chicago: Indignant Media.

Allison, Anne. 2000. *Permitted and Prohibited Desires: Mothers, Comics, and Censorship in Japan*. Berkeley: University of California Press.

Alsford, Mike. 2006. *Heroes and Villains*. Waco, TX: Baylor University Press.

Altehenger, Jennifer. 2013. "A Socialist Satire: *Manhua* Magazine and Political Cartoon Production in the PRC, 1950–1960." *Frontiers of History in China* 8, no. 1: 78–103.

Amago, Samuel, and Matthew J. Marr, eds. 2019. *Consequential Art: Comics Culture in Contemporary Spain*. Toronto: University of Toronto Press.

Amaral, Thiago de Almeida Castor do. 2016. "Migration of Comics Onomatopoeia to Other Supports." *International Journal of Comic Art* 18, no. 1 (Spring–Summer): 278–92.

Andersen, Camilla Baasch. 2021. "Musings on the Comic Book Contract Project and Legal Design Thinking." *Journal of Graphic Novels and Comics* 12, no. 1 (February): 39–45.

Andrews, Julia F. 1997. "Literature in Line: Picture Stories in the People's Republic of China." *Inks: Cartoon and Comic Art Studies* 4, no. 3 (November): 17–32.

Aragão, Octavio. 2012. "Brazilian Science Fiction and the Visual Arts: From Political Cartoons to Contemporary Comics." In *Latin American Science Fiction: Theory and Practice*, edited by M. Elizabeth Ginway and J. Andrew Brown, 185–202. New York: Palgrave Macmillan.

Arffman, Päivi. 2019. "Comics from the Underground: Publishing Revolutionary Comic Books in the 1960s and Early 1970s." *Journal of Popular Culture* 52, no. 1 (February): 169–98.

Arizpe, Evelyn. 2013. "Meaning-Making from Wordless (or Nearly Wordless) Picturebooks: What Educational Research Expects and What Readers Have to Say." *Cambridge Journal of Education* 43, no. 2 (June): 163–76.

Arnaudo, Marco. 2013. *The Myth of the Superhero.* Translated by Jamie Richards. Baltimore: Johns Hopkins University Press.

Arndt, Richard J. 2013. *Horror Comics in Black and White: A History and Catalog, 1964–2004.* Jefferson, NC: McFarland.

Ashwal, Gary, and Alex Thomas. 2018. "Are Comic Books Appropriate Health Education Formats to Offer Adult Patients?" *AMA Journal of Ethics* 20, no. 2 (February): 134–40. http://journalofethics.ama-assn.org/2018/02/ecas1-1802.html.

Asimakoulas, Dimitris. 2019. *Rewriting Humour in Comic Books: Cultural Transfer and Translation of Aristophanic Adaptations.* Cham, Switzerland: Palgrave Macmillan.

Astor, Dave. 2002. "Serious Competition in Comics Pagination." *Editor and Publisher* 135, no. 12 (March 25): 27–28.

Atkinson, Paul. 2009. "Movements within Movements: Following the Line in Animation and Comic Books." *Animation: An Interdisciplinary Journal* 4, no. 3 (November): 265–81.

Atkinson, Paul. 2010. "The Graphic Novel as Metafiction." *Studies in Comics* 1, no. 1 (April): 107–25.

Atkinson, Paul. 2018. "Between Movement and Reading: Reconceptualizing the Dynamic Picture Plane in Modernist Comics and Painting." *ImageTexT: Interdisciplinary Comics Studies* 9, no. 3. http://www.english.ufl.edu/imagetext/archives/v9_3/atkinson/.

Atkinson, Terence. 1971. *More Little "Dirty" Comics.* Vol. 2. San Diego: Socio Library.

Ault, Donald. 2005. "Preludium: Crumb, Barks, and Noomin; Re-Considering the Aesthetics of Underground Comics." *ImageTexT: Interdisciplinary Comics Studies* 1, no. 2. http://www.english.ufl.edu/imagetext/archives/v1_2/intro.shtml.

Austin, Allan W., and Patrick L. Hamilton. 2019. *All New, All Different? A History of Race and the American Superhero.* Austin: University of Texas Press.

Avery-Natale, Edward. 2013. "An Analysis of Embodiment among Six Superheroes in DC Comics." *Social Thought and Research* 32: 71–106.

Babic, Annessa Ann, ed. 2014. *Comics as History, Comics as Literature: Roles of the Comic Book in Scholarship, Society, and Entertainment.* Madison, NJ: Fairleigh Dickinson University Press.

Babic, Annessa Ann. 2018. *America's Changing Icons: Constructing Patriotic Women from World War I to the Present.* Lanham, MD: Rowman and Littlefield.

Badman, Derik A. 2010. "Talking, Thinking, and Seeing in Pictures: Narration, Focalization, and Ocularization in Comics Narratives." *International Journal of Comic Art* 12, no. 2 (Fall): 91–111.

Bae, Keung Yoon "Becky." 2017. "From Underground to the Palm of Your Hand: The Spatiality and Cultural Practice of South Korean Webtoons." *East Asian Journal of Popular Culture* 3, no. 1 (April): 73–84.

Baetens, Jan. 2001. "Revealing Traces: A New Theory of Graphic Enunciation." In *The Language of Comics: Word and Image*, edited by Robin Varnum and Christina T. Gibbons, 145–55. Jackson: University Press of Mississippi.

Baetens, Jan. 2003. "Comic Strips and Constrained Writing." *Image [&] Narrative: Online Magazine of the Visual Narrative* 4, no. 1 (October). http://www.imageandnarrative.be/inarchive/graphicnovel/janbaetens_constrained.htm.

Baetens, Jan. 2009. "A Cultural Approach of Non-Narrative Graphic Novels: A Case Study from Flanders." In *Teaching the Graphic Novel*, edited by Stephen E. Tabachnick, 281–87. New York: Modern Language Association of America.

Baetens, Jan. 2010. *Pour le roman-photo*. Brussels: Les Impressions Nouvelles.

Baetens, Jan. 2011a. "Abstraction in Comics." *SubStance* 40, no. 1: 94–113.

Baetens, Jan. 2011b. "From Black & White to Color and Back: What Does It Mean (Not) to Use Color?" *College Literature* 38, no. 3 (Summer): 111–28.

Baetens, Jan. 2013a. "The 'Photo-Graphic Novel': Hybridization and Genre Theory." In *The Cultural Dynamics of Generic Change in Contemporary Fiction: Theoretical Frameworks, Genres and Model Interpretations*, edited by Michael Basseler, Ansgar Nünning, and Christine Schwanecke, 147–62. Trier, Germany: Wissenschaftlicher Verlag Trier.

Baetens, Jan. 2013b. "The Photo-Novel: Stereotype as Surprise." *History of Photography* 37, no. 2: 137–52.

Baetens, Jan. 2015. "The Photographic Novel." In *Handbook of Intermediality: Literature–Image–Sound–Music*, edited by Gabriele Rippl, 219–39. Berlin: Walter de Gruyter.

Baetens, Jan. 2017. "Drawing Photo Novels." *ImageTexT: Interdisciplinary Comics Studies* 9, no. 2. http://imagetext.english.ufl.edu/archives/v9_2/baetens/.

Baetens, Jan. 2018a. "Hybridized Popular Literature: Fotoromanzi and Cineromanzi in Postwar Italy and France." *Inks: The Journal of the Comics Studies Society* 2, no. 3 (Fall): 271–87.

Baetens, Jan. 2018b. "The Postwar 'Drawn Novel.'" In *The Cambridge History of the Graphic Novel*, edited by Jan Baetens, Hugo Frey, and Stephen E. Tabachnick, 75–91. Cambridge: Cambridge University Press.

Baetens, Jan. 2020. "Literary Adaptations in Comics and Graphic Novels." In *The Oxford Handbook of Comic Book Studies*, edited by Frederick Luis Aldama, 611–29. Oxford: Oxford University Press.

Baetens, Jan, and Mieke Bleyen. 2010. "Photo Narrative, Sequential Photography, Photonovels." In *Intermediality and Storytelling*, edited by Marina Grishakova and Marie-Laure Ryan, 165–82. Berlin: Walter de Gruyter.

Baetens, Jan, and Hugo Frey. 2015. *The Graphic Novel: An Introduction*. Cambridge: Cambridge University Press.

Baetens, Jan, Hugo Frey, and Stephen E. Tabachnick, eds. 2018. *The Cambridge History of the Graphic Novel*. Cambridge: Cambridge University Press.

Baetens, Jan, and Ana Gonzalez. 1996. *Le Roman-photo: Actes du colloque de Calaceite (Fondation NOESIS)*. Leiden: Brill Rodopi.

Baetens, Jan, and Clémentine Mélois. 2018. *Le Roman-photo*. Brussels: Le Lombard.

Baetens, Jan, and Charlotte Pylyser. 2017. "Comics and Time." In *The Routledge Companion to Comics*, edited by Frank Bramlett, Roy T. Cook, and Aaron Meskin, 303‑10. New York: Routledge.

Bahl, Erin Kathleen, Sergio Figueiredo, and Rich Shivener, eds. 2020. "Comics and Graphic Storytelling in Technical Communication." Special issue, *Technical Communication Quarterly* 29, no. 3.

Bailey, Beth. 2002. "Sex as a Weapon: Underground Comix and the Paradox of Liberation." In *Imagine Nation: The American Counterculture of the 1960s and '70s*, edited by Peter Braunstein and Michael William Doyle, 305–24. New York: Routledge.

Bainbridge, Jason, and Craig Norris. 2010. "Hybrid Manga: Implications for the Global Knowledge Economy." In *Manga: An Anthology of Global and Cultural Perspectives*, edited by Toni Johnson-Woods, 235–52. New York: Continuum.

Bajac-Carter, Maja, Norma Jones, and Bob Batchelor, eds. 2014. *Heroines of Comic Books and Literature: Portrayals in Popular Culture*. Lanham, MD: Rowman and Littlefield.

Bake, Julika, and Michaela Zöhrer. 2017. "Telling the Stories of Others: Claims of Authenticity in Human Rights Reporting and Comics Journalism." *Journal of Intervention and Statebuilding* 11, no. 1 (February): 81–97.

Baker, Bill. 2008. "The Essential Sequential Steampunk: A Modest Survey of the Genre within the Comic Book Medium." In *Steampunk*, edited by Ann VanderMeer and Jeff VanderMeer, 359–68. San Francisco: Tachyon Publications.

Baker, Steve. 2001. *Picturing the Beast: Animals, Identity, and Representation*. Urbana: University of Illinois Press.

Bakis, Maureen. 2014. *The Graphic Novel Classroom: POWerful Teaching and Learning with Images*. Thousand Oaks, CA: Corwin Press.

Balzer, Jens. 2006. "Wam – Clonk – Chomp – Zow – Bop: On the Physics of Sound in the Comics." In *Comic Meets Theatre*, edited by Annegret Hahn and Berit Schuck, 124–27. Berlin: Theater der Zeit.

Bamberger, W. C. 2017. "Social Justice and Silver Age Superheroes." In *The Ages of the Justice League: Essays on America's Greatest Superheroes in Changing Times*, edited by Joseph J. Darowski, 50–57. Jefferson, NC: McFarland.

Banita, Georgiana. 2013. "Cosmopolitan Suspicion: Comics Journalism and Graphic Silence." In *Transnational Perspectives on Graphic Narratives: Comics at the Crossroads*, edited by Shane Denson, Christina Meyer, and Daniel Stein, 49–66. London: Bloomsbury.

Barbee, Christopher. 2008. "The Silver Age Legion: Adventure into the Classics." In *Teenagers from the Future: Essays on the Legion of Super-Heroes*, edited by Timothy Callahan, 49–58. Edwardsville, IL: Sequart Research and Literacy Organization.

Bares, William. 2008. "Panel Beat: Layout and Timing of Comic Panels." In *Smart Graphics: 6th International Symposium, Proceedings*, edited by Andreas Butz, Brian Fisher, Antonio Krüger, Patrick Olivier, and Marc Christie, 273–76. Berlin: Springer Verlag.

Baricordi, Andrea, Massimiliano de Giovanni, Andrea Pietroni, Barbara Rossi, and Sabrina Tunesi. 2000. *Anime: A Guide to Japanese Animation (1958–1988)*. Translated by Adeline D'Opera. Montreal: Protoculture.

Barker, Kenneth. 1996. "The Comic Series of the *New York Sunday Herald* 1899–1924 and the *New York Sunday Tribune* 1914–1916, 1919–1924." *Inks: Cartoon and Comic Art Studies* 3, no. 2: 10–19.

Barker, Kenneth. 1997. "An Introduction to the Canadian Newspaper Comic." *Inks: Cartoon and Comic Art Studies* 4, no. 2: 18–25.

Barker, Martin. 1989. *Comics: Ideology, Power, and the Critics*. Manchester: Manchester University Press.

Barker, Martin. (1984) 1992. *A Haunt of Fears: The Strange History of the British Horror Comics Campaign*. Jackson: University Press of Mississippi.

Baroni, Raphaël. 2016. "(Un)natural Temporalities in Comics." *European Comic Art* 9, no. 1 (March): 5–23.

Barry, Erin. 2017. "Eight-Page Eroticism: Sexual Violence and the Construction of Normative Masculinity in Tijuana Bibles." *Journal of Graphic Novels and Comics* 8, no. 3 (June): 227–37.

Bartosch, Sebastian, and Andreas Stuhlmann. 2013. "Reconsidering Adaptation as Translation: The Comic in Between." *Studies in Comics* 4, no. 1 (April): 59–74.

Bateman, John A. 2008. *Multimodality and Genre: A Foundation for the Systematic Analysis of Multimodal Documents*. Basingstoke, Hants., England: Palgrave Macmillan.

Bateman, John A. 2014. *Text and Image: A Critical Introduction to the Visual/Verbal Divide*. Abingdon, Oxon., England: Routledge.

Bateman, John A., Francisco O. D. Veloso, and Yan Ling Lau. 2021. "On the Track of Visual Style: A Diachronic Study of Page Composition in Comics and Its Functional Motivation." *Visual Communication* 20, no. 2 (May): 209–47.

Bateman, John A., Francisco O. D. Veloso, Janina Wildfeuer, Felix Hiu Laam Cheung, and Nancy Songdan Guo. 2017. "An Open Multilevel Classification Scheme for the Visual Layout of Comics and Graphic Novels: Motivation and Design." *Digital Scholarship in the Humanities* 32, no. 3 (June): 476–510.

Bateman, John A., and Janina Wildfeuer. 2014a. "Defining Units of Analysis for the Systematic Analysis of Comics: A Discourse-Based Approach." *Studies in Comics* 5, no. 2 (October): 373–403.

Bateman, John A., and Janina Wildfeuer. 2014b. "A Multimodal Discourse Theory of Visual Narrative." *Journal of Pragmatics* 74 (October): 180–208.

Batinić, Josip. 2016. "'Enhanced Webcomics': An Exploration of the Hybrid Form of Comics on the Digital Medium." *Image [&] Narrative: Online Magazine of the Visual Narrative* 17, no. 5 (January): 80–91. http://www.imageandnarrative.be/index.php/imagenarrative/article/view/1384/1114.

Batkin, Jane. 2017. *Identity in Animation: A Journey into Self, Difference, Culture and the Body*. London: Routledge.

Baudinette, Thomas. 2017. "Japanese Gay Men's Attitudes towards 'Gay Manga' and the Problem of Genre." *East Asian Journal of Popular Culture* 3, no. 1: 59–72.

Baudry, Julien. 2018. "Paradoxes of Innovation in French Digital Comics." *The Comics Grid: Journal of Comics Scholarship* 8, no. 1: 1–24. https://www.comicsgrid.com/article/id/3564/.

Bearden-White, Roy. 2009. "Closing the Gap: Examining the Invisible Sign in Graphic Narratives." *International Journal of Comic Art* 11, no. 1 (Spring): 347–62.

Beaty, Bart. 2001. "Fredric Wertham Faces His Critics: Contextualizing the Postwar Comics Debate." *International Journal of Comic Art* 3, no. 2 (Fall): 202–21.

Beaty, Bart. 2005. *Fredric Wertham and the Critique of Mass Culture.* Jackson: University Press of Mississippi.

Beaty, Bart. 2007. *Unpopular Culture: Transforming the European Comic Book in the 1990s.* Toronto: University of Toronto Press.

Beaty, Bart. 2008. "The Concept of 'Patrimoine' in Contemporary Franco-Belgian Comics Production." In *History and Politics in French-Language Comics and Graphic Novels*, edited by Mark McKinney, 69–93. Jackson: University Press of Mississippi.

Beaty, Bart. 2009. "Autobiography as Authenticity." In *A Comics Studies Reader*, edited by Jeet Heer and Kent Worcester, 226–35. Jackson: University Press of Mississippi.

Beaty, Bart. 2012. *Comics versus Art.* Toronto: University of Toronto Press.

Beaty, Bart, and Stephen Weiner, eds. 2012a. *Critical Survey of Graphic Novels: History, Theme, and Technique.* Ipswich, MA: Salem Press.

Beaty, Bart, and Stephen Weiner, eds. 2012b. *Critical Survey of Graphic Novels: Heroes and Superheroes.* Ipswich, MA: Salem Press.

Beaty, Bart, and Stephen Weiner, eds. 2012c. *Critical Survey of Graphic Novels: Independents and Underground Classics.* Ipswich, MA: Salem Press.

Beaty, Bart, and Stephen Weiner, eds. 2013. *Critical Survey of Graphic Novels: Manga.* Ipswich, MA: Salem Press.

Beaty, Bart, and Benjamin Woo. 2016. *The Greatest Comic Book of All Time: Symbolic Capital and the Field of American Comic Books.* New York: Palgrave Macmillan.

Beaty, Bart, Benjamin Woo, Brian Johnson, and Miranda Campbell. 2020. "Theorizing Comic Cons." *Journal of Fandom Studies* 8, no. 1 (March): 9–31.

Becker, Richard A. 2009. "The Crisis of Confidence in Comics Adaptations: Why Comics Are So Rarely Faithfully Adapted to the Big Screen." *International Journal of Comic Art* 11, no. 1 (Spring): 436–56.

Becker, Thomas. 2011. "Cool Premedialisation as Symbolic Capital of Innovation: On Intercultural Intermediality between Comics, Literature, Film, Manga, and Anime." In *Intercultural Crossovers, Transcultural Flows: Manga/Comics*, edited by Jaqueline Berndt, 107–17. Kyoto: Kyoto Seika University International Manga Research Center.

Belk, Russell W. 1987. "Material Values in the Comics: A Content Analysis of Comic Books Featuring Themes of Wealth." *Journal of Consumer Research* 14, no. 1 (June): 26–42.

Bell, John. 2006. *Invaders from the North: How Canada Conquered the Comic Book Universe.* Toronto: Dundurn Group.

Bendis, Brian Michael. 2014. *Words for Pictures: The Art and Business of Writing Comics and Graphic Novels*. New York: Watson-Guptill.

Benedetti, Alejo, ed. 2019. *Men of Steel, Women of Wonder: Modern American Superheroes in Contemporary Art*. Fayetteville: University of Arkansas Press.

Bennett, Jill. 1982. *Learning to Read with Picture Books*. Stroud, Glos., England: Thimble Press.

Bennett, Tamryn. 2014. "Comics Poetry: Beyond 'Sequential Art.'" *Image [&] Narrative: Online Magazine of the Visual Narrative* 15, no. 2 (July): 106–23. http://www.imageandnarrative .be/index.php/imagenarrative/article/view/544/397.

Bennett, Tamryn, and Guillermo Batiz. 2014. "Comics Poetry: Praxis and Pedagogy." *ImageTexT: Interdisciplinary Comics Studies* 7, no. 3. http://imagetext.english.ufl.edu/ archives/v7_3/bennett_and_batiz/.

Benton, Mike. 1991. *Superhero Comics of the Silver Age: The Illustrated History*. Dallas: Taylor Publishing.

Benton, Mike. 1992a. *Superhero Comics of the Golden Age: The Illustrated History*. Dallas: Taylor Publishing.

Benton, Mike. 1992b. *Science Fiction Comics: The Illustrated History*. Dallas: Taylor Publishing.

Berenstein, Ofer. 2012. "Comic Book Fans' Recommendations Ceremony: A Look at the Inter-Personal Communication Patterns of a Unique Readers/Speakers Community." *Participations: Journal of Audience and Reception Studies* 9, no. 2 (November): 74–96.

Beringer, Alex. 2015. "Transatlantic Picture Stories: Experiments in the Antebellum American Comic Strip." *American Literature* 87, no. 3 (September): 455–88.

Berlatsky, Eric. 2009. "Lost in the Gutter: Within and Between Frames in Narrative and Narrative Theory." *Narrative* 17, no. 2 (May): 162–87.

Berndt, Jaqueline. 2012a. "Manga x Museum in Contemporary Japan." In *Manhwa, Manga, Manhua: East Asian Comics Studies*, edited by Jaqueline Berndt, 141–50. Leipzig: Leipziger Universitätsverlag.

Berndt, Jaqueline, ed. 2012b. *Manhwa, Manga, Manhua: East Asian Comics Studies*. Leipzig: Leipziger Universitätsverlag.

Berndt, Jaqueline. 2013. "Ghostly: 'Asian Graphic Narratives' *Nonnonba*, and Manga." In *From Comic Strips to Graphic Novels: Contributions to the Theory and History of Graphic Narrative*, edited by Daniel Stein and Jan-Noël Thon, 363–84. Berlin: Walter de Gruyter.

Berndt, Jaqueline. 2018. "Anime in Academia: Representative Object, Media Form, and Japanese Studies." *Arts* 7, no. 4 (September): 1–13. https://www.mdpi.com/2076-0752/7/4/56.

Berndt, Jaqueline, and Bettina Kümmerling-Meibauer, eds. 2014. *Manga's Cultural Crossroads*. New York: Routledge.

Berndt, Jaqueline, and Steffi Richter, eds. 2006. *Reading Manga: Local and Global Perceptions of Japanese Comics*. Leipzig: Leipziger Universitätsverlag.

Berninger, Mark, Jochen Ecke, and Gideon Haberkorn, eds. 2010. *Comics as a Nexus of Cultures: Essays on the Interplay of Media, Disciplines and International Perspectives*. Jefferson, NC: McFarland.

Beronä, David A. 2001. "Pictures Speak in Comics without Words: Pictorial Principles in the World of Milt Gross, Hendrik Dorgathen, Eric Drooker, and Peter Kuper." In *The Language of Comics: Word and Image*, edited by Robin Varnum and Christina T. Gibbons, 19–39. Jackson: University Press of Mississippi.

Beronä, David A. 2008. *Wordless Books: The Original Graphic Novels*. New York: Harry N. Abrams.

Beronä, David A. 2013. "Woodcut Novels: Cutting a Path to the Graphic Novel." Comics Forum, May 23. https://comicsforum.org/2013/05/23/woodcut-novels-cutting-a-path -to-the-graphic-novel-by-david-a-berona/.

Berry, Dan. 2013. "Hourly Comics Day." *Studies in Comics* 4, no. 2 (October): 401–11.

Besel, Jennifer M. 2011. *The Captivating, Creative, Unusual History of Comic Books*. Mankato, MN: Capstone Press.

Best, Daniel. 2013. *The 1955 Romance Comics Trial*. Saint Peters, SA, Australia: Blaq Books.

Bevan, Paul. 2016. *A Modern Miscellany: Shanghai Cartoon Artists, Shao Xunmei's Circle and the Travels of Jack Chen, 1926–1938*. Leiden: Brill.

Bhadury, Poushali. 2018. "'There Is No Such Thing as a Straight Woman': Queer Female Representations in South Asian Graphic Narratives." *Journal of Lesbian Studies* 22, no. 4: 424–34.

Bhatia, Tej K. 2006. "Super-Heroes to Super Languages: American Popular Culture through South Asian Language Comics." *World Englishes* 25, no. 2 (May): 279–98.

Birken, Jacob. 2014. "Set Pieces: Cultural Appropriation and the Search for Contemporary Identities in Shōnen Manga." In *Representing Multiculturalism in Comics and Graphic Novels*, edited by Carolene Ayaka and Ian Hague, 146–62. New York: Routledge.

Birmingham, Elizabeth. 2013. "Girls' Fantasies, Freedom, and Brotherly Love: Incest Narratives in Shōjo Anime." *Intensities: The Journal of Cult Media*, no. 5 (Spring–Summer): 24–47. https://intensitiescultmedia.files.wordpress.com/2013/07/girls_-fantasies-free dom-and-brotherly-love-incest-narratives-in-shc58djo-anime-elizabeth-birmingham.pdf.

Black, James Eric. 2009. "Amoozin' but Confoozin': Comic Strips as a Voice of Dissent in the 1950s." *ETC: A Review of General Semantics* 66, no. 4 (October): 460–77.

Blackbeard, Bill, ed. 1995. *R. F. Outcault's "The Yellow Kid": A Centennial Celebration of the Kid Who Started the Comics*. Northampton, MA: Kitchen Sink Press.

Blackbeard, Bill. 2003. "The Four Color Paper Trail: A Look Back." *International Journal of Comic Art* 5, no. 2 (Fall): 205–15.

Bladow, Kyle. 2019. "Framing Storytelling: Indigenous Graphic Narratives." *Journal of Popular Culture* 52, no. 1 (February): 35–52.

Blanc-Hoàng, Henri-Simon. 2017. "Colonialism, Postcolonialism and Science Fiction Comics in the Southern Cone." *Studies in Comics* 8, no. 1 (July): 29–49.

Blank, Juliane. 2017. "'. . . But Is It Literature?' Graphic Adaptation in Germany in the Context of High and Popular Culture." *European Comic Art* 10, no. 1 (March): 74–93.

Blin-Rolland, Armelle, Guillaume Lecomte, and Marc Ripley, eds. 2017. "Comics and Adaptation." Special issue, *European Comic Art* 10 no. 1 (March).

Blum, Elizabeth D. 2018. "Tracing Views of Nature in the Marvel Cinematic Universe." In *Assembling the Marvel Cinematic Universe: Essays on the Social, Cultural and Geopolitical Domains*, edited by Julian C. Chambliss, William L. Svitavsky, and Daniel Fandino, 127–40. Jefferson, NC: McFarland.

Boillat, Alain. 2017. "Perspectives on Cinema and Comics: Adapting Feature Films into French-Language Comics Serials during the Post-War Years." *European Comic Art* 10, no. 1 (March): 9–23.

Bolling, Ben, and Matthew J. Smith, eds. 2014. *It Happens at Comic-Con: Ethnographic Essays on a Pop Culture Phenomenon*. Jefferson, NC: McFarland.

Bolton, Ben. 2012. "The U.S. HIV/AIDS Crisis and the Negotiation of Queer Identity in Superhero Comics; or, Is Northstar Still a Fairy?" In *Comic Books and American Cultural History: An Anthology*, edited by Matthew Pustz, 202–19. New York: Continuum.

Bolton, Christopher. 2018. *Interpreting Anime*. Minneapolis: University of Minnesota Press.

Bolton, Matthew. 2011. "Fidelity and Period Aesthetics in Comics Adaptation." *ImageTexT: Interdisciplinary Comics Studies* 6, no. 1. http://imagetext.english.ufl.edu/archives/v6_1/ bolton/.

Bongco, Mila. 2000. *Reading Comics: Language, Culture, and the Concept of the Superhero in Comic Books*. New York: Garland Publishing.

Bonifazio, Paola. 2017. "Political Photoromances: The Italian Communist Party, *Famiglia Cristiana*, and the Struggle for Women's Hearts." *Italian Studies* 72, no. 4 (November): 393–413.

Bonifazio, Paola. 2020. *The Photoromance: A Feminist Reading of Popular Culture*. Cambridge, MA: MIT Press.

Booker, M. Keith. 2014. *Comics through Time: A History of Icons, Idols, and Ideas*. Santa Barbara, CA: Greenwood.

Booth, Paul. 2015. *Playing Fans: Negotiating Fandom and Media in the Digital Age*. Iowa City: University of Iowa Press.

Borggreen, Gunhild. 2015. "Drawing Disaster: Manga Response to the Great Eastern Japan Earthquake." In *Comics and Power: Representing and Questioning Culture, Subjects and Communities*, edited by Rikke Platz Cortsen, Erin La Cour, and Anne Magnussen, 263–84. Newcastle upon Tyne: Cambridge Scholars Publishing.

Borkent, Mike. 2017. "Mediated Characters: Multimodal Viewpoint Construction in Comics." *Cognitive Linguistics* 28, no. 3: 539–63.

Borodo, Michał. 2015. "Multimodality, Translation and Comics." *Perspectives* 23, no. 1: 22–41.

Boschenhoff, Sandra Eva. 2014. *Tall Tales in Comic Diction, from Literature to Graphic Fiction: An Intermedial Analysis of Comic Adaptations of Literary Texts*. Trier, Germany: Wissenschaftlicher Verlag Trier.

Bounegru, Liliana, and Charles Forceville. 2011. "Metaphors in Editorial Cartoons Representing the Global Financial Crisis." *Visual Communication* 10, no. 2 (May): 209–29.

Bourdaa, Mélanie. 2013. "'Following the Pattern': The Creation of an Encyclopaedic Universe with Transmedia Storytelling." *Adaptation* 6, no. 2 (August): 202–14.

Bowden, Jonathan. 2013. *Pulp Fascism: Right-Wing Themes in Comics, Graphic Novels, and Popular Literature*. San Francisco: Counter-Currents.

Bowkett, Steve, and Tony Hitchman. 2012. *Using Comic Art to Improve Speaking, Reading and Writing*. Abingdon, Oxon., England: Routledge.

Boykin, Jessica. 2019. "Filling in the Gutters: Graphic Biographies Disrupting Dominant Narratives of the Civil Rights Movement." *Journal of Multimodal Rhetorics* 3, no. 1 (Spring): 68–85. http://journalofmultimodalrhetorics.com/files/documents/3e 1da5ea-f18e-4dc0-abda-96dbf877eb3e.pdf.

Brabant, Sarah, and Linda A. Mooney. 1997. "Sex Role Stereotyping in the Sunday Comics: A Twenty Year Update." *Sex Roles: A Journal of Research* 37, nos. 3–4 (May): 269–81.

Bradley, Drew. 2015. "Small Press Month: A Brief History of Underground Comix." *Multiversity Comics*, February 3. http://www.multiversitycomics.com/news-columns/ small-press-month-a-brief-history-of-underground-comix/.

Bramlett, Frank. 2018. "Linguistic Discourse in Web Comics: Extending Conversation and Narrative into Alt-Text and Hidden Comics." In *The Language of Popular Culture*, edited by Valentin Werner, 72–91. New York: Routledge.

Bramlett, Frank, Roy T. Cook, and Aaron Meskin, eds. 2017. *The Routledge Companion to Comics*. New York: Routledge.

Brandl, Mark Staff. 2007. "Panels, Cover, and Viewers: My Mongrels of Painting, Installation, and Comics." *International Journal of Comic Art* 9, no. 2 (Fall): 43–57.

Braund, Steve. 2015. "The Itinerant Illustration: Creating Storyworlds in the Reader's Space." *Journal of Illustration* 2, no. 2 (December): 267–85.

Brenner, Robin E. 2007. *Understanding Manga and Anime*. Westport, CT: Libraries Unlimited.

Brent, Ruth S. 1991. "Nonverbal Design Language in Comics." *The Journal of American Culture* 14, no. 1 (March): 57–61.

Bresler, Liora. 2009. "University Faculty as Intellectual Entrepreneurs: Vision, Experimental Learning, and Animation." *Visual Arts Research* 35, no. 1 (Summer): 12–23.

Bresnahan, Mary Jiang, Yasuhiro Inoue, and Naomi Kagawa. 2006. "Players and Whiners? Perceptions of Sex Stereotyping in Animé in Japan and the US." *Asian Journal of Communication* 16, no. 2: 207–17.

Brialey, Leonie. 2013. "Sincerity and Speech Balloons: The Shape and Weight of Words in Autobiographical Comics." In *Cultural Excavation and Formal Expression in the Graphic Novel*, edited by Jonathan C. Evans and Thomas Giddens, 217–24. Oxford: Oxford University Press.

Brienza, Casey. 2010. "Producing Comics Culture: A Sociological Approach to the Study of Comics." *Journal of Graphic Novels and Comics* 1, no. 2 (December): 105–19.

Brienza, Casey. 2013. "Objects of *Otaku* Affection: Animism, *Anime* Fandom, and the Gods of . . . Consumerism?" In *The Handbook of Contemporary Animism*, edited by Graham Harvey, 479–90. Abingdon, Oxon., England: Routledge.

Brienza, Casey. 2016. *Manga in America: Transnational Book Publishing and the Domestication of Japanese Comics*. London: Bloomsbury.

Brooker Will. 2013. "Fandom and Authorship." In *The Superhero Reader*, edited by Charles Hatfield, Jeet Heer, and Kent Worcester, 61–71. Jackson: University Press of Mississippi.

Brown, Jeffrey A. 1997. "Comic Book Fandom and Cultural Capital." *Journal of Popular Culture* 30, no. 4 (Spring): 13–31.

Brown, Jeffrey A. 1999. "Comic Book Masculinity and the New Black Superhero." *African American Review* 33, no. 1 (Spring): 25–42.

Brown, Jeffrey A. 2000. *Black Superheroes, Milestone Comics, and Their Fans.* Jackson: University Press of Mississippi.

Brown, Jeffrey A. 2011a. *Dangerous Curves: Action Heroines, Gender, Fetishism, and Popular Culture.* Jackson: University Press of Mississippi.

Brown, Jeffrey A. 2011b. "Supermoms? Maternity and the Monstrous-Feminine in Superhero Comics." *Journal of Graphic Novels and Comics* 2, no. 1 (January): 77–87.

Brown, Jeffrey A. 2012. "Ethnography: Wearing One's Fandom." In *Critical Approaches to Comics: Theories and Methods*, edited by Matthew J. Smith and Randy Duncan, 280–90. New York: Routledge.

Brown, Jeffrey A. 2015. *Beyond Bombshells: The New Action Heroine in Popular Culture.* Jackson: University Press of Mississippi.

Brown, Jeffrey A. 2017. *The Modern Superhero in Film and Television: Popular Genre and American Culture.* New York: Routledge.

Brown, Kieron Michael. 2013. "Musical Sequences in Comics." *The Comics Grid: Journal of Comics Scholarship* 3, no. 1 (November): 1–6. https://www.comicsgrid.com/article/id/3499/.

Brown, Kieron Michael. 2018. "Comics, Materiality, and the Limits of Media Combinations." *ImageTexT: Interdisciplinary Comics Studies* 9, no. 3. http://www.english.ufl.edu/imagetext/archives/v9_3/brown/.

Brown, Lisa. 2013. "The Speaking Animal: Nonhuman Voices in Comics." In *Speaking for Animals: Animal Autobiographical Writing*, edited by Margo DeMello, 73–77. New York: Routledge.

Brown, Lyndsay. 2013. "Pornographic Space-Time and the Potential of Fantasy in Comics and Fan Art." *Transformative Works and Cultures*, no. 13. https://journal.transformativeworks.org/index.php/twc/article/view/465/396.

Brown, Michelle P. 1994. *Understanding Illuminated Manuscripts: A Guide to Technical Terms.* Los Angeles: J. Paul Getty Museum.

Brownie, Barbara, and Danny Graydon. 2016. *The Superhero Costume: Identity and Disguise in Fact and Fiction.* London: Bloomsbury.

Brozo, William G., Gary Moorman, and Carla K. Meyer. 2013. *Wham! Teaching with Graphic Novels across the Curriculum.* New York: Teachers College Press.

Brunetti, Ivan. 2006. "Cartooning Will Destroy You." *Schizo*, no. 4.

Brunetti, Ivan. 2011. *Cartooning: Philosophy and Practice.* New Haven, CT: Yale University Press.

Bryan, Peter Cullen. 2018. "Geeking Out and Hulking Out: Toward an Understanding of Marvel Fan Communities." In *Age of the Geek: Depictions of Nerds and Geeks in Popular Media*, edited by Kathryn E. Lane, 149–65. Cham, Switzerland: Palgrave Macmillan.

Buchanan, Rebekah. 2012. "Zines in the Classroom: Reading Culture." *English Journal* 102, no. 2 (November): 71–77.

Buchenberger, Stefan. 2011. "Comic Book Super Villains and the Loss of Humanity." *International Journal of Comic Art* 13, no. 2 (Fall): 539–52.

Bucher, Hans-Jürgen, and Bettina Boy. "How Informative are Information Comics in Science Communication? Empirical Results from an Eye-Tracking Study and Knowledge Testing." In *Empirical Comics Research: Digital, Multimodal, and Cognitive Methods*, edited by Alexander Dunst, Jochen Laubrock, and Janina Wildfeuer, 176–96. New York: Routledge.

Buhle, Paul. 2003. "The New Scholarship of Comics." *Chronicle of Higher Education*, May 16, B7–B9.

Buhle, Paul. 2009. "Eco-Comics, Then and Now." *Capitalism, Nature, Socialism* 20, no. 3 (September): 68–73.

Bukatman, Scott. 2006. "Comics and the Critique of Chronophotography; or, 'He Never Knew When It Was Coming!'" *Animation* 1, no. 1: 83–103.

Burke, Liam. 2012. "Special Effect: Have Film Adaptations Changed Mainstream Comics?" *SCAN: Journal of Media Arts Culture* 9, no. 1 (June). http://scan.net.au/scn/journal/vol9number1/Liam-Burke.html.

Burke, Liam. 2015. *The Comic Book Film Adaptation: Exploring Modern Hollywood's Leading Genre*. Jackson: University Press of Mississippi.

Burke, Liam, Ian Gordon, and Angela Ndalianis, eds. 2020. *The Superhero Symbol: Media, Culture, and Politics*. New Brunswick, NJ: Rutgers University Press.

Busch, Lenja. 2017. "Onomatopoeia in Comics: On the A-Human Theatre of Expression in Graphic Representations." *Thewis*, Gesellschaft für Theaterwissenschaft. http://www.theater-wissenschaft.de/miszellen-onomatopoeia-in-comics/.

Cadieux, Lee. 2011. "Digital Thought Balloons: Electronic Delivery and the Comic Book." *International Journal of the Book* 8, no. 4: 135–42.

Calafat, Marie-Charlotte, and Frédérique Deschamps, eds. 2017. *Photo-roman*. Paris: Textuel/Mucem.

Caldwell, Joshua. 2012. "Comic Panel Layout: A Peircean Analysis." *Studies in Comics* 2, no. 2 (January): 317–38.

Calvert, Sheena. 2011. "Materia Secunda: Text-as-Image." *Book 2.0* 1, no. 2 (March): 139–61.

Camden, Vera J. 2020. "The Thought Balloon and Its Vicissitudes in Contemporary Comics." *American Imago* 77, no. 3 (Fall): 603–38.

Campbell, Bruce. 2009. *¡Viva la Historieta! Mexican Comics, NAFTA, and the Politics of Globalization*. Jackson: University Press of Mississippi.

Campbell, Joseph. (1949) 2009. *The Hero with a Thousand Faces*. Novato, CA: New World Library.

Campbell, T. 2006. *A History of Webcomics: "The Golden Age," 1993–2005.* San Antonio: Antarctic Press.

Cañero, Julio, and Esther Claudio, eds. 2015. *On the Edge of the Panel: Essays on Comics Criticism.* Newcastle upon Tyne: Cambridge Scholars Publishing.

Cappello, Daniela. 2019. "Comics and Science Fiction in West Bengal." *Interdisziplinäre Zeitschrift für Südasienforschung,* no. 5. https://crossasia-journals.ub.uni-heidelberg.de/ index.php/izsa/article/view/10442.

Carlin, John, and Sheena Wagstaff, eds. 1983. *The Comic Art Show: Cartoons in Paintings and Popular Culture.* New York: Whitney Museum of American Art.

Carmack, Betty J. 1997. "Realistic Representations of Companion Animals in Comic Art in the USA." *Anthrozoös* 10, nos. 2–3: 108–20.

Carney, Sean. 2005. "The Function of the Superhero at the Present Time." *Iowa Journal of Cultural Studies* 6, no. 1 (Spring): 100–117.

Carney, Sean. 2008. "The Ear of the Eye; or, Do Drawings Make Sounds?" *English Language Notes* 46, no. 2 (Fall–Winter): 193–209.

Carrasco, Jorge Catalá, Paulo Drinot, and James Scorer, eds. 2017. *Comics and Memory in Latin America.* Pittsburgh: University of Pittsburgh Press.

Carrier, David. 2000. *The Aesthetics of Comics.* University Park: Pennsylvania State University Press.

Carter, James Bucky. 2008. "Comics, the Canon, and the Classroom." In *Teaching Visual Literacy: Using Comic Books, Graphic Novels, Anime, Cartoons, and More to Develop Comprehension and Thinking Skills,* edited by Nancy Frey and Douglas Fisher, 47–60. Thousand Oaks, CA: Corwin Press.

Carter, James Bucky. 2011. "Graphic Novels, Web Comics, and Creator Blogs: Examining Product and Process." *Theory into Practice* 50, no. 3 (Summer): 190–97.

Carter, James Bucky, and Erik A. Evensen. 2011. *Super-Powered Word Study: Teaching Words and Word Parts through Comics.* Mankato, MN: Maupin House.

Cary, Stephen. 2004. *Going Graphic: Comics at Work in the Multilingual Classroom.* Portsmouth, NH: Heinemann.

Casey, Jim. 2009. "Silver Age Comics." In *The Routledge Companion to Science Fiction,* edited by Mark Bould, Andrew M. Butler, Adam Roberts, and Sherryl Vint, 123–33. Abingdon, Oxon., England: Routledge.

Castaldi, Simone. 2004. "Adult Fumetti and the Postmodern: Poetics of Italian Sequential Art in the 1970s and 1980s." *Word and Image: A Journal of Verbal/Visual Enquiry* 20, no. 4: 271–82.

Castaldi, Simone. 2012. *Drawn and Dangerous: Italian Comics of the 1970s and 1980s.* Jackson: University Press of Mississippi.

Cates, Isaac. 2011. "The Diary Comic." In *Graphic Subjects: Critical Essays on Autobiography and Graphic Novels,* edited by Michael A. Chaney, 209–26. Madison: University of Wisconsin Press.

Cavalier, Stephen. 2011. *The World History of Animation*. Berkeley: University of California Press.

Cavallaro, Dani. 2007. *Anime Intersections: Tradition and Innovation in Theme and Technique*. Jefferson, NC: McFarland.

Cavallaro, Dani. 2009. *Anime and Memory: Aesthetic, Cultural and Thematic Perspectives*. Jefferson, NC: McFarland.

Cavallaro, Dani. 2010a. *Anime and the Art of Adaptation: Eight Famous Works from Page to Screen*. Jefferson, NC: McFarland.

Cavallaro, Dani. 2010b. *Anime and the Visual Novel: Narrative Structure, Design and Play at the Crossroads of Animation and Computer Games*. Jefferson, NC: McFarland.

Cavallaro, Dani. 2010c. *Magic as Metaphor in Anime: A Critical Study*. Jefferson, NC: McFarland.

Cavallaro, Dani. 2011. *The Fairy Tale and Anime: Traditional Themes, Images and Symbols at Play on Screen*. Jefferson, NC: McFarland.

Cavallaro, Dani. 2012. *Art in Anime: The Creative Quest as Theme and Metaphor*. Jefferson, NC: McFarland.

Cavallaro, Dani. 2013. *Japanese Aesthetics and Anime: The Influence of Tradition*. Jefferson, NC: McFarland.

Chambliss, Julian. 2012. "Superhero Comics: Artifacts of the U.S. Experience." *Juniata Voices* 12 (Fall): 149–55. https://www.juniata.edu/offices/juniata-voices/media/chambliss-superhero-comics.pdf.

Chambliss, Julian, William Svitavsky, and Thomas Donaldson, eds. 2013. *Ages of Heroes, Eras of Men: Superheroes and the American Experience*. Newcastle upon Tyne: Cambridge Scholars Publishing.

Chaney, Michael A. 2011a. "Animal Subjects of the Graphic Novel." *College Literature: A Journal of Critical Literary Studies* 38, no. 3 (Summer): 129–49.

Chaney, Michael A., ed. 2011b. *Graphic Subjects: Critical Essays in Autobiography and Graphic Novels*. Madison: University of Wisconsin Press.

Chaney, Michael A. 2011c. "Terrors of the Mirror and the *Mise en Abyme* of Graphic Novel Autobiography." *College Literature: A Journal of Critical Literary Studies* 38, no. 3: 21–44.

Chaney, Michael A. 2013. "Not Just a Theme: Transnationalism and Form in Visual Narratives of US Slavery." In *Transnational Perspectives on Graphic Narratives: Comics at the Crossroads*, edited by Shane Denson, Christina Meyer, and Daniel Stein, 15–31. London: Bloomsbury.

Chaney, Michael A. 2016. *Reading Lessons in Seeing: Mirrors, Masks, and Mazes in the Autobiographical Graphic Novel*. Jackson: University Press of Mississippi.

Chaney, Michael A., and Sara B. Chaney. 2020. "Bakhtinian Laughter and Recent Political Editorial Cartoons." In *The Oxford Handbook of Comic Book Studies*, edited by Frederick Luis Aldama, 165–89. Oxford: Oxford University Press.

Chapman, Jane, and Daniel Ellin. 2012. "Multi-Panel Comic Narratives in Australian First World War Trench Publications as Citizen Journalism." *Australian Journal of Communication* 39, no. 3 (November): 1–22.

Chapman, Jane, Anna Hoyles, Andrew Kerr, and Adam Sherif. 2015. *Comics and the World Wars: A Cultural Record*. Basingstoke, Hants., England: Palgrave Macmillan.

Chase, Alisia. 2013. "You Must Look at the Personal Clutter: Diaristic Indulgence, Female Adolescence, and Feminist Autobiography." In *Drawing from Life: Memory and Subjectivity in Comic Art*, edited by Jane Tolmie, 207–40. Jackson: University Press of Mississippi.

Chase, Gregory. 2012. "In the Gutter: Comix Theory." *Studies in Comics* 3, no. 1: 107–28.

Chavanne, Renaud. 2010. *Composition de la bande dessinée*. Montrouge, France: Éditions PLG.

Chavanne, Renaud. 2015. "The Composition of Comics." Translated by Ann Miller. *European Comic Art* 8, no. 1 (Spring): 111–44.

Chen, Jin-Shiow. 2007. "A Study of Fan Culture: Adolescent Experiences with Animé/Manga Doujinshi and Cosplay in Taiwan." *Visual Arts Research* 33, no. 1: 14–24.

Chiarello, Mark, and Todd Klein. 2013. *The DC Comics Guide to Coloring and Lettering Comics*. New York: Watson-Guptill.

Chiba, Naoki, and Hiroko Chiba. 2007. "Words of Alienation, Words of Flight: Loanwords in Science Fiction Anime." In *Robot Ghosts and Wired Dreams: Japanese Science Fiction from Origins to Anime*, edited by Christopher Bolton, Istvan Csicsery-Ronay Jr., and Takayuki Tatsumi, 148–71. Minneapolis: University of Minnesota Press.

Chie, Yamanaka. 2013. "*Manhwa* in Korea: (Re-)Nationalizing Comics Culture." In *Manga's Cultural Crossroads*, edited by Jaqueline Berndt and Bettina Kümmerling-Meibauer, 85–99. New York: Routledge.

Chiu, Monica, ed. 2015. *Drawing New Color Lines: Transnational Asian American Graphic Narratives*. Hong Kong: Hong Kong University Press.

Christiansen, Hans-Christian. 2000. "Comics and Film: A Narrative Perspective." In *Comics and Culture: Analytical and Theoretical Approaches to Comics*, edited by Anne Magnussen and Hans-Christian Christiansen, 107–22. Copenhagen: Museum Tusculanum Press.

Chu, Kin Wai. 2018. "The Institutional Support for Hong Kong Independent Comics." In *Comics Studies Here and Now*, edited by Frederick Luis Aldama, 131–43. New York: Routledge.

Chua, Karl Ian Uy Cheng. 2016. "Boy Meets World: The Worldview of *Shōnen Kurabu* in the 1930s." *Japan Forum* 28, no. 1: 74–98.

Chun, Bong-Kyung, Dong-Sung Ryu, Won-Il Hwang, and Hwan-Gue Cho. 2006. "An Automated Procedure for Word Balloon Placement in Cinema Comics." In *Advances in Visual Computing: Second International Symposium, ISVC 2006, Proceedings*, part 2, edited by George Bebis, Richard Boyle, Bahram Parvin, Dario Koracin, Paolo Remagnino, Ara Nefian, Gopi Meenakshisundaram, Valerio Pascucci, Jiri Zara, Jose Molineros, Holger Theisel, and Thomas Malzbender, 576–85. Berlin: Springer Verlag.

Chute, Hillary L. 2008. "Comics as Literature? Reading Graphic Narrative." *PMLA* 123, no. 2 (March): 452–65.

Chute, Hillary L. 2010. *Graphic Women: Life Narrative and Contemporary Comics*. New York: Columbia University Press.

Chute, Hillary L. 2011. "Comics Form and Narrating Lives." *Profession* 1: 107–17.

Chute, Hillary L. 2016. *Disaster Drawn: Visual Witness, Comics, and Documentary Form.* Cambridge, MA: Harvard University Press.

Chute, Hillary L. 2017. *Why Comics? From Underground to Everywhere.* New York: HarperCollins.

Chute, Hillary L., and Marianne DeKoven. 2006. "Introduction: Graphic Narrative." *Modern Fiction Studies* 52, no. 4 (Winter): 767–82.

Chute, Hillary L., and Patrick Jagoda, eds. 2014. "Comics and Media." Special issue, *Critical Inquiry* 40, no. 3 (Spring).

Cicci, Matthew A. 2016. "Marvel Team-Up: Hawkeye, Loki, and the Inescapable, Innate Resistance of the Female Superhero Comic Fan." *The Journal of Comics and Culture* 1 (Spring): 95–122.

Cioffi, Frank L. 2009. "Graphic Fictions and Graphic Subjects: Teaching the Illustrated Medical Narrative." In *Teaching the Graphic Novel,* edited by Stephen E. Tabachnick, 179–88. New York: Modern Language Association of America.

Clark, Spencer. 2013. "'Your Credibility Could Be Shot': Preservice Teachers' Thinking about Nonfiction Graphic Novels, Curriculum Decision Making, and Professional Acceptance." *Social Studies* 104, no. 1: 38–45.

Clarke, M. J. 2014. "The Production of the *Marvel Graphic Novel* Series: The Business and Culture of the Early Direct Market." *Journal of Graphic Novels and Comics* 5, no. 2 (April): 192–210.

Clayton, Aaron. 2010. "Bloody Hell: Realism in American War Comics." *International Journal of Comic Art* 12, no. 1 (Spring): 370–87.

Click, Melissa A., and Suzanne Scott, eds. 2018. *The Routledge Companion to Media Fandom.* New York: Routledge.

Close, Samantha. 2015. "The Absent Presence of Gender in Webcomics." *Feminist Media Studies* 15, no. 3 (June): 533–38.

Cocca, Carolyn. 2014. "The 'Broke Back Test': A Quantitative and Qualitative Analysis of Portrayals of Women in Mainstream Superhero Comics, 1993–2013." *Journal of Graphic Novels and Comics* 5, no. 4 (December): 411–28.

Cocca, Carolyn. 2016. *Superwomen: Gender, Power, and Representation.* London: Bloomsbury.

Cohen, Doron, Geoffrey Beattie, and Heather Shovelton. 2010. "Nonverbal Indicators of Deception: How Iconic Gestures Reveal Thoughts That Cannot Be Suppressed." *Semiotica,* no. 182 (October): 133–74.

Cohen, Karl F. 1997. *Forbidden Animation: Censored Cartoons and Blacklisted Animators in America.* Jefferson, NC: McFarland.

Cohen, Martin S. 1977. "The Novel in Woodcuts: A Handbook." *Journal of Modern Literature* 6, no. 2 (April): 171–95.

Cohn, Jesse. 2009. "Mise-en-Page: A Vocabulary for Page Layouts." In *Teaching the Graphic Novel,* edited by Stephen E. Tabachnick, 44–57. New York: Modern Language Association of America.

Cohn, Neil. 2005. "Un-Defining 'Comics': Separating the Cultural from the Structural in 'Comics.'" *International Journal of Comic Art* 7, no. 2 (Fall): 236–48.

Cohn, Neil. 2007. "A Visual Lexicon." *Public Journal of Semiotics* 1, no. 1 (January): 35–56. https://journals.lub.lu.se/pjos/article/view/8814/7895.

Cohn, Neil. 2010. "The Limits of Time and Transitions: Challenges to Theories of Sequential Image Comprehension." *Studies in Comics* 1, no. 1 (April): 127–47.

Cohn, Neil. 2011. "A Different Kind of Cultural Frame: An Analysis of Panels in American Comics and Japanese Manga." *Image [&] Narrative: Online Magazine of the Visual Narrative* 12, no. 1 (March): 120–34. http://ojs.arts.kuleuven.be/index.php/imagenarrative/article/view/128.

Cohn, Neil. 2013a. "Beyond Speech Balloons and Thought Bubbles: The Integration of Text and Image." *Semiotica*, no. 197 (October): 35–63.

Cohn, Neil. 2013b. "Navigating Comics: An Empirical and Theoretical Approach to Strategies of Reading Comic Page Layouts." *Frontiers in Psychology* 4, no. 186 (April): 1–15. https://www.frontiersin.org/articles/10.3389/fpsyg.2013.00186/full.

Cohn, Neil. 2013c. *The Visual Language of Comics: Introduction to the Structure and Cognition of Sequential Images*. London: Bloomsbury.

Cohn, Neil. 2014. "Building a Better 'Comic Theory': Shortcomings of Theoretical Research on Comics and How to Overcome Them." *Studies in Comics* 5, no. 1: 57–75.

Cohn, Neil. 2016. "A Multimodal Parallel Architecture: A Cognitive Framework for Multimodal Interactions." *Cognition: International Journal of Cognitive Science* 146 (January): 304–23.

Cohn, Neil. 2019. "Being Explicit about the Implicit: Inference Generating Techniques in Visual Narrative." *Language and Cognition* 11, no. 1 (April): 66–97. https://www.cambridge.org/core/journals/language-and-cognition/article/being-explicit-about-the-implicit-inference-generating-techniques-in-visual-narrative/AEBDBD7A09A3892D860463AB57588112.

Cohn, Neil, Jessika Axnér, Michaela Diercks, Rebecca Yeh, and Kaitlin Pederson. 2017. "The Cultural Pages of Comics: Cross-Cultural Variation in Page Layouts." *Journal of Graphic Novels and Comics* 10, no. 1 (February): 67–86.

Cohn, Neil, and Hannah Campbell. 2015. "Navigating Comics II: Constraints on the Reading Order of Comic Page Layouts." *Applied Cognitive Psychology* 29, no. 2 (March–April): 193–99.

Cohn, Neil, and Stephen Maher. 2015. "The Notion of Motion: The Neurocognition of Motion Lines in Visual Narratives." *Brain Research* 1601 (January): 73–84.

Cohn, Neil, Ryan Taylor, and Kaitlin Pederson. 2017. "A Picture Is Worth More Words over Time: Multimodality and Narrative Structure across Eight Decades of American Superhero Comics." *Multimodal Communication* 6, no. 1 (January): 19–37.

Cohn, Neil, Amaro Taylor-Weiner, and Suzanne Grossman. 2012. "Framing Attention in Japanese and American Comics: Cross-Cultural Differences in Attentional Structure."

Frontiers in Psychology 3, no. 349. https://www.frontiersin.org/articles/10.3389/fpsyg
.2012.00349/full.

Cohn, Neil, and Eva Wittenberg. 2015. "Action Starring Narratives and Events: Structure
and Inference in Visual Narrative Comprehension." *Journal of Cognitive Psychology* 27,
no. 7 (May): 812–28.

Collver, Jordan, and Emma Weitkamp. 2018. "Alter Egos: An Exploration of the Perspectives
and Identities of Comic Creators." *Journal of Science Communication* 17, no. 1 (January):
1–22. https://jcom.sissa.it/archive/17/01/JCOM_1701_2018_A01.

Comtois, Pierre, John Romita Sr., Gene Colan, and Gil Kane. 2011. *Marvel Comics in the
1970s: An Issue-by-Issue Field Guide to a Pop Culture Phenomenon*. Vol. 3. Raleigh, NC:
TwoMorrows Publishing.

Conard, Sébastien, and Tom Lambeens. 2012. "Duration in Comics." *European Comic Art*
5, no. 2 (December): 92–113.

Condis, Megan. 2001. "Surveying the Field: Recent Scholarship on Superheroines."
ImageTexT: Interdisciplinary Comics Studies 6, no. 1. http://www.english.ufl.edu/image
text/archives/v6_1/condis/.

Condry, Ian. 2013. *The Soul of Anime: Collaborative Creativity and Japan's Media Success Story*.
Durham, NC: Duke University Press.

Conners, Joan L. 2005. "Visual Representations of the 2004 Presidential Campaign:
Political Cartoons and Popular Culture References." *American Behavioral Scientist* 49,
no. 3 (November): 479–87.

Conners, Joan L. 2007. "Popular Culture in Political Cartoons: Analyzing Cartoonist
Approaches." *PS: Political Science and Politics* 40, no. 2 (April): 261–65.

Coogan, Peter. 2006. *Superhero: The Secret Origin of a Genre*. Austin, TX: MonkeyBrain Books.

Coogan, Peter. 2010. "From Love to Money: The First Decade of Comics Fandom."
International Journal of Comic Art 12, no. 1 (Spring): 50–67.

Cook, Malcolm. 2013. "The Lightning Cartoon: Animation from Music Hall to Cinema."
Early Popular Visual Culture 11, no. 3 (August): 137–254.

Cook, Roy T. 2012. "Why Comics Are Not Films: Metacomics and Medium-Specific
Conventions." In *The Art of Comics: A Philosophical Approach*, edited by Aaron Meskin
and Roy T. Cook, 165–87. Chichester, W. Susx., England: Wiley-Blackwell.

Cook, Roy T. 2013. "Canonicity and Normativity in Massive, Serialized, Collaborative Fiction."
Journal of Aesthetics and Art Criticism 71, no. 3 (Summer): 271–76.

Cook, Roy T. 2015. "Judging a Comic Book by Its Cover: Marvel Comics, Photo-Covers, and the
Objectivity of Photography." *Image [&] Narrative: Online Magazine of the Visual Narrative*
16, no. 2 (July): 14–27. http://www.imageandnarrative.be/index.php/imagenarrative/
article/view/805/610.

Cook, Roy T., and Aaron Meskin. 2015. "Comics, Prints, and Multiplicity." *Journal of Aesthetics
and Art Criticism* 73, no. 1 (January): 57–67.

Cooke, Stephanie. 2019. "A Glossary of Comic Book Terminology." Creator Resource. http://
www.creatorresource.com/a-glossary-of-comic-book-terminology/.

Cools, Valérie. 2011. "The Phenomenology of Contemporary Mainstream Manga." *Image [&] Narrative: Online Magazine of the Visual Narrative* 12, no. 1 (March). http://www .imageandnarrative.be/index.php/imagenarrative/article/view/126/97.

Cornilliat, François. 2011. "How Do You Pronounce a Pictogram? On 'Visible Writing' in Comics." In *Visible Writings: Cultures, Forms, Readings*, edited by Marija Dalbello and Mary Shaw, 195–210. New Brunswick, NJ: Rutgers University Press.

Cornog, Martha, and Erin Byrne. 2009. "Censorship of Graphic Novels in Libraries." In *Graphic Novels beyond the Basics: Insights and Issues for Libraries*, edited by Martha Cornog and Timothy Perper, 211–32. Santa Barbara, CA: Libraries Unlimited.

Costello, Matthew J. 2009. *Secret Identity Crisis: Comic Books and the Unmasking of Cold War America*. London: Bloomsbury.

Costello, Matthew J. 2013. "The Super Politics of Comic Book Fandom." *Transformative Works and Cultures*, no. 13. https://journal.transformativeworks.org/index.php/twc/article/view/528/398.

Costello, Matthew J. 2015. "U.S. Superpower and Superpowered Americans in Science Fiction and Comic Books." In *The Cambridge Companion to American Science Fiction*, edited by Eric Carl Link and Gerry Canavan, 125–38. Cambridge: Cambridge University Press.

Couch, Christopher N. C. 2000. "The Publication and Formats of Comics, Graphic Novels, and Tankōbon." *Image [&] Narrative: Online Magazine of the Visual Narrative* 1, no. 1 (January). http://www.imageandnarrative.be/inarchive/narratology/chriscouch.htm.

Coughlan, David. 2009. "The Naked Hero and Model Man: Costumed Identity in Comic Book Narratives." In *Heroes of Film, Comics and American Culture: Essays on Real and Fictional Defenders of Home*, edited by Lisa M. DeTora, 234–52. Jefferson, NC: McFarland.

Couperie, Pierre, and Maurice C. Horn. 1968. *A History of the Comic Strip*. Translated by Eileen B. Hennessy. New York: Crown Publishers.

Couser, G. Thomas. 2018. "Is There a Body in This Text? Embodiment in Graphic Somatography." *a/b: Auto/Biography Studies* 33, no. 2 (Spring): 347–73.

Crafton, Donald. 1979. "Animation Iconography: The 'Hand of the Artist.'" *Quarterly Review of Film Studies* 4, no. 4 (Fall): 409–28.

Crafton, Donald. 1993. *Before Mickey: The Animated Film, 1898–1928*. Chicago: University of Chicago Press.

Crafton, Donald. 2012. *Shadow of a Mouse: Performance, Belief, and World-Making in Animation*. Berkeley: University of California Press.

Craig, Jane Ann. 1991. *Drawing on Your Rights: Using Editorial Cartoons to Teach about the Bill of Rights*. Austin, TX: Law Focused Education.

Creekmur, Corey K. 2014. "Comics." In *The Oxford Handbook of Science Fiction*, edited by Rob Latham, 212–25. Oxford: Oxford University Press.

Croissant, Doris. 2008. "Prince Genji in Manga, Gender, Pop and Parody." In *Ga-Netchū! The Manga Anime Syndrome*, edited by Hans-Peter Reichmann and Stephan von der Schulenburg, 158–65. Frankfurt am Main: Deutsches Filmmuseum / Deutsches Film-institut.

Crucifix, Benoît. 2017. "Cut-Up and Redrawn: Reading Charles Burns's Swipe Files." *Inks: Journal of the Comics Studies Society* 1, no. 3 (Fall): 309–33.

Crucifix, Benoît. 2020. "Drawing, Redrawing, and Undrawing." In *The Oxford Handbook of Comic Book Studies*, edited by Frederick Luis Aldama, 148–64. Oxford: Oxford University Press.

Crucifix, Benoît, and Björn-Olav Dozo. 2018. "E-Graphic Novels." In *The Cambridge History of the Graphic Novel*, edited by Jan Baetens, Hugo Frey, and Stephen E. Tabachnick, 574–90. Cambridge: Cambridge University Press.

Cuccolini, Giulio C. 2010. "A Two-Sided Narration through Words and Images." *International Journal of Comic Art* 12, no. 1 (Spring): 124–34.

Cunningham, Phillip Lamarr. 2010. "The Absence of Black Supervillains in Mainstream Comics." *Journal of Graphic Novels and Comics* 1, no. 1 (January): 51–62.

Curtis, Neal. 2016. *Sovereignty and Superheroes.* Manchester: Manchester University Press.

Curtis, Neal, and Valentina Cardo. 2018. "Superheroes and Third-Wave Feminism." *Feminist Media Studies* 18, no. 3 (June): 381–96.

Curto, Gemma. 2020. "Floods in Contemporary Biocentric Graphic Novels." *Green Letters: Studies in Ecocriticism* 24, no. 1 (March): 6–22.

Cutter, Martha J., and Cathy J. Schlund-Vials, eds. 2018. *Redrawing the Historical Past: History, Memory, and Multiethnic Graphic Novels.* Athens: University of Georgia Press.

Czerwiec, M. K., and Michelle N. Huang. 2017. "Hospice Comics: Representations of Patient and Family Experience of Illness and Death in Graphic Novels." *Journal of Medical Humanities* 38, no. 2 (June): 95–113.

Czerwiec, M. K., Ian Williams, Susan Merrill Squier, Michael J. Green, Kimberly R. Myers, and Scott T. Smith. 2015. *Graphic Medicine Manifesto.* University Park: Pennsylvania State University Press.

D'Amore, Laura Mattoon. 2008. "Invisible Girl's Quest for Visibility: Early Second Wave Feminism and the Comic Book Superheroine." *Americana: Journal of American Popular Culture* 7, no. 2 (Fall). https://www.americanpopularculture.com/journal/articles/fall_2008/d%27amore.htm.

Daniels, Les. 1971. *Comix: A History of Comic Books in America.* New York: Outerbridge and Dienstfrey.

Danky, James, and Denis Kitchen, eds. 2009. *Underground Classics: The Transformation of Comics into Comix.* New York: Harry N. Abrams.

Danziger-Russell, Jacqueline. 2013. *Girls and Their Comics: Finding a Female Voice in Comic Book Narrative.* Lanham, MD: Scarecrow Press.

Dar, Jehanzeb. 2018. "Holy Islamophobia, Batman! Demonization of Muslims and Arabs in Mainstream Comic Books." In *Islam and Popular Culture*, edited by Anna Piela, 99–110. London: Routledge.

D'Arcy, Geraint. 2020. *Mise en Scène, Acting, and Space in Comics.* Cham, Switzerland: Palgrave Macmillan.

Darowski, Joseph J. 2014. "Improbability of Assignment: Arriving at a Golden Age of Comic Books." In *Critical Insights: The American Comic Book*, edited by Joseph Michael Sommers, 90–103. Ipswich, MA: Salem Press.

Darowski, Joseph J. 2017. "The Brave and Bold Beginning of the Silver Age Superteam." In *The Ages of the Justice League: Essays on America's Greatest Superheroes in Changing Times*, edited by Joseph J. Darowski, 5–17. Jefferson, NC: McFarland.

Davenport, Christian. 1997. "Black Is the Color of My Comic Book Character: An Examination of Ethnic Stereotypes." *Inks: Cartoon and Comic Arts Studies* 4, no. 1 (Spring): 20–28.

Davidson, Sol. 2008. "Educational Comics: A Family Tree." *ImageTexT: Interdisciplinary Comics Studies* 4, no. 2. http://www.english.ufl.edu/imagetext/archives/v4_2/davidson/.

Davies, Dominic. 2019. *Urban Comics: Infrastructure and the Global City in Contemporary Graphic Narratives*. New York: Routledge.

Davies, Dominic, and Candida Rifkind, eds. 2020. *Documenting Trauma in Comics: Traumatic Pasts, Embodied Histories, and Graphic Reportage*. Cham, Switzerland: Palgrave Macmillan.

Davies, Paul Fisher. 2013. "'Animating' the Narrative in Abstract Comics." *Studies in Comics* 4, no. 2 (October): 251–76.

Davies, Paul Fisher. 2018. "Goffman's Frame Analysis, Modality and Comics." *Studies in Comics* 9, no. 2 (December): 279–95.

Davies, Paul Fisher. 2019a. *Comics as Communication: A Functional Approach*. Cham, Switzerland: Palgrave Macmillan.

Davies, Paul Fisher. 2019b. "New Choices of the Comics Creator." *The Comics Grid: Journal of Comics Scholarship* 9, no. 1 (February): 1–9. https://www.comicsgrid.com/article/id/3581/.

Davis, Blair. 2015. "Bare Chests, Silver Tiaras, and Removable Afros: The Visual Design of Black Comic Book Superheroes." In *The Blacker the Ink: Constructions of Black Identity in Comics and Sequential Art*, edited by Frances Gateward and John Jennings, 193–212. New Brunswick, NJ: Rutgers University Press.

Davis, Blair. 2018. *Comic Book Movies*. New Brunswick, NJ: Rutgers University Press.

De Assis, Érico Gonçalves. 2015. "The Letterer as a Translator in Comics Translation." In *Comics: Übersetzungen und Adaptionen*, edited by Nathalie Mälzer, 251–68. Berlin: Frank & Timme.

DeForest, Tim. 2004. *Storytelling in the Pulps, Comics, and Radio: How Technology Changed Popular Fiction in America*. Jefferson, NC: McFarland.

Del Rey Cabero, Enrique. 2019. "Beyond Linearity: Holistic, Multidirectional, Multilinear and Translinear Reading in Comics." *The Comics Grid: Journal of Comics Scholarship* 9, no. 1 (February): 1–21. https://www.comicsgrid.com/article/id/3583/.

Deluliis, David. 2013. "Culturally Gatekeeping the Black Comic Strip." In *Black Comics: Politics of Race and Representation*, edited by Sheena C. Howard and Ronald L. Jackson II, 239–50. London: Bloomsbury.

Deman, J. Andrew 2015. *The Margins of Comics: The Construction of Woman, Minorities, and the Geek in Graphic Narrative*. St. Catharines, Ont., Canada: Nuada Press.

De Masi, Vincenzo, and Chwen Chwen Chen. 2010. "The Growth of *Manhua* in China: An Overview." *China Media Observatory Newsletter*, no. 6 (November): 7–10.

Denison, Rayna. 2011. "Transcultural Creativity in Anime: Hybrid Identities in the Production, Distribution, Texts and Fandom of Japanese Anime." *Creative Industries Journal* 3, no. 3: 221–35.

Denison, Rayna. 2015. *Anime: A Critical Introduction*. London: Bloomsbury.

Denson, Shane. 2012. "Frame, Sequence, Medium: Comics in Plurimedial and Transnational Perspective." In *Transnational American Studies*, edited by Udo J. Hebel, 561–80. Heidelberg: Universitätsverlag Winter.

Denson, Shane. 2013. "Afterword: Framing, Unframing, Reframing; Retconning the Transnational Work of Comics." In *Transnational Perspectives on Graphic Narratives: Comics at the Crossroads*, edited by Shane Denson, Christina Meyer, and Daniel Stein, 271–84. London: Bloomsbury.

De Rothewelle, Jonathan Comyn. 2019. "Comics and Medical Narrative: A Visual Semiotic Dissection of Graphic Medicine." *Journal of Graphic Novels and Comics* 10, nos. 5–6 (October–December): 562–88.

De Syon, Guillaume. 2004. "Don't Read Those 'Toons! French Comics, Government Censorship, and Perceptions of American Military Aviation." *Contemporary French Civilization* 25, no. 2: 273–91.

De Valdés, Rosalva. 1972. "A Short History of Mexican Comic Books." *Artes de México*, no. 158: 84–86.

Dey, Subir, and Prasad Bokil. 2015. "Sound Symbolism in India Comic Books." In *ICoRD '15: Research into Design across Boundaries*. Vol. 1: *Theory, Research Methodology, Aesthetics, Human Factors and Education*, edited by Amaresh Chakrabarti, 227–36. Berlin: Springer Verlag.

Dey, Subir, and Prasad Bokil. 2016. "Syntax of Sound Symbolic Words: A Study of the Hindi Comic Books in India." *International Journal of Comic Art* 18, no. 1 (Spring–Summer): 260–77.

Diamond, Matthew. 2002. "No Laughing Matter: Post–September 11 Political Cartoons in Arab/Muslim Newspapers." *Political Communication* 19, no. 2 (November): 251–72.

Dickinson, Hannah, and Maggie M. Werner. 2015. "Beyond Talking Heads: Sourced Comics and the Affordances of Multimodality." *Composition Studies* 43, no. 1 (Spring): 51–74. https://compositionstudiesjournal.files.wordpress.com/2020/05/43.1-full-issue.pdf.

Dicks, Andrew. 2015. "Stories from Below: Subject-Generated Comics." *Visual Anthropology* 28, no. 2 (March): 137–54.

Dierick, Charles, and Pascal Lefèvre, eds. 1998. *Forging a New Medium: The Comic Strip in the Nineteenth Century*. Brussels: Vrije Universiteit Brussel University Press.

DiPaolo, Marc. 2011. *War, Politics, and Superheroes: Ethics and Propaganda in Comics and Film*. Jefferson, NC: McFarland.

Di Ricco, Massimo. 2015. "Drawing for a New Public: Middle Eastern 9th Art and the Emergence of a Transnational Graphic Movement." In *Postcolonial Comics: Texts, Events, Identities*, edited by Binita Mehta and Pia Mukherji, 187–203. New York: Routledge.

Dittmar, Jakob F. 2012. "Digital Comics." *Scandinavian Journal of Comic Art* 1, no. 2 (Autumn): 82–91. http://sjoca.com/wp-content/uploads/2013/01/SJoCA-1-2-Forum-Dittmar.pdf.

Dittmar, Jakob F. 2013. "Comics and History: Myth-Making in Nazi References." *International Journal of Comic Art* 15, no. 1 (Spring): 270–86.

Dittmar, Jakob F. 2015. "Experiments in Comics Storytelling." *Studies in Comics* 6, no. 1 (July): 157–67.

Dittmer, Jason. 2007. "The Tyranny of the Serial: Popular Geopolitics, the Nation, and Comic Book Discourse." *Antipode* 39, no. 2 (March): 247–68.

Dittmer, Jason. 2010. "Comic Book Visualities: A Methodological Manifesto on Geography, Montage and Narration." *Transactions of the Institute of British Geographers*, n.s., 35, no. 2 (April): 222–36.

Dittmer, Jason, ed. 2014a. *Comic Book Geographies*. Stuttgart: Franz Steiner Verlag.

Dittmer, Jason. 2014b. "Serialization and Displacement in Graphic Narrative." In *Serialization in Popular Culture*, edited by Rob Allen and Thijs van den Berg, 125–40. New York: Routledge.

Dittmer, Jason, and Alan Latham. 2015. "The Rut and the Gutter: Space and Time in Graphic Narrative." *Cultural Geographies* 22, no. 3 (July): 427–44.

Dixon, Wheeler Winston, and Richard Graham. 2017. *A Brief History of Comic Book Movies*. Cham, Switzerland: Palgrave Macmillan.

Dobbs, G. Michael. 2007. *Escape! How Animation Broke into the Mainstream in the 1990s*. Albany, GA: BearManor Media.

Dobrin, Sidney I., ed. 2020. *EcoComix: Essays on the Environment in Comics and Graphic Novels*. Jefferson, NC: McFarland.

Dolle-Weinkauff, Bernd. 2013. "Types of Violence in Sequential Art: The Mise en Scène of Violent Action Comics, Graphic Novels and Manga." In *Films, Graphic Novels and Visuals: Developing Multiliteracies in Foreign Language Education; An Interdisciplinary Approach*, edited by Daniela Elsner, Sissy Helff, and Britta Viebrock, 87–104. Münster, Germany: LIT Verlag.

Dolle-Weinkauff, Bernd. 2018. "What Are 'Historical Comics'? On Historical Storytelling in Comics, Manga and Graphic Novels." In *Geschichte im Comic: Befunde–Theorien– Erzählweisen*, edited by Bernd Dolle-Weinkauff, 11–28. Berlin: Christian A. Bachmann Verlag.

Dong, Lan, ed. 2012. *Teaching Comics and Graphic Narratives: Essays on Theory, Strategy and Practice*. Jefferson, NC: McFarland.

Donovan, Courtney. 2014. "Representations of Health, Embodiment, and Experience in Graphic Memoir." *Configurations* 22, no. 2 (Spring): 237–53.

Donovan, John. 2012. "Parody and Propaganda: Fighting American and the Battle against Crime and Communism in the 1950s." In *Comic Books and American Cultural History: An Anthology*, edited by Matthew Pustz, 110–19. New York: Continuum.

Donovan, Robert J., Lynda Fielder, Patrick Donovan, and Claire Handley. 2009. "Is Trivialisation of Alcohol Consumption a Laughing Matter? Alcohol Incidence in a

Metropolitan Daily Newspaper's Comic Strips." *Drug and Alcohol Review* 28, no. 3 (May): 257–62.

Dony, Christophe. 2014. "The Rewriting Ethos of the Vertigo Imprint: Critical Perspectives on Memory-Making and Canon Formation in the American Comics Field." *Comicalités: Études de Culture Graphique.* https://journals.openedition.org/comicalites/1918.

Dony, Christophe, Tanguy Habrand, and Gert Meesters, eds. 2014. *La bande dessinée en dissidence / Comics in Dissent: Alternative, indépendance, auto-édition / Alternative, Independence, Self-Publishing.* Liège: Presses Universitaires de Liège.

Dooley, Michael, and Steven Heller, eds. 2005. *The Education of a Comics Artist: Visual Narrative in Cartoons, Graphic Novels, and Beyond.* New York: Allworth Press.

Dowd, Douglas Bevan. 2004. "Strands of a Single Cord: Comics and Animation." In *Strips, Toons, and Bluesies: Essays in Comics and Culture*, edited by Douglas Bevan Dowd and Todd M. Hignite, 8–33. New York: Princeton Architectural Press.

Dowers, Michael. 2010. *Newave! The Underground Mini Comix of the 1980s.* Seattle: Fantagraphics Books.

Dowling, Jennifer. 2009. "'Oy Gevalt!' A Peek at the Development of Jewish Superheroines." In *The Contemporary Comic Book Superhero*, edited by Angela Ndalianis, 184–203. New York: Routledge.

Doyle, Peter. 2008. "If Walls Could Talk: Spatialising Narrative in the Museum." *SCAN: Journal of Media Arts Culture* 5, no. 2 (September): 1–11. http://scan.net.au/scan/journal/display.php?journal_id=119.

Drennig, Georg. 2010. "Otherness and the European as Villain and Antihero in American Comics." In *Comics as a Nexus of Cultures: Essays on the Interplay of Media, Disciplines and International Perspectives*, edited by Mark Berninger, Jochen Ecke, and Gideon Haberkorn, 127–39. Jefferson, NC: McFarland.

Drew, Jenny. 2016. *Cartooning Teen Stories: Using Comics to Explore Key Life Issues with Young People.* London: Jessica Kingsley Publishers.

Drucker, Johanna. 2008. "What Is Graphic about Graphic Novels?" *English Language Notes* 46, no. 2 (Fall–Winter): 39–55.

Duffy, Damian. 2015. "Hyper/Comics/Con/Text: Institutional Contexts and Interface Design in Online Educational Hypercomics." *Networking Knowledge: Journal of the MeCCSA Postgraduate Network* 8, no. 4 (June). https://ojs.meccsa.org.uk/index.php/netknow/article/view/390.

Duffy, Damian. 2020. "Comics Studies as Practitioner-Scholar." In *The Oxford Handbook of Comic Book Studies*, edited by Frederick Luis Aldama, 671–86. Oxford: Oxford University Press.

Duffy, Damian, and John Jennings. 2010. *Black Comix: African American Independent Comics, Art and Culture.* Brooklyn: Mark Batty Publisher.

Dufner, Gary, and Joo Kim. 2014. "Text and Images: Varying Sizes of Word Balloons in Comics." *International Journal of Comic Art* 16, no. 1 (Spring): 445–57.

Duggan, Jennifer. 2016. "Traumatic Origins: Orphanhood and the Superhero." In *Good Grief! Children and Comics: A Collection of Companion Essays*, edited by Michelle Ann Abate and Joe Sutliff Sanders, 47–97. Columbus: Ohio State University Libraries.

Duggan, Michael. 2008. *Web Comics for Teens*. Boston: Cengage Learning.

Duin, Steve, and Mike Richardson. 1998. *Comics: Between the Panels*. Milwaukie, OR: Dark Horse.

Dunaway, Finis. 2008. "Gas Masks, Pogo, and the Ecological Indian: Earth Day and the Visual Politics of American Environmentalism." *American Quarterly* 60, no. 1 (March): 67–99.

Duncan, Randy, and Matthew J. Smith. 2009. *The Power of Comics: History, Form, and Culture*. New York: Continuum.

Duncan, Randy, and Matthew J. Smith. 2013. *Icons of the American Comic Book: From Captain America to Wonder Woman*. Santa Barbara, CA: Greenwood.

Duncan, Randy, and Matthew J. Smith. 2020. "Next Issue: Anticipation and Promise in Comics Studies." In *The Oxford Handbook of Comic Book Studies*, edited by Frederick Luis Aldama, 642–55. Oxford: Oxford University Press.

Duncan, Randy, Michael Ray Taylor, and David Stoddard. 2016. *Creating Comics as Journalism, Memoir, and Nonfiction*. New York: Routledge.

Duncombe, Stephen. 1997. *Notes from Underground: Zines and the Politics of Alternative Culture*. Brooklyn: Verso.

Dunst, Alexander, Jochen Laubrock, and Janina Wildfeuer, eds. 2018. *Empirical Comics Research: Digital, Multimodal, and Cognitive Methods*. New York: Routledge.

Dyer, Ben, ed. 2009. *Supervillains and Philosophy: Sometimes, Evil Is Its Own Reward*. Chicago: Open Court.

Earle, Harriet E. H. 2013a. "Comics and the Chronotope: Time-Space Relationships in Traumatic Sequential Art." *HARTS and Minds: The Journal of Humanities and Arts* 1, no. 2 (Autumn): 2–13.

Earle, Harriet E. H. 2013b. "Comics and Page Bleeds." *Alluvium* 2, no. 5 (October). https://www.alluvium-journal.org/2013/10/09/comics-and-page-bleeds/.

Earle, Harriet E. H. 2013c. "Panel Transitions in Trauma Comics." *Alluvium* 2, no. 1 (January). https://www.alluvium-journal.org/2013/01/12/panel-transitions-in-trauma-comics/.

Earle, Harriet E. H. 2014. "Framing Comics Words." *Alluvium* 3, no. 2 (October). http://dx.doi.org/10.7766/alluvium.v3.2.02.

Earle, Harriet E. H. 2020. *Comics: An Introduction*. Abingdon, Oxon., England: Routledge.

Earle, Monalesia. 2019. *Writing Queer Women of Color: Representation and Misdirection in Contemporary Fiction and Graphic Narratives*. Jefferson, NC: McFarland.

Easton, Lee. 2013. "Saying No to Hetero-Masculinity: The Villain in the Superhero Film." *Cinephile: The University of British Columbia's Film Journal* 9, no. 2: 39–44.

Easton, Lee, and Richard Harrison. 2010. *Secret Identity Reader: Essays on Sex, Death and the Superhero*. Hamilton, Ont., Canada: Wolsak and Wynn.

Eckard, Sandra, ed. 2017. *Comic Connections: Analyzing Hero and Identity*. Lanham, MD: Rowman and Littlefield.

Ecke, Jochen, 2010. "Spatializing the Movie Screen: How Mainstream Cinema Is Catching Up on the Formal Potentialities of the Comic Book Page." In *Comics as a Nexus of Cultures: Essays on the Interplay of Media, Disciplines and International Perspectives*, edited by Mark Berninger, Jochen Ecke, and Gideon Haberkorn, 7–20. Jefferson, NC: McFarland.

Ecke, Jochen. 2019. *The British Comic Book Invasion: Alan Moore, Warren Ellis, Grant Morrison and the Evolution of the American Style*. Jefferson, NC: McFarland.

Eco, Umberto. 1990. *The Limits of Interpretation*. Bloomington: Indiana University Press.

Edidin, Rachel. 2008. "Four-Color Invasion: How Comics Crashed the Canon." *Gulf Coast: A Journal of Literature and Fine Arts* 20, no. 2 (Summer–Fall): 295–302.

Edwards, Janis L., and Laura Ware. 2005. "Representing the Public in Campaign Media: A Political Cartoon Perspective." *American Behavioral Scientist* 49, no. 3 (November): 466–78.

Edwards, Louise. 2013. "Drawing Sexual Violence in Wartime China: Anti-Japanese Propaganda Cartoons." *Journal of Asian Studies* 72, no. 3 (August): 563–86.

Edwards, Natalie, Amy L. Hubbell, and Ann Miller, eds. 2011. *Textual and Visual Selves: Photography, Film, and Comic Art in French Autobiography*. Lincoln: University of Nebraska Press.

Eedy, Sean. 2014. "Reimagining GDR Comics: *Kultur*, Children's Literature and the Socialist Personality." *Journal of Graphic Novels and Comics* 5, no. 3 (September): 245–56.

Eisner, Will. (1985) 2008a. *Comics and Sequential Art: Principles and Practices from the Legendary Cartoonist*. New York: W. W. Norton.

Eisner, Will. 2008b. *Expressive Anatomy for Comics and Narrative: Principles and Practices from the Legendary Cartoonist*. New York: W. W. Norton.

Eisner, Will. (1996) 2008c. *Graphic Storytelling and Visual Narrative: Principles and Practices from the Legendary Cartoonist*. New York: W. W. Norton.

Elmslie, Matthew. 2008. "Diversity and Evolution in the Reboot Legion." In *Teenagers from the Future: Essays on the Legion of Super-Heroes*, edited by Timothy Callahan, 242–60. Edwardsville, IL: Sequart Research and Literacy Organization.

El Refaie, Elisabeth. 2003. "Understanding Visual Metaphor: The Example of Newspaper Cartoons." *Visual Communication* 2, no. 1: 75–95.

El Refaie, Elisabeth. 2009a. "Metaphor in Political Cartoons: Exploring Audience Responses." In *Multimodal Metaphor*, edited by Charles J. Forceville and Eduardo Urios-Aparisi, 173–96. Berlin: Mouton de Gruyter.

El Refaie, Elisabeth. 2009b. "Multiliteracies: How Readers Interpret Political Cartoons." *Visual Communication* 8, no. 2: 181–205.

El Refaie, Elisabeth. 2010. "Visual Modality versus Authenticity: The Example of Autobiographical Comics." *Visual Studies* 25, no. 2 (September): 162–74.

El Refaie, Elisabeth. 2011. "The Pragmatics of Humor Reception: Young People's Responses to a Newspaper Cartoon." *Humor: International Journal of Humor Research* 24, no. 1: 87–108.

El Refaie, Elisabeth. 2012. *Autobiographical Comics: Life Writing in Pictures*. Jackson: University Press of Mississippi.

El Refaie, Elisabeth. 2015. "Reconsidering 'Image Metaphor' in the Light of Perceptual Simulation Theory." *Metaphor and Symbol* 30, no. 1 (January–March): 63–76.

El Refaie, Elisabeth. 2019. *Visual Metaphor and Embodiment in Graphic Illness Narratives*. Oxford: Oxford University Press.

Epskamp, Kees. 1992. "Cross-Cultural Interpretations of Cartoons and Drawings." In *The Empowerment of Culture: Development, Communication, and Popular Media*, edited by Ad Boeren and Kees Epskamp, 79–93. The Hague: Centre for the Study of Education in Developing Countries.

Estren, Mark James. (1974) 1993. *A History of Underground Comics*. Oakland: Ronin.

Etter, Lukas. 2016. "Visible Hand? Subjectivity and Its Stylistic Markers in Graphic Narratives." In *Subjectivity across Media: Interdisciplinary and Transmedial Perspectives*, edited by Maike Sarah Reinerth and Jan-Noël Thon, 92–110. New York: Routledge.

Eury, Michael. 2017. *Hero-a-Go-Go: Campy Comic Books, Crimefighters, and Culture of the Swinging Sixties*. Raleigh, NC: TwoMorrows Publishing.

Evans, Janet. 2013. "From Comics, Graphic Novels and Picturebooks to Fusion Texts: A New Kid on the Block!" *Education 3–13: International Journal of Primary, Elementary, and Early Years Education* 41, no. 2: 233–48.

Evans, Jonathan. 2016. "More than Simply a Flash of Colour: The True Rhetorical Power of Superhero Style." In *Framescapes: Graphic Narrative Intertexts*, edited by Mikhail Peppas and Sanabelle Ebrahim, 3–13. Oxford: Inter-Disciplinary Press.

Evans, Jonathan. 2019. "Challenging Adaptation Studies: A Review of Comics and Adaptation." *The Comics Grid: Journal of Comics Scholarship* 9, no. 1: 1–7. https://www.comicsgrid.com/article/id/3579/.

Eveleth, Kyle. 2014. "Rust and Revitalization: The So-Called Bronze and Modern Ages of Comics." In *Critical Insights: The American Comic Book*, edited by Joseph Michael Sommers, 119–35. Ipswich, MA: Salem Press.

Fagence, Brian. 2011. "Writing Art: Revealing Distinctive Modes." *Journal of Writing in Creative Practice* 4, no. 2: 177–88.

Falardeau, Mira. 2018. *A History of Women Cartoonists*. Oakville, Ont., Canada: Mosaic Press.

Falgas, Julien. 2020. "Not All Fans Leave a Trace: The Case of a Digital Comic Serial Inspired by Television Series." In *French Perspectives on Media, Participation and Audiences*, edited by Céline Ségur, 149–64. Cham, Switzerland: Palgrave Macmillan.

Fall, Juliet Jane. 2014. "Put Your Body on the Line: Autobiographical Comics, Empathy and Plurivocality." In *Comic Book Geographies*, edited by Jason Dittmer, 91–108. Stuttgart: Franz Steiner Verlag.

Farinella, Matteo. 2018a. "Of Microscopes and Metaphors: Visual Analogy as a Scientific Tool." *The Comics Grid: Journal of Comics Scholarship* 8, no. 1: 1–16. https://www.comicsgrid.com/article/id/3578/.

Farinella, Matteo. 2018b. "The Potential of Comics in Science Communication." *Journal of Science Communication* 17, no. 1 (January). https://jcom.sissa.it/sites/default/files/documents/JCOM_1701_2018_Y01.pdf.

Faris, Michael J. 2019. "Sex-Education Comics: Feminist and Queer Approaches to Alternative Sex Education." *Journal of Multimodal Rhetorics* 3, no. 1: 86–114. http://journalofmulti modalrhetorics.com/files/documents/3e1da5ea-f18e-4dc0-abda-96dbf877eb3e.pdf.

Farmer, Clark. 2006. "Comic Book Color and the Digital Revolution." *International Journal of Comic Art* 8, no. 2 (Fall): 330–46.

Farrelly, Liz. 2001. *Zines*. London: Booth-Clibborn Editions.

Fawaz, Ramzi. 2011. "'Where No X-Man Has Gone Before!' Mutant Superheroes and the Cultural Politics of Popular Fantasy in Postwar America." *American Literature* 83, no. 2 (June): 355–88.

Fawaz, Ramzi. 2016. *The New Mutants: Superheroes and the Radical Imagination of American Comics*. New York: New York University Press.

Feiffer, Jules. (1965) 2003. *The Great Comic Book Heroes*. Rev. ed. Seattle: Fantagraphics Books.

Fein, Ofer, and Asa Kasher. 1996. "How to Do Things with Words and Gestures in Comics." *Journal of Pragmatics* 26, no. 6 (December): 793–808.

Fennel, Jack. 2012. "The Aesthetics of Supervillainy." *Law Text Culture* 16: 305–18.

Fenty, Sean, Trena Houp, and Laurie Taylor. 2004. "Webcomics: The Influence and Continuation of the Comix Revolution." *ImageTexT: Interdisciplinary Comics Studies* 1, no. 2. http://www.english.ufl.edu/imagetext/archives/v1_2/group/index.shtml.

Fingeroth, Danny. 2007. *Disguised as Clark Kent: Jews, Comics, and the Creation of the Superhero*. New York: Continuum.

Fink, Moritz. 2018. "Of *Maus* and *Gen*: Author Avatars in Nonfiction Comics." *International Journal of Comic Art* 20, no. 1 (Spring–Summer): 267–96.

Fischer, Roger A. 1996. *Them Damned Pictures: Explorations in American Political Cartoon Art*. North Haven, CT: Archon Books.

Fishelov, David. 1990. "Types of Character, Characteristics of Types." *Style* 24, no. 3: 422–39.

Flinn, Margaret C. 2013. "High Comics Art: The Louvre and the Bande Dessinée." *European Comic Art* 6, no. 2 (December): 69–94.

Flora, Cornelia Butler. 1980a. "Fotonovelas: Message Creation and Reception." *Journal of Popular Culture* 14, no. 3 (Winter): 524–34.

Flora, Cornelia Butler. 1980b. "Women in Latin American Fotonovelas: From Cinderella to Mata Hari." *Women's Studies International Quarterly* 3, no. 1: 95–104.

Flora, Cornelia Butler. 1984. "Roasting Donald Duck: Alternative Comics and Photonovels in Latin America." *Journal of Popular Culture* 18, no. 1 (Summer): 163–83.

Flora, Cornelia Butler. 1989. "The Political Economy of Fotonovela Production in Latin America." *Studies in Latin American Popular Culture* 8: 215–30.

Flora, Cornelia Butler, and Jan L. Flora. 1978. "The Fotonovela as a Tool for Class and Cultural Domination." *Latin American Perspectives* 5, no. 1 (Winter): 134–50.

Flores, Emil Francis M. 2013. "Up in the Sky, Feet on the Ground: Cultural Identity in Filipino Superhero Komiks." In *Cultural Excavation and Formal Expression in the Graphic Novel,* edited by Jonathan C. Evans and Thomas Giddens, 73–86. Oxford: Oxford University Press.

Fludernik, Monika. 2015. "Blending in Cartoons: The Production of Comedy." In *The Oxford Handbook of Cognitive Literary Studies,* edited by Lisa Zunshine, 155–75. Oxford: Oxford University Press.

Forceville, Charles. 2013. "Creative Visual Variation in Comics Balloons." In *Creativity and the Agile Mind: A Multi-Disciplinary Study of a Multi-Faceted Phenomenon,* edited by Tony Veale, Kurt Feyaerts, and Charles Forceville, 253–73. Berlin: Mouton de Gruyter.

Forceville, Charles. 2016. "Conceptual Metaphor Theory, Blending Theory and Other Cognitivist Perspectives on Comics." In *The Visual Narrative Reader,* edited by Neil Cohn, 89–114. London: Bloomsbury.

Forceville, Charles, Elisabeth El Refaie, and Gert Meesters. 2014. "Stylistics and Comics." In *The Routledge Handbook of Stylistics,* edited by Michael Burke, 485–99. Abingdon, Oxon., England: Routledge.

Forceville, Charles, and Marloes Jeulink. 2011. "The Flesh and Blood of Embodied Understanding: The Source-Path-Goal Schema in Animation Film." *Pragmatics and Cognition* 19, no. 1 (August): 37–59.

Forceville, Charles, Tony Veale, and Kurt Feyaerts. 2010. "Balloonics: The Visuals of Balloons in Comics." In *The Rise and Reason of Comics and Graphic Literature: Critical Essays on the Form,* edited by Joyce Goggin and Dan Hassler-Forest, 56–73. Jefferson, NC: McFarland.

Foss, Chris, Jonathan W. Gray, and Zach Whalen, eds. 2016. *Disability in Comic Books and Graphic Narratives.* Basingstoke, Hants., England: Palgrave Macmillan.

Foster, David William. 2016. *El Eternauta, Daytripper, and Beyond: Graphic Narrative in Argentina and Brazil.* Austin: University of Texas Press.

Foster, John. 1991. "From 'Ulla Dulla Mogo' to 'Serene Azure Vault in Heaven': Literary Style in Australian Children's Comic Books." *Journal of Popular Culture* 25, no. 3 (Winter): 63–77.

Foster, John. 2011. "Picture Books as Graphic Novels and Vice Versa: The Australian Experience." *Bookbird: A Journal of International Children's Literature* 49, no. 4: 68–75.

Foster, William, III. 2002. "The Image of Blacks (African Americans) in Underground Comix: New Liberal Agenda or Same Racist Stereotypes?" *International Journal of Comic Art* 4, no. 2 (Fall): 168–85.

Foster, William, III. 2005. *Looking for a Face Like Mine: The History of African Americans in Comics.* Waterbury, CT: Fine Tooth Press.

Fox, Abram. 2014. "The Color and the Shape: Procedural Rhetoric in Works by David Mazzucchelli and Daniel Clowes." *International Journal of Comic Art* 16, no. 2 (Fall–Winter): 300–312.

Fox, Celina. 1988. *Graphic Journalism in England during the 1830s and 1840s.* New York: Garland Publishing.

Frahm, Ole. 2000. "Weird Signs: Comics as a Means of Parody." In *Comics and Culture: Analytical and Theoretical Approaches to Comics*, edited by Anne Magnussen and Hans-Christian Christiansen, 177–91. Copenhagen: Museum Tusculanum Press.

Francis, Fred. 2016. "'Footnotes to Miller and Moore': Monomyth and Transnationality in the 1986 Superhero Comics." *Comparative American Studies: An International Journal* 14, nos. 3–4 (September–December): 289–301.

Franklin, Morris E., III. 2001. "Coming Out in Comic Books: Letter Columns, Readers, and Gay and Lesbian Characters." In *Comics and Ideology*, edited by Matthew P. McAllister, Edward H. Sewell Jr., and Ian Gordon, 221–50. New York: Peter Lang.

Freedman, Ariela. 2015. "Comics and the Canon: Introduction to the Forum." *Partial Answers: Journal of Literature and the History of Ideas* 13, no. 2 (June): 251–54.

Freeman, Matthew. 2014. "Branding Consumerism: Cross-Media Characters and Story-Worlds at the Turn of the 20th Century." *International Journal of Cultural Studies* 18, no. 6 (November): 629–44.

Frey, Nancy, and Douglas Fisher, eds. 2008. *Teaching Visual Literacy: Using Comic Books, Graphic Novels, Anime, Cartoons, and More to Develop Comprehension and Thinking Skills.* Thousand Oaks, CA: Corwin Press.

Friedenthal, Andrew J. 2017. *Retcon Game: Retroactive Continuity and the Hyperlinking of America.* Jackson: University Press of Mississippi.

Friedenthal, Andrew J. 2019. *The World of DC Comics.* New York: Routledge.

Friesen, Jan, John T. Van Stan II, and Skander Elleuche. 2018. "Communicating Science through Comics: A Method." *Publications* 6, no. 3 (August). https://www.mdpi.com/2304-6775/6/3/38.

Frome, Jonathan. 1999. "Identification in Comics." *Comics Journal*, no. 211 (April): 82–86.

Furniss, Maureen. 2016. *A New History of Animation.* London: Thames and Hudson.

Gabilliet, Jean-Paul. 2010. *Of Comics and Men: A Cultural History of American Comic Books.* Translated by Bart Beaty and Nick Nguyen. Jackson: University Press of Mississippi.

Gabilliet, Jean-Paul. 2016. "Reading Facsimile Reproductions of Original Artwork: The Comics Fan as Connoisseur." *Image [&] Narrative: Online Magazine of the Visual Narrative* 17, no. 4 (November): 16–25. http://www.imageandnarrative.be/index.php/imagenarrative/article/view/1318/1069.

Gabilliet, Jean-Paul. 2018. "Underground Comix and the Invention of Autobiography, History, and Reportage." In *The Cambridge History of the Graphic Novel*, edited by Jan Baetens, Hugo Frey, and Stephen E. Tabachnick, 155–70. Cambridge: Cambridge University Press.

Galewitz, Herb, ed. 1972. *Great Comics: Syndicated by the "Daily News"—"Chicago Tribune."* New York: Crown Publishers.

Gallacher, Lesley-Anne. 2011. "(Fullmetal) Alchemy: The Monstrosity of Reading Words and Pictures in Shōnen Manga." *Cultural Geographies* 18, no. 4 (October): 457–73.

Garbot, Dave, and Walter Foster. 2016. *The Big Book of Cartooning: An Adventurous Journey into the Amazing and Awesome World of Cartooning.* London: Quarto Group.

García, Carmen Valero. 2008. "Onomatopoeia and Unarticulated Language in the Translation of Comic Books: The Case of Comics in Spanish." In *Comics in Translation*, edited by Federico Zanettin, 237–50. Manchester: St. Jerome.

García, Enrique. 2018. "The Latina Superheroine: Protecting the Reader from the Comic Book Industry's Racial, Gender, Ethnic, and Nationalistic Biases." In *Comic Studies Here and Now*, edited by Frederick Luis Aldama, 163–79. New York: Routledge.

García, Santiago. 2015. *On the Graphic Novel*. Translated by Bruce Campbell. Jackson: University Press of Mississippi.

Gardner, Jared. 2006. "Archives, Collectors, and the New Media Work of Comics." *Modern Fiction Studies* 52, no. 4 (Winter): 787–806.

Gardner, Jared. 2008. "Autography's Biography, 1972–2007." *Biography: An Interdisciplinary Quarterly* 31, no. 1 (Winter): 1–26.

Gardner, Jared. 2012. *Projections: Comics and the History of Twenty-First-Century Storytelling*. Stanford, CA: Stanford University Press.

Gardner, Jared. 2013. "A History of the Narrative Comic Strip." In *From Comic Strips to Graphic Novels: Contributions to the Theory and History of Graphic Narrative*, edited by Daniel Stein and Jan-Noël Thon, 241–53. Berlin: Walter de Gruyter.

Gardner, Jared. 2014. "Film + Comics: A Multimodal Romance in the Age of Transmedial Convergence." In *Storyworlds across Media: Toward a Media-Conscious Narratology*, edited by Marie-Laure Ryan and Jan-Noël Thon, 193–210. Lincoln: University of Nebraska Press.

Gardner, Jared. 2017. "Antebellum Popular Serialities and the Transatlantic Birth of 'American' Comics." In *Media of Serial Narrative*, edited by Frank Kelleter, 37–52. Columbus: Ohio State University Press.

Gardner, Jared, and David Herman. 2011. "Graphic Narratives and Narrative Theory." *SubStance* 40, no. 1: 3–13.

Gardner, Jeanne Emerson. 2012a. "'Dreams May End, But Love Never Does': Marriage and Materialism in American Romance Comics, 1947–1954." In *Comic Books and American Cultural History: An Anthology*, edited by Matthew Pustz, 94–109. New York: Continuum.

Gardner, Jeanne Emerson. 2012b. "Girls Who Sinned in Secret and Paid in Public: Romance Comics, 1949–1954." In *Comic Books and the Cold War, 1946–1962: Essays on Graphic Treatment of Communism, the Code and Social Concerns*, edited by Chris York and Rafiel York, 92–102. Jefferson, NC: McFarland.

Gardner, Jeanne Emerson. 2013. "She Got Her Man, But Could She Keep Him? Love and Marriage in American Romance Comics, 1947–1954." *Journal of American Culture* 36, no. 1 (March): 16–24.

Garrett, Greg. 2008. *Holy Superheroes! Exploring the Sacred in Comics, Graphic Novels, and Film*. Louisville: Westminster John Knox Press.

Garrity, Shaenon. 2011. "The History of Webcomics." *Comics Journal*, July 15. http://www.tcj .com/the-history-of-webcomics/.

Garvey, Ellen Gruber. 2002. "Out of the Mainstream and into the Streets: Small Press Magazines, the Underground Press, Zines, and Artists' Books." In *Perspectives on*

American Book History: Artifacts and Commentary, edited by Scott E. Casper, Joanne D. Chaison, and Jeffrey D. Groves, 367–402. Amherst: University of Massachusetts Press.

Gateward, Frances, and John Jennings, eds. 2015. *The Blacker the Ink: Constructions of Black Identity in Comics and Sequential Art*. New Brunswick, NJ: Rutgers University Press.

Gaudreault, André. 2009. *From Plato to Lumière: Narration and Monstration in Literature and Cinema*. Translated by Timothy Barnard. Toronto: University of Toronto Press.

Gavaler, Chris. 2015. *On the Origin of Superheroes: From the Big Bang to Action Comics no. 1*. Iowa City: University of Iowa Press.

Gavaler, Chris. 2017. "Refining the Comics Form." *European Comic Art* 10, no. 2 (December): 1–23.

Gavaler, Chris. 2018a. *Superhero Comics*. London: Bloomsbury.

Gavaler, Chris. 2018b. "Undemocratic Layout: Eight Methods of Accentuating Images." *The Comics Grid: Journal of Comics Scholarship* 8, no. 1: 1–24. https://www.comicsgrid.com/article/id/3568/.

Gavaler, Chris. 2019. "Three of a Perfect Pair: Image, Text, and Image-Text Narrators." *Image [&] Narrative: Online Magazine of the Visual Narrative* 20, no. 1 (April): 67–84. http://www.imageandnarrative.be/index.php/imagenarrative/article/view/2076/1626.

Gavaler, Chris, and Leigh Ann Beavers. 2020. "Clarifying Closure." *Journal of Graphic Novels and Comics* 11, no. 2 (April): 182–211.

Gearino, Dan. 2017. *Comic Shop: The Retail Mavericks Who Gave Us a New Geek Culture*. Athens, OH: Swallow Press.

Gedin, David. 2019. "Format Codings in Comics: The Elusive Art of Punctuation." *Inks: Journal of the Comics Studies Society* 3, no. 3 (Fall): 298–314.

Gerety, Rowan Moore. 2016. "Comics without Captions." *Virginia Quarterly Review* 92, no. 1 (Winter): 140–53.

Geyh, Paula. 2017. "Between Word and Image." In *The Cambridge Companion to Postmodern American Fiction*, edited by Paula Geyh, 163–80. Cambridge: Cambridge University Press.

Ghosal, Torsa. 2018. "The Page Is Local: Planetarity and Embodied Metaphor in Anglophone Graphic Narratives from South Asia." In *Comics Studies Here and Now*, edited by Frederick Luis Aldama, 180–90. New York: Routledge.

Gibson, Mel. 2010a. "Graphic Novels, Comics and Picturebooks." In *Routledge Companion to Children's Literature*, edited by David Rudd, 100–111. Abingdon, Oxon., England: Routledge.

Gibson, Mel. 2010b. "What Bunty Did Next: Exploring Some of the Ways in Which the British Girls' Comic Protagonists Were Revisited and Revised in Late Twentieth-Century Comics and Graphic Novels." *Journal of Graphic Novels and Comics* 1, no. 2 (December): 121–35.

Gibson, Mel. 2018. "'It's All Come Flooding Back': Memories of Childhood Comics." In *Comics Memory: Archives and Styles*, edited by Maaheen Ahmed and Benoît Crucifix, 37–56. Cham, Switzerland: Palgrave Macmillan.

Gibson, Mel, David Huxley, and Joan Ormrod, eds. 2014. *Superheroes and Identities*. Abingdon, Oxon., England: Routledge.

Gibson, Mel, Golnar Nabizadeh, and Kay Sambell. 2014. "Watch This Space: Childhood, Picturebooks and Comics." *Journal of Graphic Novels and Comics* 5, no. 3 (September): 241–44.

Gibson, Melanie Elizabeth. 2020. "Rising from the Ashes: Making Spaces for New Children's Comics Cultures in Britain in the 21st Century." *Journal of Graphic Novels and Comics* 11, no. 2 (April): 201–25.

Giddens, Thomas. 2012. "Comics, Law, and Aesthetics: Towards the Use of Graphic Fiction in Legal Studies." *Law and Humanities* 6, no. 1: 85–109.

Giddens, Thomas, ed. 2015. *Graphic Justice: Intersections of Comics and Law*. Abingdon, Oxon., England: Routledge.

Giddens, Thomas. 2016. "What Is Graphic Justice?" *The Comics Grid: Journal of Comics Scholarship* 6, no. 1 (Summer): 1–5. https://www.comicsgrid.com/article/id/3540/.

Giddens, Thomas. 2018. *On Comics and Legal Aesthetics: Multimodality and the Haunted Mask of Knowing*. Abingdon, Oxon., England: Routledge.

Giesen, Rolf. 2015. *Chinese Animation: A History and Filmography, 1922–2012*. Jefferson, NC: McFarland.

Gifford, Denis. 1971. *The History of the British Newspaper Comic Strip*. Princes Risborough, Bucks., England: Shire Publications.

Gifford, Denis. 1975. *Victorian Comics*. Westport, CT: Greenwood Press.

Gifford, Denis. 2003. "Popular Literature: Comics, Dime Novels, Pulps and Penny Dreadfuls." In *International Companion Encyclopedia of Children's Literature*, edited Peter Hunt, 363–85. Abingdon, Oxon., England: Routledge.

Gilmore, James, and Matthias Stork, eds. 2014. *Superhero Synergies: Comic Book Characters Go Digital*. Lanham, MD: Rowman and Littlefield.

Glascock, Jack, and Catherine Preston-Schreck. 2004. "Gender and Racial Stereotypes in Daily Newspaper Comics: A Time-Honored Tradition?" *Sex Roles* 51, no. 7 (October): 423–31.

Glaser, Jennifer. 2014. "Of Superheroes and Synecdoche: Holocaust Exceptionalism, Race, and the Rhetoric of Jewishness in America." In *Jewish Rhetorics: History, Theory, Practice*, edited by Michael Bernard-Donals and Janice W. Fernheimer, 231–48. Waltham, MA: Brandeis University Press.

Glazer, Sarah. 2015. "Graphic Medicine: Comics Turn a Critical Eye on Health Care." *Hastings Center Report* 45, no. 3 (May–June): 15–19.

Goggin, Joyce. 2010. "Of Gutters and Guttersnipes: Hogarth's Legacy." In *The Rise and Reason of Comics and Graphic Literature: Critical Essays on the Form*, edited by Joyce Goggin and Dan Hassler-Forest, 6–24. Jefferson, NC: McFarland.

Gökçen, Başaran İnce. 2015. "The Free Republican Party in the Political Cartoons of the 1930s." *New Perspectives on Turkey* 53 (Fall): 93–136.

Goldsmith, Francisca. 2005. *Graphic Novels Now: Building, Managing, and Marketing a Dynamic Collection*. Chicago: American Library Association.

Gombrich, E. H. 1972. "The Mask and the Face: The Perception of Physiognomic Likeness in Life and in Art." In *Art, Perception, and Reality*, by E. H. Gombrich, Julian Hochberg, and Max Black, edited by Maurice Mandelbaum, 1–46. Baltimore: Johns Hopkins University Press.

Gombrich, E. H. (1960) 2000. *Art and Illusion: A Study in the Psychology of Pictorial Representation*. Rev. ed. Princeton, NJ: Princeton University Press.

Gomes, Mario, and Jan Peuckert. 2010. "Memento Mori: A Portuguese Style of Melancholy." In *Comics as a Nexus of Cultures: Essays on the Interplay of Media, Disciplines and International Perspectives*, edited by Mark Berninger, Jochen Ecke, and Gideon Haberkorn, 116–26. Jefferson, NC: McFarland.

Gomez, Christopher. 2014. "Teaching Physical Geography at University with Cartoons and Comic Strips: Motivation, Construction and Usage." *New Zealand Geographer* 70, no. 2 (August): 140–45.

Gomez Romero, Luis, and Ian Dahlman, eds. 2012. "Justice Framed: Law in Comics and Graphic Novels." Special issue, *Law Text Culture* 16, no. 1. https://ro.uow.edu.au/ltc/vol16/iss1/.

González, Jesús A. 2014. "'Living in the Funnies': Metafiction in American Comic Strips." *Journal of Popular Culture* 47, no. 4 (August): 838–56.

Goodbrey, Daniel Merlin. 2013a. "Digital Comics: New Tools and Tropes." *Studies in Comics* 4, no. 1: 185–97.

Goodbrey, Daniel Merlin. 2013b. "From Comic to Hypercomic." In *Cultural Excavation and Formal Expression in the Graphic Novel*, edited by Jonathan C. Evans and Thomas Giddens, 291–302. Oxford: Oxford University Press.

Goodbrey, Daniel Merlin. 2015a. "Game Comics: An Analysis of an Emergent Hybrid Form." *Journal of Graphic Novels and Comics* 6, no. 1 (March): 3–14.

Goodbrey, Daniel Merlin. 2015b. "The Sound of Digital Comics." *Writing Visual Culture* 7, no. 1 (October): 1–17. https://www.herts.ac.uk/__data/assets/pdf_file/0004/293278/TVAD_WVC-Volume-7.pdf.

Goodbrey, Daniel Merlin, and Jayms Clifford Nichols, eds. 2015. "Digital Comics." Special issue, *Networking Knowledge: Journal of the MeCCSA Postgraduate Network* 8, no. 4 (June). https://ojs.meccsa.org.uk/index.php/netknow/issue/view/47.

Goodrum, Michael, Tara Prescott, and Philip Smith, eds. 2018. *Gender and the Superhero Narrative*. Jackson: University Press of Mississippi.

Gordon, Ian. 1993. *Comic Strips and Consumer Culture, 1890–1945*. Washington, DC: Smithsonian Institution Press.

Gordon, Ian. 2000. "Beyond the Funnies: Comic Books, History, and Hegemony." *American Quarterly* 52, no. 1 (March): 145–50.

Gordon, Ian. 2013. "Comics, Creators, and Copyright: On the Ownership of Serial Narratives by Multiple Authors." In *A Companion to Media Authorship*, edited by Jonathan Gray and Derek Johnson, 221–36. Chichester, W. Susx., England: Wiley-Blackwell.

Gordon, Ian. 2016. *Kid Comic Strips: A Genre across Four Countries*. New York: Palgrave Macmillan.

Gordon, Ian. 2020. "Comics Studies in America: The Making of a Field of Scholarship?" In *The Oxford Handbook of Comic Book Studies*, edited by Frederick Luis Aldama, 631–41. Oxford: Oxford University Press.

Gordon, Ian, Mark Jancovich, and Matthew P. McAllister, eds. 2007. *Film and Comic Books*. Jackson: University Press of Mississippi.

Gorman, Michele. 2007. *Getting Graphic! Comics for Kids*. Columbus, OH: Linworth Books.

Goulart, Ron. 1986. *The Great Comic Book Artists*. New York: St. Martin's Press.

Goulart, Ron. 1998. "Comic Book Noir." In *The Big Book of Noir*, edited by Ed Gorman, Lee Server, and Martin H. Greenberg, 337–45. New York: Carroll and Graf.

Goulart, Ron. 2008. *Good Girl Art*. New Castle, PA: Hermes Press.

Grail, Ivan. 2007. "The Truly Un-Canny Samurai: Classical Literature and Parody in the Kibyoshi." *International Journal of Comic Art* 9, no. 1 (Spring): 61–78.

Grant, Barry Keith, and Scott Henderson, eds. 2019. *Comics and Pop Culture: Adaptation from Panel to Frame*. Austin: University of Texas Press.

Gravett, Paul. 1998. "The Cartoonist's Progress: The Inventors of Comics in Great Britain." In *Forging a New Medium: The Comic Strip in the Nineteenth Century*, edited by Charles Dierick and Pascal Lefèvre, 81–103. Brussels: Vrije Universiteit Brussel University Press.

Gravett, Paul. 2004. *Manga: Sixty Years of Japanese Comics*. London: Laurence King.

Gravett, Paul. 2013. *Comics Art*. London: Tate Publishing.

Gravett, Paul. 2017. *Mangasia: The Definitive Guide to Asian Comics*. London: Thames and Hudson.

Gray, Brenna Clarke. 2016. "Border Studies in the Gutter: Canadian Comics and Structural Borders." *Canadian Literature: A Quarterly of Criticism and Review* 228–29 (Spring–Summer): 170–87.

Gray, Brenna Clarke, and Peter Wilkins. 2016. "The Case of the Missing Author: Toward an Anatomy of Collaboration in Comics." In *Cultures of Comics Work*, edited by Casey Brienza and Paddy Johnston, 115–30. New York: Palgrave Macmillan.

Green, Michael J., and Kimberly R. Myers. 2010. "Graphic Medicine: Use of Comics in Medical Education and Patient Care." *BMJ: British Medical Journal* 340, no. 7746 (March): 574–77.

Gregov, R. J. 2008. "The Re-Illustration of Comic Book Heroes." *International Journal of Comic Art* 10, no. 1 (Spring): 471–81.

Grennan, Simon. 2017. *A Theory of Narrative Drawing*. New York: Palgrave Macmillan.

Grennan, Simon. 2018. "The Influence of Manga on the Graphic Novel." In *The Cambridge History of the Graphic Novel*, edited by Jan Baetens, Hugo Frey, and Stephen E. Tabachnick, 320–36. Cambridge: Cambridge University Press.

Gresh, Lois H., and Robert Weinberg. 2002. *The Science of Superheroes*. Hoboken, NJ: John Wiley and Sons.

Gresh, Lois H., and Robert Weinberg. 2004. *The Science of Supervillains*. Hoboken, NJ: John Wiley and Sons.

Greyson, Devon. 2007. "GLBTQ Content in Comics/Graphic Novels for Teens." *Collection Building* 26, no. 4 (October): 130–34.

Gries, Laurie. 2015. "Obama Zombies and Rhetorical (Dis)Identifications in an Era of Dog Whistle Politics and Political Polarization." *ImageTexT: Interdisciplinary Comics Studies* 8, no. 1. http://imagetext.english.ufl.edu/archives/v8_1/gries/.

Groene, Samantha L., and Vanessa E. Hettinger. 2016. "Are You 'Fan' Enough? The Role of Identity in Media Fandoms." *Psychology of Popular Media Culture* 5, no. 4: 324–39.

Groensteen, Thierry. 1993. "Fully-Painted-Artwork: Seduction by Images." In *Couleur directe: Chefs d'oeuvres de la nouvelle bande dessinée française / Mesiterwerke des neuen französischen Comics / Masterworks of the New French Comics*, edited by Didier Moulin, 10–75. Thurn, Austria: Edition Kunst der Comics.

Groensteen, Thierry. 1997. "Comic Strip and Newspaper Cartoons: The Dawn of a Revolution." In *The Sixties: Britain and France, 1962–1973; The Utopian Years*, edited by David Alan Mellor and Laurent Gervereau, 132–48. London: Philip Wilson Publishers.

Groensteen, Thierry. 2007. *The System of Comics*. Translated by Bart Beaty and Nick Nguyen. Jackson: University Press of Mississippi.

Groensteen, Thierry. 2009. "Why Are Comics Still in Search of Cultural Legitimization?" In *A Comics Studies Reader*, edited by Jeet Heer and Kent Worcester, 3–11. Jackson: University Press of Mississippi.

Groensteen, Thierry. 2010. "The Monstrator, the Recitant, and the Shadow of the Narrator." *European Comic Art* 3, no. 1 (March): 1–21.

Groensteen, Thierry. 2013. *Comics and Narration*. Translated by Ann Miller. Jackson: University Press of Mississippi.

Groensteen, Thierry. 2016. "The Art of Braiding: A Clarification." *European Comic Art* 9, no. 1 (Spring): 88–98.

Groß, Florian. 2013. "Lost in Translation: Narratives of Transcultural Displacement in the Wordless Graphic Novel." In *Transnational Perspectives on Graphic Narratives: Comics at the Crossroads*, edited by Shane Denson, Christina Meyer, and Daniel Stein, 197–210. London: Bloomsbury.

Groth, Gary. 1988. "Grown-Up Comics: Breakout from the Underground." *Print* 42, no. 6 (November–December): 98–111.

Groth, Gary. 2001. "Independent Spirits: A Comics Perspective." In *Below Critical Radar: Fanzines and Alternative Comics from 1976 to Now*, edited by Roger Sabin and Teal Triggs, 17–32. Brighton and Hove, E. Susx., England: Slab-O-Concrete.

Grove, Laurence. 1999. "Visual Cultures, National Visions: The Ninth Art of France." In *New Directions in Emblem Studies*, edited by Amy Wygant, 43–57. Glasgow: Glasgow Emblem Studies.

Grove, Laurence. 2005. *Text/Image Mosaics in French Culture: Emblems and Comic Strips*. Farnham, Surrey, England: Ashgate Publishing.

Grove, Laurence. 2010. *Comics in French: The European Bande Dessinée in Context*. New York: Berghahn Books.

Grünewald, Dietrich. 2012. "The Picture Story Principle." *International Journal of Comic Art* 14, no. 1 (Spring): 171–97.

Grunzke, Andrew. 2017. "Using Multimodal Literacy to Teach Gender History through Comic Books; or, How 'The Wonder Women of History' Became 'Marriage à la Mode.'" In *Educating through Popular Culture: You're Not Cool Just Because You Teach with Comics*, edited by Edward Janak and Ludovic A. Sourdot, 243–63. Lanham, MD: Lexington Books.

Gunawan, Iwan. 2014. "Visual Design for the Universe of Wayang Comics." *International Journal of Comics Art* 16, no. 2 (Fall–Winter): 528–45.

Gunning, Tom. 2014. "The Art of Succession: Reading, Writing, and Watching Comics." *Critical Inquiry* 40, no. 3 (Spring): 36–51.

Gutierrez, Anna Katrina. 2014. "American Superheroes, Manga Cuteness and the Filipino Child: the Emergence of Glocal Philippine Comics and Picturebooks." *Journal of Graphic Novels and Comics* 5, no. 3 (September): 344–60.

Guynes, Sean A. 2014. "Four-Color Sound: A Peircean Semiotics of Comic Book Onomatopoeia." *Public Journal of Semiotics* 6, no. 1 (January): 58–72. https://journals.lub .lu.se/pjos/article/view/11916/10586.

Guynes, Sean A., and Martin Lund, eds. 2020. *Unstable Masks: Whiteness and American Superhero Comics*. Columbus: Ohio State University Press.

Hague, Ian. 2012. "Beyond the Visual: The Roles of the Senses in Contemporary Comics." *Scandinavian Journal of Comic Art* 1, no. 1 (Spring): 97–110. http://sjoca.com/wp-content/ uploads/2012/06/SJoCA-1-1-Article-Hague.pdf.

Hague, Ian. 2014. *Comics and the Senses: A Multisensory Approach to Comics and Graphic Novels*. New York: Routledge.

Hajdu, David. 2008. *The Ten-Cent Plague: The Great Comic-Book Scare and How It Changed America*. New York: Farrar, Straus and Giroux.

Hall, Justin, ed. 2012. *No Straight Lines: Four Decades of Queer Comics*. Seattle: Fantagraphics Books.

Hammond, Heidi. 2009. *Graphic Novels and Multimodal Literacy: A Reader Response Study*. Chișinău: Lambert Academic Publishing.

Hammontree, David R. 2017. "Extreme Transitions: Trends and Trepidations from 1992 to 1996." In *The Ages of the Justice League: Essays on America's Greatest Superheroes in Changing Times*, edited by Joseph J. Darowski, 142–50. Jefferson, NC: McFarland.

Han, Jung-Sun N. 2006. "Empire of Comic Visions: Japanese Cartoon Journalism and Its Political Statements on Korea, 1867–1910." *Japanese Studies* 26, no. 3: 283–302.

Hanley, Richard. 2005. "Identity Crisis: Time Travel and Metaphysics in the DC Multiverse." In *Superheroes and Philosophy: Truth, Justice, and the Socratic Way*, edited by Tom Morris and Matt Morris, 237–49. Chicago: Open Court.

Hanley, Tim. 2018. "The Evolution of Female Readership: Letter Columns in Superhero Comics." In *Gender and the Superhero Narrative*, edited by Michael Goodrum, Tara Prescott, and Philip Smith, 221–50. Jackson: University Press of Mississippi.

Harbi, Amine. 2016. "'He Isn't an Animal, He Isn't a Human; He Is Just Different': Exploring the Medium of Comics in Empowering Children's Critical Thinking." *Journal of Graphic Novels and Comics* 7, no. 4 (December): 431–44.

Harkham, Sammy, and Dan Nadel. 2010. "New Art Comics Panel." In *The Best American Comics Criticism*, edited by Ben Schwartz, 343–48. Seattle: Fantagraphics Books.

Harnett, John. 2016. "Framing the Subconscious: Envisioning the Polysemic Narrative of the Graphic Novel as a Reference Point for Psychoanalytical and Semiotic Discourse." In *Framescapes: Graphic Narrative Intertexts*, edited by Mikhail Peppas and Sanabelle Ebrahim, 73–83. Oxford: Inter-Disciplinary Press.

Harnett, John. 2019. "Cognitive Pathfinders: Highlighting Cross-Modal Interaction and the Orchestration of Memory in Comics." In *Multimodality: Disciplinary Thoughts and the Challenge of Diversity*, edited by Janina Wildfeuer, Jana Pflaeging, John Bateman, Ognyan Seizov, and Chiao-I Tseng, 171–94. Berlin: Walter de Gruyter.

Harris-Fain, Darren. 2018. "The Superhero Graphic Novel." In *The Cambridge History of the Graphic Novel*, edited by Jan Baetens, Hugo Frey, and Stephen E. Tabachnick, 492–508. Cambridge: Cambridge University Press.

Hart, Christopher. 2001. *Manhwa Mania: How to Draw Korean Comics.* New York: Watson-Guptill.

Hart, John Patrick. 2008. *Art of the Storyboard: A Filmmaker's Introduction.* Burlington, MA: Focal Press.

Hart, Melissa. 2010. *Using Graphic Novels in the Classroom, Grades 4–8.* Garden Grove, CA: Teacher Created Resources.

Harvey, Colin B. 2015. *Fantastic Transmedia: Narrative, Play and Memory across Science Fiction and Fantasy Storyworlds.* Basingstoke, Hants., England: Palgrave Macmillan.

Harvey, Robert C. 1979. "The Aesthetics of the Comic Strip." *Journal of Popular Culture* 12, no. 4 (Spring): 640–52.

Harvey, Robert C. 1994. *The Art of the Funnies: An Aesthetic History.* Jackson: University Press of Mississippi.

Harvey, Robert C. 1996. *The Art of the Comic Book: An Aesthetic History.* Jackson: University Press of Mississippi.

Harvey, Robert C. 2001. "Comedy at the Juncture of Word and Image: The Emergence of the Modern Magazine Gag Cartoon Reveals the Vital Blend." In *The Language of Comics: Word and Image*, edited by Robin Varnum and Christina T. Gibbons, 75–96. Jackson: University Press of Mississippi.

Harvey, Robert C. 2009. "How Comics Came to Be: Through the Juncture of Word and Image from Magazine Gag Cartoons to Newspaper Strips, Tools for Critical Appreciation Plus Rare Seldom Witnessed Historical Facts." In *A Comics Studies Reader*, edited by Jeet Heer and Kent Worcester, 25–45. Jackson: University Press of Mississippi.

Harvey, Robert C. 2014. *Insider Histories of Cartooning: Rediscovering Forgotten Famous Comics and Their Creators.* Jackson: University Press of Mississippi.

Harvey, Robert C., Richard V. West, and Brian Walker. 1998. *Children of the Yellow Kid: The Evolution of the American Comic Strip*. Seattle: Frye Art Museum / University of Washington Press.

Haslem, Wendy, Elizabeth Macfarlane, and Sarah Richardson, eds. 2019. *Superhero Bodies: Identity, Materiality, Transformation*. New York: Routledge.

Hassler-Forest, Dan. 2012. *Capitalist Superheroes: Caped Crusaders in the Neoliberal Age*. Alresford, Hants., England: Zero Books.

Hassoun, Dan. 2013. "Sequential Outliers: The Role of Spoilers in Comic Book Reading." *Journal of Graphic Novels and Comics* 4, no. 2 (April): 346–58.

Hatfield, Charles. 2005. *Alternative Comics: An Emerging Literature*. Jackson: University Press of Mississippi.

Hatfield, Charles. 2006. "Comic Art, Children's Literature, and the New Comics Studies." *Lion and the Unicorn* 30, no. 3 (September): 360–82.

Hatfield, Charles. 2009a. "An Art of Tensions." In *A Comics Studies Reader*, edited by Jeet Heer and Kent Worcester, 132–48. Jackson: University Press of Mississippi.

Hatfield, Charles. 2009b. "Defining Comics in the Classroom; or, The Pros and Cons of Unfixability." In *Teaching the Graphic Novel*, edited by Stephen E. Tabachnick, 19–27. New York: Modern Language Association of America.

Hatfield, Charles. 2009c. "Superheroes and the Silver Age." In *Faster than a Speeding Bullet: The Art of the Superhero*, edited by Ben Saunders. Eugene, OR: Jordan Schnitzer Museum of Art.

Hatfield, Charles. 2010. "Indiscipline; or, The Condition of Comics Studies." *Transatlantica: Revue d'Etudes Américaines / American Studies Journal*, no. 1 (September). https://journals.openedition.org/transatlantica/4933.

Hatfield, Charles. 2014. "Do Independent Comics Still Exist in the US and Canada?" In *La bande dessinée en dissidence / Comics in Dissent: Alternative, indépendance, auto-édition / Alternative, Independence, Self-Publishing*, edited by Christophe Dony, Tanguy Habrand, and Gert Meesters, 59–78. Liège: Presses Universitaires de Liège.

Hatfield, Charles, Jeet Heer, and Kent Worcester, eds. 2013. *The Superhero Reader*. Jackson: University Press of Mississippi.

Hays, Anne. 2017. "Reading the Margins: Embedded Narratives in Feminist Personal Zines." *Journal of Popular Culture* 50, no. 1 (February): 86–108.

Hayton, Christopher J. 2014. "Evolving Sub-Texts in the Visual Exploitation of the Female Form: Good Girl and Bad Girl Comic Art Pre– and Post–Second Wave Feminism." *ImageTexT: Interdisciplinary Comics Studies* 7, no. 4. http://imagetext.english.ufl.edu/archives/v7_4/hayton/.

Healey, Karen. 2009. "When Fangirls Perform: The Gendered Fan Identity in Superhero Comics Fandom." In *The Contemporary Comic Book Superhero*, edited by Angela Ndalianis, 158–77. New York: Routledge.

Heer, Jeet, and Kent Worcester, eds. 2004. *Arguing Comics: Literary Masters on a Popular Medium*. Jackson: University Press of Mississippi.

Heer, Jeet, and Kent Worcester, eds. 2009. *A Comics Studies Reader*. Jackson: University Press of Mississippi.

Heifler, Sydney Phillips. 2020. "Romance Comics, Dangerous Girls, and the Importance of Fathers." *Journal of Graphic Novels and Comics* 11, no. 4 (August): 376–93.

Heimerl, Theresia. 2017. "Rampant Lechers, Chaste Heroes: (De-)Sexualised Violence in Comic Book Screen Adaptations." *Journal for Religion, Film and Media* 3, no. 1: 45–57. https://jrfm.eu/index.php/ojs_jrfm/article/view/79.

Heintjes, Tom. 2020. "'We Crack the Door Open, but We're Still Just Peeking In': Three African American Cartoonists Discuss the Challenges of Working in Syndicated Cartooning." *Hogan's Alley: The Magazine of the Cartoon Arts* 22: 44–57. https://www.hoganmag.com/blog/2021/2/9/we-crack-the-door-open-but-were-still-just-peeking-in-a-black-cartoonist-roundtable?rq=Heintjes%20tom.

Helsel, Philip Browning. 2018. "Comics and In-Between Kids: Immigration-Themed Graphic Novels as a Resource for Second-Generation Adolescents." *Pastoral Psychology* 67 (April): 125–39.

Helvie, Forrest C. 2014. "Comic Fandom throughout the Ages." In *Critical Insights: The American Comic Book*, edited by Joseph Michael Sommers, 186–99. Ipswich, MA: Salem Press.

Hembrough, Tara. 2019. "Rural and Native American Students' Utilization of Auto-biographical Comic Strips to Explore Their Identities through Digital Storytelling in the Multimodal Writing Classroom." *Journal of Multimodal Rhetorics* 3, no. 1: 115–60. http://journalofmultimodalrhetorics.com/3-1-issue-hembrough.

Hemovich, Vanessa. 2018. "From Princess to Protagonist: Redesigning the Video Game Superhero." In *Gender and Superhero Narrative*, edited by Michael Goodrum, Tara Prescott, and Philip Smith, 205–20. Jackson: University Press of Mississippi.

Herald, Nathan. 2011. *Graphic Novels for Young Readers: A Genre Guide for Ages 4–14*. Santa Barbara, CA: Libraries Unlimited.

Heritage Auctions. 2004. "Glossary of Comic Terms." https://comics.ha.com/c/ref/glossary.zx.

Herman, Daniel. 2004. *Silver Age: The Second Generation of Comic Book Artists*. New Castle, PA: Hermes Press.

Herman, David. 2004. "Toward a Transmedial Narratology." In *Narrative across Media: The Languages of Storytelling*, edited by Marie-Laure Ryan, 47–75. Lincoln: University of Nebraska Press.

Herman, David. 2010. "Word-Image / Utterance-Gesture: Case Studies in Multimodal Storytelling." In *New Perspectives on Narrative and Multimodality*, edited by Ruth Page, 78–98. New York: Routledge.

Herman, David. 2011. "Storyworld/Umwelt: Nonhuman Experiences in Graphic Narratives." *SubStance* 40, no. 1: 156–81.

Herman, David. 2012. "Toward a Zoonarratology: Storytelling and Species Difference in Animal Comics." In *Narrative, Interrupted: The Plotless, the Disturbing, and the Trivial in*

Literature, edited by Markku Lehtimäki, Laura Karttunen, and Maria Mäkelä, 91–119. Berlin: Walter de Gruyter.

Herman, David, ed. 2018. *Animal Comics: Multispecies Storyworlds in Graphic Narratives*. London: Bloomsbury.

Herrmann, Andrew F. 2018. "Communication and Ritual at the Comic Book Shop: The Convergence of Organizational and Popular Cultures." *Journal of Organizational Ethnography* 7, no. 3: 285–301.

Hescher, Achim. 2016. *Reading Graphic Novels: Genre and Narration*. Berlin: Walter de Gruyter.

Hewitson, Mark. 2012. "Black Humour: Caricature in Wartime." *Oxford German Studies* 41, no. 2: 213–35.

Hicks, Marianne. 2009. "'Teh Futar': The Power of the Webcomic and the Potential of Web 2.0." In *Drawing the Line: Using Cartoons as Historical Evidence*, edited by Richard Scully and Marian Quartly, 11.1–11.20. Clayton, Vic., Australia: Monash University ePress.

Hignite, Todd M. 2006. *In the Studio: Visits with Contemporary Cartoonists*. New Haven, CT: Yale University Press.

Hill, Jane H., and Carole Browner. 1982. "Gender Ambiguity and Class Stereotyping in the Mexican *Fotonovela*." *Studies in Latin American Popular Culture* 1: 43–64.

Hills, Matt. 2002. *Fan Cultures*. London: Routledge.

Hinds, Harold E., Jr., and Charles M. Tatum. 1992. *Not Just for Children: The Mexican Comic Book in the Late 1960s and 1970s*. Westport, CT: Greenwood Press.

Hirohito, Miyamoto. 2002. "The Formation of an Impure Genre: On the Origins of *Manga*." Translated by Jennifer Prough. *Review of Japanese Culture and Society* 14 (December): 39–48.

Hoberek, Andrew. 2019. "Building and Unbuilding a Comics Canon." *PMLA* 134, no. 3 (May): 614–19.

Hodge, James J. 2019. *Sensations of History: Animation and New Media Art*. Jackson: University Press of Mississippi.

Høigilt, Jacob. 2018. *Comics in Contemporary Arab Culture: Politics, Language and Resistance*. London: I. B. Tauris.

Holbo, John. 2012. "Redefining Comics." In *The Art of Comics: A Philosophical Approach*, edited by Aaron Meskin and Roy T. Cook, 3–30. Chichester, W. Susx., England: Wiley-Blackwell.

Hopkins, Susan. 2002. *Girl Heroes: The New Force in Popular Culture*. London: Pluto Press.

Horn, Maurice. 2000. "American Comic Strips and Silent Seriable: A Parallel." *International Journal of Comic Art* 2, no. 1 (Spring): 85–89.

Horn, Pierre L. 2001. "American Graffiti—French Style: Three Comics Strip Artists Look at Pre-War America." *International Journal of Comic Art* 3, no. 1 (Spring): 86–92.

Horsman, Yasco. 2014. "Infancy of Art: Comics, Childhood and Picture Books." *Journal of Graphic Novels and Comics* 5, no. 3 (September): 323–35.

Horstkotte, Silke. 2013. "Zooming In and Out: Panels, Frames, Sequences, and the Building of Graphic Storyworlds." In *From Comic Strips to Graphic Novels: Contributions to the*

Theory and History of Graphic Narrative, edited by Daniel Stein and Jan-Noël Thon, 27–48. Berlin: Walter de Gruyter.

Horstkotte, Silke, and Nancy Pedri. 2011. "Focalization in Graphic Narrative." *Narrative* 19, no. 3 (October): 330–57.

Horstkotte, Silke, and Nancy Pedri. 2016. "The Body at Work: Subjectivity in Graphic Memoir." In *Subjectivity across Media: Interdisciplinary and Transmedial Perspectives*, edited by Maike Sarah Reinerth and Jan-Noël Thon, 87–101. New York: Routledge.

Horton, Ian. 2007. "Colonial Stereotypes in Innovative European Comic Books." In *Bilderwelten – Textwelten – Comicwelten: Romanistische Begegnungen mit der Neunten Kunst*, edited by Frank Leinen and Guido Rings, 125–41. Munich: Martin Meidenbauer.

Hosler, Jay, and K. B. Boomer. 2011. "Are Comic Books an Effective Way to Engage Nonmajors in Learning and Appreciating Science?" *CBE: Life Sciences Education* 10, no. 3 (September). http://www.lifescied.org/content/10/3/309.full.

Hou, Charles, and Cynthia Hou. 1998. *The Art of Decoding Political Cartoons: A Teacher's Guide*. Vancouver: Moody's Lookout Press.

Howard, Sheena C. 2017. *Encyclopedia of Black Comics*. Golden, CO: Fulcrum Publishing.

Howard, Sheena C., and Ronald L. Jackson II, eds. 2013. *Black Comics: Politics of Race and Representation*. London: Bloomsbury.

Howard, Yetta. 2018. "Unsuitable for Children? Adult-erated Age in Underground Graphic Narratives." *American Literature* 90, no. 2 (June): 283–313.

Howe, Sean. 2012a. *Marvel Comics: The Untold Story*. New York: HarperCollins.

Howe, Sean. 2012b. "A Short History of Comic Book Superteams and How We Got *The Avengers*." *Vulture*, May 4. https://www.vulture.com/2012/05/how-comic-book-super teams-begat-the-avengers.html.

Howell, Jennifer. 2015. *The Algerian War in French-Language Comics: Postcolonial Memory, History, and Subjectivity*. Lanham, MD: Lexington Books.

Howell, Peter. 2001. "Strategy and Style in English and French Translations of Japanese Comic Books." *Edinburgh Working Papers in Applied Linguistics*, no. 11: 59–66.

Hu, Tze-Yue G. 2010. *Frames of Anime: Culture and Image Building*. Hong Kong: Hong Kong University Press.

Hughes, Janette Michelle, Alyson King, Peggy Perkins, and Victor Fuke. 2011. "Adolescents and 'Autographics': Reading and Writing Coming-of-Age Graphic Novels." *Journal of Adolescent and Adult Literacy* 54, no. 8 (May): 601–12.

Humphrey, Aaron. 2018. "Emotion and Secrecy in Australian Asylum-Seeker Comics: The Politics of Visual Style." *International Journal of Cultural Studies* 21, no. 5 (September): 457–85. https://digital.library.adelaide.edu.au/dspace/bitstream/2440/105304/3/hdl_105304.pdf.

Hurtado, David. 2016. *Flipping Out: The Art of Flip Book Animation*. Lake Forest, CA: Walter Foster Publishing.

Huska, Melanie. 2014. "Image and Text in Service of the Nation: Historically Themed Comic Books as Civic Education in 1980s Mexico." In *Comics as History, Comics as Literature:*

Roles of the Comic Book in Scholarship, Society, and Entertainment, edited by Annessa Ann Babic, 65–78. Madison, NJ: Fairleigh Dickinson University Press.

Huxley, David. 2002. *Nasty Tales: Sex, Drugs, Rock 'n' Roll and Violence in the British Underground*. Manchester: Critical Vision.

Huxley, David. 2018. *Lone Heroes and the Myth of the American West in Comic Books, 1945–1962*. Cham, Switzerland: Palgrave Macmillan.

Hyman, David. 2017. *Revision and the Superhero Genre*. Cham, Switzerland: Palgrave Macmillan.

Iaccino, James F. 1997. "Jungian Archetypes in American Comic Strips." In *Understanding the Funnies: Critical Interpretations of Comic Strips*, edited by Gail W. Pieper with Kenneth D. Nordin and Joseph Ursitti, 62–76. Lisle, IL: Procopian Press.

Iadonisi, Richard, ed. 2012. *Graphic History: Essays on Graphic Novels and/as History*. Newcastle upon Tyne: Cambridge Scholars Publishing.

Inge, M. Thomas. 1990. *Comics as Culture*. Jackson: University Press of Mississippi.

Inge, M. Thomas. 1991. "Form and Function in Metacomics: Self-Reflexivity in the Comic Strip." *Studies in Popular Culture* 13, no. 2: 1–10.

Inge, M. Thomas. 2016. "Origins of Early Comics and Proto-Comics." In *The Routledge Companion to Comics*, edited by Frank Bramlett, Roy T. Cook, and Aaron Meskin, 25–31. New York: Routledge.

Ingulsrud, John E., and Kate Allen. 2009. *Reading Japan Cool: Patterns of Manga Literacy and Discourse*. Lanham, MD: Lexington Books.

Inose, Hiroko. 2012. "Translating Japanese Onomatopoeia and Mimetic Words in Manga into Spanish and English." In *Translationswissenschaft: Alte und neue Arten der Translation in Theorie und Praxis*, edited by Lew N. Zybatow, Alena Petrova, and Michael Ustaszewski, 97–116. Bern: Peter Lang.

Ioannidou, Elisavet. 2013. "Adapting Superhero Comics for the Big Screen: Subculture for the Masses." *Adaptation* 6, no. 2 (August): 230–38.

Ito, Kinko. 1994. "Images of Women in Weekly Male Comic Magazines in Japan." *Journal of Popular Culture* 27, no. 4 (March): 81–95.

Ito, Kinko. 1995. "Sexism in Japanese Weekly Comic Magazines for Men." In *Asian Popular Culture*, edited by John A. Lent, 127–37. Boulder, CO: Westview Press.

Ito, Kinko. 2002a. "The *Manga* Culture in Japan." *Japan Studies Review* 7: 1–16.

Ito, Kinko. 2002b. "The World of Japanese Ladies' Comics: From Romantic Fantasy to Lustful Perversion." *Journal of Popular Culture* 36, no. 1 (August): 68–85.

Ito, Kinko. 2005. "A History of *Manga* in the Context of Japanese Culture and Society." *Journal of Popular Culture* 38, no. 3 (February): 456–75.

Jackson, Tim. 2016. *Pioneering Cartoonists of Color*. Jackson: University Press of Mississippi.

Jacobs, Dale. 2007a. "Beyond Visual Rhetoric: Multimodal Rhetoric and Newspaper Comic Strips." *International Journal of Comic Art* 9, no. 1 (Spring): 502–14.

Jacobs, Dale. 2007b. "More than Words: Comics as a Means of Teaching Multiple Literacies." *English Journal* 96, no. 3 (January): 19–25.

Jacobs, Dale. 2013. *Graphic Encounters: Comics and the Sponsorship of Multimodal Literacy.* London: Bloomsbury.

Jacobs, Dale. 2014. "Webcomics, Multimodality, and Information Literacy." *ImageTexT: Interdisciplinary Comics Studies* 7, no. 3. http://www.english.ufl.edu/imagetext/archives/v7_3/jacobs/.

Jacobs, Dale. 2020. "Comics Studies as Interdiscipline." In *The Oxford Handbook of Comic Book Studies,* edited by Frederick Luis Aldama, 656–70. Oxford: Oxford University Press.

Janson, Klaus. 2013a. *The DC Comics Guide to Inking Comics.* New York: Watson-Guptill.

Janson, Klaus. 2013b. *The DC Comics Guide to Pencilling Comics.* New York: Watson-Guptill.

Jaquith, James R. 1973. "Tabooed Words in Comic Strips: A Transparent Mask." In *You and Others: Readings in Introductory Anthropology,* edited by A. Kimball Romney and Paul L. DeVore, 448–51. Cambridge, MA: Winthrop Publishers.

Jee, Benjamin D., and Florencia K. Anggoro. 2012. "Comic Cognition: Exploring the Potential Cognitive Impacts of Science Comics." *Journal of Cognitive Education and Psychology* 11, no. 2: 196–208.

Jeffries, Dru H. 2017. *Comic Book Film Style: Cinema at 24 Panels per Second.* Austin: University of Texas Press.

Jenkins, Henry. 2009. "'Just Men in Tights': Rewriting Silver Age Comics in an Era of Multiplicity." In *The Contemporary Comic Book Superhero,* edited by Angela Ndalianis, 16–43. New York: Routledge.

Jenkins, Henry. 2011. "Acafandom and Beyond: Week Two, Part One." Confessions of an Aca-Fan. http://henryjenkins.org/blog/2011/06/acafandom_and_beyond_week_two.html.

Jenkins, Henry. 2020. *Comics and Stuff.* New York: New York University Press.

Jensen, Darin. 2017. "Bronze Age: A Life in Comics and Teaching." *Writing on the Edge* 27, no. 2 (Spring): 60–71.

Johnson, Fred. 2012. "Film School for Slideware: Film, Comics, and Slideshows as Sequential Art." *Computers and Composition* 29, no. 2 (June): 124–36.

Johnson-Woods, Toni, ed. 2010. *Manga: An Anthology of Global and Cultural Perspectives.* New York: Continuum.

Johnston, Phillip. 2016. "Wordless! Music for Comics and Graphic Novels Turns Time into Space (and Back Again)." *Southerly* 76, no. 1: 96–110.

Johnston, W. Robert. 1989. "Splash Panel Adventures!" *Smithsonian Studies in American Art* 3, no. 3 (Summer): 39–53.

Jones, Clint. 2020. *Apocalyptic Ecology in the Graphic Novel: Life and the Environment after Societal Collapse.* Jefferson, NC: McFarland.

Jones, David Annwn. 2014. "'Graphic Resurgence': The Return of the Early Gothic Comic Strip in Trans-Medial Discourse." *Studies in Comics* 5, no. 1 (April): 31–56.

Jones, Gerard. 2002. *Killing Monsters: Why Children Need Fantasy, Super Heroes, and Make-Believe Violence.* New York: Basic Books.

Jones, Gerard. 2004. *Men of Tomorrow: Geeks, Gangsters, and the Birth of the Comic Book.* New York: Basic Books.

Jones, Gerard, and Will Jacobs, eds. 1996. *The Comic Book Heroes: The First History of Modern Comic Books from the Silver Age to the Present.* Rocklin, CA: Prima Lifestyles.

Jones, Leslie. 2005. "Cracking the Comics Canon." *Art on Paper* 10, no. 2 (November–December): 44–49.

Jones, Matthew. 2009. *Found in Translation: Structural and Cognitive Aspects of the Adaptation of Comic Art to Film.* Saarbrücken: VDM Verlag Dr. Müller.

Jüngst, Heike Elisabeth. 2000. "Educational Comics: Text-Type, or Text-Types in a Format?" *Image [&] Narrative: Online Magazine of the Visual Narrative* 1, no. 1 (January). http://www.imageandnarrative.be/inarchive/narratology/heikeelisabethjuengst.htm.

Jüngst, Heike Elisabeth. 2010. *Information Comics: Knowledge Transfer in a Popular Format.* Frankfurt am Main: Peter Lang.

Junid, Iman, and Eriko Yamato. 2019. "Manga Influences and Local Narratives: Ambiguous Identification in Comics Production." *Creative Industries Journal* 12, no. 1 (March): 66–85.

Juricevic, Igor. 2018. "Analysis of Pictorial Metaphors in Comicbook Art: Test of the LA-MOAD Theory." *Journal of Graphic Novels and Comics* 9, no. 4 (August): 329–49.

Juricevic, Igor, and Alicia J. Horvath. 2016. "Analysis of Motions in Comic Book Cover Art: Using Pictorial Metaphors." *The Comics Grid: Journal of Comics Scholarship* 6, no. 1: 1–15. https://www.comicsgrid.com/article/id/3532/.

Kacsuk, Zoltan. 2018. "Re-Examining the 'What Is Manga' Problematic: The Tension and Interrelationship between the 'Style' versus 'Made in Japan' Positions." *Arts* 7, no. 3 (July). https://www.mdpi.com/2076-0752/7/3/26.

Kaenel, Philippe. 2005. *Le métier d'illustrateur, 1830–1880: Rodolphe Töpffer, J.-J. Grandville, Gustave Doré.* Geneva: Librairie Droz.

Kaindl, Klaus. 2004. "Multimodality in the Translation of Humour in Comics." In *Perspectives and Multimodality*, edited by Eija Ventola, Cassily Charles, and Martin Kaltenbacher, 173–92. Amsterdam: John Benjamins.

Kannemeyer, Anton. 2019. "As I Please: A Personal Reflection on Censorship." *International Journal of Comic Art* 21, no. 1 (Spring–Summer): 52–61.

Kannenberg, Gene, Jr. 2001. "Graphic Text, Graphic Context: Interpreting Custom Fonts and Hands in Contemporary Comics." In *Illuminating Letters: Typography and Literary Interpretation*, edited by Paul C. Gutjahr and Megan L. Benton, 163–92. Amherst: University of Massachusetts Press.

Kaplan, Arie. 2003a. "How the Jews Created the Comic Book Industry, part 1: The Golden Age (1933–1955)." *Reform Judaism* 32, no. 1 (Fall): 14–23.

Kaplan, Arie. 2003b. "How the Jews Created the Comic Book Industry, part 2: The Silver Age (1956–1978)." *Reform Judaism* 32, no. 2 (Winter): 10–16.

Karaminas, Vicki. 2007. "Australian Gothic: Black Light Angels, Fashion, and Subcultural Style." *International Journal of Comic Art* 9, no. 1 (Spring): 438–52.

Karasik, Paul, and Mark Newgarden. 2017. *How to Read "Nancy": The Elements of Comics in Three Easy Panels.* Seattle: Fantagraphics Books.

Kashtan, Aaron. 2018. *Between Pen and Pixel: Comics, Materiality and the Book of the Future.* Columbus: Ohio State University Press.

Kashtan, Aaron. 2019. "Comic Books from the 1980s to the 2010s." In *The Cambridge History of Science Fiction,* edited by Gerry Canavan and Eric Carl Link, 616–31. Cambridge: Cambridge University Press.

Kasthuri, Raghavi Ravi, and Sathyaraj Venkatesan. 2015. "Picturing Illness: History, Poetics, and Graphic Medicine." *Research and Humanities in Medical Education* 2 (November): 11–17. https://www.rhime.in/ojs/index.php/rhime/article/view/9/pdf_4.

Katz, Jill S. 2008. "Women and Mainstream Comic Books." *International Journal of Comic Art* 10, no. 2 (Spring): 101–47.

Katz, Maya Balakirsky. 2013. "The De-Politicization of Israeli Political Cartoons." *Israel Studies* 18, no. 1 (Spring): 1–30.

Kaur, Raminder. 2012. "Atomic Comics: Parabolic Mimesis and the Graphic Fictions of Science." *International Journal of Cultural Studies* 15, no. 4 (July): 329–47.

Kawa, Abraham. 2009. "Comics since the Silver Age." In *The Routledge Companion to Science Fiction,* edited by Mark Bould, Andrew M. Butler, Adam Roberts, and Sherryl Vint, 163–73. Abingdon, Oxon., England: Routledge.

Keen, Suzanne. 2011. "Fast Tracks to Narrative Empathy: Anthropomorphism and Dehumanization in Graphic Narratives." *SubStance* 40, no. 1: 135–55.

Kelp-Stebbins, Katherine. 2020. "Reading Spaces: The Politics of Page Layout." In *The Oxford Handbook of Comic Book Studies,* edited by Frederick Luis Aldama, 75–93. Oxford: Oxford University Press.

Kempson, Michelle. 2014. "'My Version of Feminism': Subjectivity, DIY, and the Feminist Zine." *Social Movement Studies* 14, no. 4 (July): 459–72.

Kempson, Michelle. 2018. "Researching Zine Culture Using In-Depth Participant Interviews." *SAGE Research Methods Cases.* https://www.doi.org/10.4135/9781526429803.

Kendall, L. N., Quentin Raffaelli, Alan Kingstone, and Rebecca M. Todd. 2016. "Iconic Faces Are Not Real Faces: Enhanced Emotion Detection and Altered Neural Processing as Faces Become More Iconic." *Cognitive Research: Principles and Implications* 1, no. 1. http://link.springer.com/article/10.1186/s41235-016-0021-8.

Kennedy, John M. 1982. "Metaphor in Pictures." *Perception* 11, no. 5: 589–605.

Kern, Adam L. 2006. *Manga from the Floating World: Comicbook Culture and the "Kibyōshi" of Edo Japan.* Cambridge, MA: Harvard University Asia Center.

Khoury, George. 2007. *Image Comics: The Road to Independence.* Raleigh, NC: TwoMorrows Publishing.

Kidder, Orion Ussner. 2008. "Show and Tell: Notes towards a Theory of Metacomics." *International Journal of Comic Art* 10, no. 1 (Spring): 248–67.

Kidman, Shawna Feldmar. 2015. "Self-Regulation through Distribution: Censorship and the Comic Book Industry in 1954." *The Velvet Light Trap,* no. 75 (Spring): 21–37.

Kidman, Shawna Feldmar. 2019. *Comic Books Incorporated: How the Business of Comics Became the Business of Hollywood.* Berkeley: University of California Press.

Kilgore, Christopher D. 2015. "Unnatural Graphic Narration: The Panel and the Sublime." *JNT: Journal of Narrative Theory* 45, no. 1: 18–45.

King, Edward, and Joanna Page. 2017. *Posthumanism and the Graphic Novel in Latin America.* London: University College London Press.

King, Frank. 2014. *Gasoline Alley: The Complete Sundays.* Vol. 2: *1923–1925.* Milwaukie, OR: Dark Horse.

King, Frank, and Dick Moores. 2012. *Gasoline Alley: Daily Comics.* Vol. 1: *1964–1966.* San Diego: IDW Publishing.

Kinsella, Sharon. 1998. "Japanese Subculture in the 1990s: *Otaku* and the Amateur *Manga* Movement." *Journal of Japanese Studies* 24, no. 2 (Summer): 289–316.

Kinsella, Sharon. 2000. *Adult Manga: Culture and Power in Contemporary Japanese Society.* Abingdon, Oxon., England: Routledge.

Kirchoff, Jeffrey S. J. 2012. "Beyond Remediation: Comic Book Captions and Silent Film Intertitles as the Same Genre." *Studies in Comics* 3, no. 1 (August): 25–46.

Kirchoff, Jeffrey S. J. 2013. "It's Just Not the Same as Print (and It Shouldn't Be): Rethinking the Possibilities of Digital Comics." *Technoculture: An Online Journal of Technology in Society* 3. https://tcjournal.org/vol3/kirchoff.

Kirchoff, Jeffrey S. J., and Mike P. Cook, eds. 2019. *Perspectives on Digital Comics: Theoretical, Critical and Pedagogical Essays.* Jefferson, NC: McFarland.

Kirtley, Susan E. 2018. "'A Word to You Feminist Women': The Parallel Legacies of Feminism and Underground Comics." In *The Cambridge History of the Graphic Novel*, edited by Jan Baetens, Hugo Frey, and Stephen E. Tabachnick, 269–85. Cambridge: Cambridge University Press.

Kirtley, Susan E., Antero Garcia, and Peter E. Carlson, eds. 2020. *With Great Power Comes Great Pedagogy: Teaching, Learning, and Comics.* Jackson: University Press of Mississippi.

Kirtz, Jaime Lee. 2014. "Computers, Comics and Cult Status: A Forensics of Digital Graphic Novels." *Digital Humanities Quarterly* 8, no. 3. http://www.digitalhumanities.org/dhq/vol/8/3/000185/000185.html.

Klaehn, Jeffery, ed. 2007. *Inside the World of Comic Books.* Montreal: Black Rose Books.

Klanten, Robert, Adeline Mollard, and Matthias Hubner, eds. 2011. *Behind the Zines: Self-Publishing Culture.* Berlin: Gestalten Verlag.

Klausen, Jytte. 2009. *The Cartoons that Shook the World.* New Haven, CT: Yale University Press.

Kleefeld, Sean. 2020. *Webcomics.* London: Bloomsbury.

Kling, Bernt. 1977. "On SF Comics: Some Notes for a Future Encyclopedia." *Science Fiction Studies* 4, no. 3 (November): 277–82.

Klock, Geoff. 2002. *How to Read Superhero Comics and Why.* New York: Continuum.

Kneece, Mark. 2015. *The Art of Comic Book Writing: The Definitive Guide to Outlining, Scripting, and Pitching Your Sequential Art Stories.* New York: Watson-Guptill.

Knight, Gladys L. 2010. *Female Action Heroes: A Guide to Women in Comics, Video Games, Film, and Television.* Santa Barbara, CA: Greenwood.

Knowles, Christopher. 2007. *Our Gods Wear Spandex: The Secret History of Comic Book Heroes*. San Francisco: Red Wheel/Weiser.

Knox, Katelyn E. 2016. *Race on Display in 20th- and 21st-Century France*. Liverpool: Liverpool University Press.

Kocmarek, Ivan. 2016. "Truth, Justice, and the Canadian Way: The War-Time Comics of Bell Features Publications." *Canadian Review of Comparative Literature* 43, no. 1 (March): 148–65. https://journals.library.ualberta.ca/crcl/index.php/crcl/article/view/29171.

Kocmarek, Ivan. 2018. "Alternatives within an Alternative Form: Canadian Wartime Creators Bus Griffiths, Avrom Yanovsky, 'Ab Normal,' Tedd Steele, and Jack Tremblay." In *The Canadian Alternative: Cartoonists, Comics, and Graphic Novels*, edited by Dominick Grace and Eric Hoffman, 3–15. Jackson: University Press of Mississippi.

Køhlert, Frederik Byrn. 2017. "Comics, Form, and Anarchy." *SubStance* 46, no. 2: 11–32.

Køhlert, Frederik Byrn. 2019. *Serial Selves: Identity and Representation in Autobiographical Comics*. New Brunswick, NJ: Rutgers University Press.

Kokanović, Renata, and Jacinthe Flore. 2017. "Subjectivity and Illness Narratives." *Subjectivity* 10, no. 4 (December): 329–39. https://link.springer.com/article/10.1057/s41286-017-0038-6.

Kopf, Johannes, and Dani Lischinski. 2012. "Digital Reconstruction of Halftoned Color Comics." *Association of Computing Machinery (ACM) Transactions on Graphics* 31, no. 6 (November): 1–10.

Kořínek, Pavel. 2020. "Self-Regulation and Self-Censorship: Comics Creators in Czechoslovakia and Communist Eastern Bloc." In *The Oxford Handbook of Comic Book Studies*, edited by Frederick Luis Aldama, 256–67. Oxford: Oxford University Press.

Kothenschulte, Daniel. 2008. "Opulence and Limitation: The Styles of Early Anime." In *Ga-Netchū! The Manga Anime Syndrome*, edited by Hans-Peter Reichmann and Stephan von der Schulenburg, 50–63. Frankfurt am Main: Deutsches Filmmuseum / Deutsches Filminstitut.

Krantz, Gunnar. 2015. "Teaching Comics in Class: Between Mainstream and the Alternative." *Studies in Comics* 6, no. 1 (July): 179–89.

Krantz, Gunnar. 2018. "Fanzines and Swedish Comics Memory." In *Comics Memory: Archives and Styles*, edited by Maaheen Ahmed and Benoît Crucifix, 267–76. Cham, Switzerland: Palgrave Macmillan.

Kripal, Jeffrey J. 2011. *Mutants and Mystics: Science Fiction, Superhero Comics, and the Paranormal*. Chicago University of Chicago Press.

Kuechenmeister, Bobby. 2009. "Reading Comics Rhetorically: Orality, Literacy, and Hybridity in Comic Narratives." *SCAN: Journal of Media Arts Culture* 6, no. 1 (June). http://scan.net.au/scan/journal/display.php?journal_id=132.

Kukkonen, Karin. 2008. "Beyond Language: Metaphor and Metonymy in Comics Storytelling." *English Language Notes* 46, no. 2 (Fall–Winter): 89–98.

Kukkonen, Karin. 2009. "Textworlds and Metareference in Comics." In *Metareference across Media: Theory and Case Studies*, edited by Werner Wolf with Katharina Bantleon and Jeff Thoss, 499–514. Amsterdam: Editions Rodopi.

Kukkonen, Karin. 2010. "Navigating Infinite Earths: Readers, Mental Models, and the Multiverse of Superhero Comics." *Storyworlds: A Journal of Narrative Studies* 2 no. 1 (January): 39–58.

Kukkonen, Karin. 2011a. "Comics as a Test Case for Transmedial Narratology." *SubStance* 40, no. 1: 34–52.

Kukkonen, Karin. 2011b. "Metalepsis in Comics and Graphic Novels." In *Metalepsis in Popular Culture*, edited by Karin Kukkonen and Sonja Klimek, 213–31. Berlin: Walter de Gruyter.

Kukkonen, Karin. 2013a. *Contemporary Comics Storytelling*. Lincoln: University of Nebraska Press.

Kukkonen, Karin. 2013b. "Space, Time, and Causality in Graphic Narratives." In *From Comic Strips to Graphic Novels: Contributions to the Theory and History of Graphic Narrative*, edited by Daniel Stein and Jan-Noël Thon, 49–66. Berlin: Walter de Gruyter.

Kukkonen, Karin. 2013c. *Studying Comics and Graphic Novels*. Chichester, W. Susx., England: Wiley-Blackwell.

Kukkonen, Karin. 2014. "Web Comics." In *The Johns Hopkins Guide to Digital Media*, edited by Marie-Laure Ryan, Lori Emerson, and Benjamin J. Robertson, 521–24. Baltimore: Johns Hopkins University Press.

Kukkonen, Karin. 2018. "Genre Fiction in the Graphic Novel: The Case of Science Fiction." In *The Cambridge History of the Graphic Novel*, edited by Jan Baetens, Hugo Frey, and Stephen E. Tabachnick, 476–91. Cambridge: Cambridge University Press.

Kümmerling-Meibauer, Bettina. 2015. "From Baby Books to Picturebooks for Adults: European Picturebooks in the New Millennium." *Word and Image* 31, no. 3 (July): 249–64.

Kümmerling-Meibauer, Bettina. 2018. *The Routledge Companion to Picturebooks*. Abingdon, Oxon., England: Routledge.

Kunert-Graf, Rachel. 2018a. "Comics and Narratological Perspective: (Witnessing) Bias in Direct Experience." *ImageTexT: Interdisciplinary Comics Studies* 10, no. 1. http://imagetext .english.ufl.edu/archives/v10_1/kunert/.

Kunert-Graf, Rachel. 2018b. "Lynching Iconography: Looking in Graphic Narrative." *Inks: Journal of the Comics Studies Society* 2, no. 3 (Fall): 312–33.

Kunka, Andrew J. 2018. *Autobiographical Comics*. London: Bloomsbury.

Kunzle, David. 1973. *The History of the Comic Strip*. Vol. 1: *The Early Comic Strip: Narrative Strips and Picture Stories in the European Broadsheet from c. 1450 to 1825*. Berkeley: University of California Press.

Kunzle, David. 1983. "Between Broadsheet Caricature and 'Punch': Cheap Newspaper Cuts for the Lower Classes in the 1830s." *Art Journal* 43, no. 4 (Winter): 339–46.

Kunzle, David. 1990. *The History of the Comic Strip*. Vol. 2: *The Nineteenth Century*. Berkeley: University of California Press.

Kunzle, David. 1998. "Precursors in American Weeklies to the American Newspaper Comic Strip: A Long Gestation and a Transoceanic Cross-Breeding." In *Forging a New Medium: The Comic Strip in the Nineteenth Century*, edited by Charles Dierick and Pascal Lefèvre, 157–86. Brussels: Vrije Universiteit Brussel University Press.

Kvaran, Kara M. 2014. "SuperGay! Depictions of Homosexuality in Mainstream Superhero Comics." In *Comics as History, Comics as Literature: Roles of the Comic Book in Scholarship, Society, and Entertainment,* edited by Annessa Ann Babic, 141–56. Madison, NJ: Fairleigh Dickinson University Press.

Kwa, Shiamin. 2020a. "In Box: Rethinking Text in the Digital Age." In *The Oxford Handbook of Comic Book Studies,* edited by Frederick Luis Aldama, 36–52. Oxford: Oxford University Press.

Kwa, Shiamin. 2020b. *Regarding Frames: Thinking with Comics in the Twenty-First Century.* Rochester, NY: Rochester Institute of Technology Press.

Labarre, Nicolas. 2020. *Understanding Genres in Comics.* Cham, Switzerland: Palgrave Macmillan.

Labarre, Nicolas, Robin Barnard, and Gary Northfield. 2012. "Redrawing the Page: Reinterpretation, Recreation, Refinement." *Studies in Comics* 3, no. 2 (December): 371–79.

Labio, Catherine. 2011. "What's in a Name? The Academic Study of Comics and the 'Graphic Novel.'" *Cinema Journal* 50, no. 3 (Spring): 123–26.

Labio, Catherine. 2015. "The Architecture of Comics." *Critical Inquiry* 41, no. 2 (Winter): 312–43.

Lacassin, Francis. 1972. "The Comic Strip and Film Language." *Film Quarterly* 26, no. 1 (Autumn): 11–23.

Lackaff, Derek, and Michael Sales. 2013. "Black Comics and Social Media Economics: New Media, New Production Models." In *Black Comics: Politics of Race and Representation,* edited by Sheena C. Howard and Ronald L. Jackson II, 65–78. London: Bloomsbury.

Lackmann, Ron. 2004. *Comic Strips and Comic Books of Radio's Golden Age: A Biography of All Radio Shows Based on Comics.* Albany, GA: BearManor Media.

La Cour, Erin. 2016. "Comics as a Minor Literature." *Image [&] Narrative: Online Magazine of the Visual Narrative* 17, no. 4 (November): 79–90. http://www.imageandnarrative.be/index.php/imagenarrative/article/view/1336.

Lafky, Sue A., and Bonnie Brennan. 1995. "For Better or for Worse: Coming Out in the Funny Pages." *Studies in Popular Culture* 18, no. 1 (October): 23–47.

Lamarre, Thomas. 2002. "From Animation to Anime: Drawing Movements and Moving Drawings." *Japan Forum* 14, no. 2 (March): 329–67.

Lamarre, Thomas. 2008. "Speciesism, Part I: Translating Races into Animals in Wartime Animation." *Mechademia: Second Arc* 3, no. 1 (Fall): 75–95.

Lamarre, Thomas. 2009. *The Anime Machine: A Media Theory of Animation.* Minneapolis: University of Minnesota Press.

Lamarre, Thomas. 2011. "Speciesism, Part III: Neoteny and the Politics of Life." *Mechademia: Second Arc* 6, no. 1 (Fall): 110–36.

Lamb, Christopher. 1996. "Drawing the Line: An Absolute Defense for Political Cartoons." *Inks: Cartoon and Comic Arts Studies* 3, no. 3 (Fall): 2–11.

Lambeens, Tom, and Kris Pint. 2015. "The Interaction of Image and Text in Modern Comics." In *Texts, Transmissions, Receptions: Modern Approaches to Narratives,* edited by André Lardinois, Sophie Levie, Hans Hoeken, and Christoph Lüthy, 240–56. Leiden: Brill.

Lambert, Josh. 2009. "'Wait for the Next Pictures': Intertextuality and Cliffhanger Continuity in Early Cinema and Comic Strips." *Cinema Journal* 48, no. 2 (Winter): 3–25.

Lamerichs, Nicolle. 2016. "Euromanga: Hybrid Styles and Stories in Transcultural Manga Production." In *Global Manga: "Japanese" Comics without Japan?*, edited by Casey Brienza, 75–95. Abingdon, Oxon., England: Routledge.

Lamerichs, Nicolle. 2018. *Productive Fandom: Intermediality and Affective Response in Fan Cultures.* Amsterdam: Amsterdam University Press.

Lang, Jeffrey S., and Patrick Trimble. 1988. "Whatever Happened to the Man of Tomorrow? An Examination of the American Monomyth and the Comic Book Superhero." *Journal of Popular Culture* 22, no. 3 (Winter): 157–73.

Lannon, Keegan. 2013. "Visualizing Words: The Function of Words in Comics." *International Journal of Comic Art* 15, no. 1 (Spring–Summer): 287–305.

Laplante, Kevin de. 2005. "Making the Abstract *Concrete*: How a Comic Can Bring to Life the Central Problems of Environmental Philosophy." In *Comics as Philosophy*, edited by Jeff McLaughlin, 153–72. Jackson: University Press of Mississippi.

Larsen, Louise C. 2015. "Comics Composition; or, When Kierkegaard and Cartoon Art Took to the Streets." *International Journal of Comic Art* 17, no. 1 (Spring–Summer): 57–73.

Lavin, Michael R. 1998. "Comics Publishers in Decline: A Tale of Two Companies." *Serials Review* 24, nos. 3–4 (December): 94–106.

Lavin, Michael R. 1999. "A Librarian's Guide to Independent Comics: Part One, Publisher Profiles." *Serials Review* 25, no. 1 (June): 29–47.

Lavin, Michael R., and Joel Hahn. 1999. "A Librarian's Guide to Independent Comics: Part Two, Comic Book Reviews." *Serials Review* 25, no. 1 (June): 49–73.

Lawrence, Chris, Josh Johnson, Rodolfo Muraguchi, and Alex Ross. 2016. *The Art of Painted Comics.* Mount Laurel, NJ: Dynamite Entertainment.

Lawson, Daniel. 2014. "The Rhetorical Construction and Negotiation of Cultural Difference in American Nonfiction Comics." In *Critical Insights: The American Comic Book*, edited by Joseph Michael Sommers, 53–71. Ipswich, MA: Salem Press.

Leber-Cook, Alice, and Roy T. Cook. 2013. "Stigmatization, Multimodality and Metaphor: Comics in the Adult English as a Second Language Classroom." In *Graphic Novels and Comics in the Classroom: Essays on the Educational Power of Sequential Art*, edited by Carrye Kay Syma and Robert G. Weiner, 23–34. Jefferson, NC: McFarland.

Ledden, Sean, and Fred Fejes. 1987. "Female Gender Role Patterns in Japanese Comic Magazines." *Journal of Popular Culture* 21, no. 1 (Summer): 155–76.

Lee, Hye-Kyung. 2009. "Between Fan Culture and Copyright Infringement: Manga Scanlation." *Media, Culture and Society* 31, no. 6 (November): 1011–22.

Lee, Stan. 1974. *Origins of Marvel Comics.* New York: Simon and Schuster.

Lee, Stan, and John Buscema. 1984. *How to Draw Comics the Marvel Way.* New York: Atria Books.

Lee, Stan, Steve Ditko, Gil Kane, Jack Kirby, and Alex Ross. 2011. *Stan Lee's How to Write Comics: From the Legendary Co-Creator of Spider-Man, the Incredible Hulk, Fantastic Four, X-Men, and Iron Man.* Mount Laurel, NJ: Dynamite Entertainment.

Lee, Sung-Ae, and John Stephen. 2016. "Gynoids and Male Fantasy in East Asian Film and Anime." In *Critical Perspectives on Artificial Humans in Children's Literature*, edited by Sabine Planka, 185–202. Würzburg, Germany: Königshausen and Neumann.

Lefèvre, Pascal. 2000a. "Narration in Comics." *Image [&] Narrative: Online Magazine of the Visual Narrative* 1, no. 1 (January). http://www.imageandnarrative.be/inarchive/narratology/pascallefevre.htm.

Lefèvre, Pascal. 2000b. "The Importance of Being 'Published': A Comparative Study of Different Comics Formats." In *Comics and Culture: Analytical and Theoretical Approaches to Comics*, edited by Anne Magnussen and Hans-Christian Christiansen, 91–105. Copenhagen: Museum Tusculanum Press.

Lefèvre, Pascal. 2006. "The Battle over the Balloon: The Conflictual Institutionalization of the Speech Balloon in Various European Cultures." *Image [&] Narrative: Online Magazine of the Visual Narrative* 7, no. 14 (July). http://www.imageandnarrative.be/inarchive/painting/pascal_levevre.htm.

Lefèvre, Pascal. 2009a. "The Conquest of Space: Evolution of Panel Arrangements and Page Layouts in Early Comics Published in Belgium (1880–1929)." *European Comic Art* 2, no. 2 (December): 227–52.

Lefèvre, Pascal. (2007) 2009b. "The Construction of Space in Comics." In *A Comics Studies Reader*, edited by Jeet Heer and Kent Worcester, 157–62. Jackson: University Press of Mississippi.

Lefèvre, Pascal. 2011a. "Not Just Black and White: Divergent Colonial Period Representations of Africans in French and Belgian Broadsheets (1880–1914)." *Signs: Studies in Graphic Narrative: International Journal for the History of Early Comics and Sequential Art* 2, no. 2 (December): 3–14.

Lefèvre, Pascal. 2011b. "Some Medium-Specific Qualities of Graphic Sequences." *SubStance* 40, no. 1: 14–33.

Lefèvre, Pascal. 2013a. "The Modes of Documentary Comics / Die Modi dokumentarisher Comics." In *Der dokumentarische Comic: Reportage und Biografie*, edited by Hans-Joachim Backe and Dietrich Grünewald, 30–60. Berlin: Christian A. Bachmann Verlag.

Lefèvre, Pascal. 2013b. "Narration in the Flemish Dual Publication System: The Crossover Genre of the Humoristic Adventure." In *From Comic Strips to Graphic Novels: Contributions to the Theory and History of Graphic Narrative*, edited by Daniel Stein and Jan-Noël Thon, 255–70. Berlin: Walter de Gruyter.

Lefèvre, Pascal. 2015. "Gatekeeping at Two Main Belgian Comics Publishers, Dupuis and Lombard, at a Time of Transition (in the 1980s)." *Studies in Comics* 6, no. 1 (July): 109–19.

Lefèvre, Pascal. 2016. "No Content without Form: Graphic Style as the Primary Entrance to a Story." In *The Visual Narrative Reader*, edited by Neil Cohn, 67–87. London: Bloomsbury.

Lefèvre, Pascal. 2017. "Mixed Visual Media from the Standpoint of the Reader/Spectator." *ImageTexT: Interdisciplinary Comics Studies* 9, no. 2. http://imagetext.english.ufl.edu/archives/v9_2/lefevre/.

Lefèvre, Pascal, ed. 2018. "More than 100 Comics-Related Words in 8 Languages." https://sites.google.com/site/lefevrepascal/morethan100comics-relatedwordsin8languag.

Lefèvre, Pascal, and Morgan Di Salvia. 2011. "A Creative Culture Where It Is Hard to Make a Living: The Socio-Economic Situation of Comics Authors and Illustrators in Belgium." *European Comic Art* 4, no. 1 (March): 59–80.

Lefèvre, Pascal, and Gert Meesters. 2018. "Interpretation of an Evolving Line Drawing." In *Empirical Comics Research: Digital, Multimodal, and Cognitive Methods*, edited by Alexander Dunst, Jochen Laubrock, and Janina Wildfeuer, 197–214. New York: Routledge.

Legrady, Georges. 2000. "Modular Structure and Image/Text Sequences: Comics and Interactive Media." In *Comics and Culture: Analytical and Theoretical Approaches to Comics*, edited by Anne Magnussen and Hans-Christian Christiansen, 79–90. Copenhagen: Museum Tusculanum Press.

Lendrum, Rod. 2005a. "The Super Black Macho, One Baaad Mutha: Black Superhero Masculinity in 1970s Mainstream Comic Books." *Extrapolation* 46, no. 3 (Fall): 360–72.

Lendrum, Rod. 2005b. "Queering Super-Manhood: Superhero Masculinity, Camp and Public Relations as a Textual Framework." *International Journal of Comic Art* 7, no. 1 (Spring): 287–303.

Lent, John A. 1994. *Animation, Caricature, and Gag and Political Cartoons in the United States and Canada: An International Bibliography*. Westport, CT: Greenwood Press.

Lent, John A. 1995. "Comics in East Asian Countries: A Contemporary Survey." *Journal of Popular Culture* 29, no. 1 (Summer): 185–98.

Lent, John A., ed. 1999a. *Pulp Demons: International Dimensions of the Postwar Anti-Comics Campaign*. Madison, NJ: Fairleigh Dickinson University Press.

Lent, John A., ed. 1999b. *Themes and Issues in Asian Cartooning: Cute, Cheap, Mad and Sexy*. Bowling Green, OH: Bowling Green State University Popular Press.

Lent, John A. 2000. "East European Cartooning: Differences over Time and Space." *International Journal of Comic Art* 2, no. 1 (Spring): 102–8.

Lent, John A., ed. 2001. *Illustrating Asia: Comics, Humor Magazines and Picture Books*. Honolulu: University of Hawai'i Press.

Lent, John A. 2002. "New Zealand: Exporter of Mainstream Cartoonists, Haven for Alternative Comics." *International Journal of Comic Art* 4, no. 1 (Spring): 170–204.

Lent, John A., ed. 2005. *Cartooning in Latin America*. Cresskill, NJ: Hampton Press.

Lent, John A. 2008. "Comic Art in Asian Cultural Context." In *Med@sia: Global Media/tion in and out of Context*, edited by Todd Joseph Miles Holden and Timothy J. Scrase, 224–42. Abingdon, Oxon., England: Routledge.

Lent, John A., ed. 2014. *Southeast Asian Cartoon Art: History, Trends and Problems*. Jefferson, NC: McFarland.

Lent, John A. 2015. *Asian Comics*. Jackson: University Press of Mississippi.

Lent, John A., and Xu Ying. 2017. *Comics Art in China*. Jackson: University Press of Mississippi.

Leong, Tim. 2013. *Super Graphic: A Visual Guide to the Comic Book Universe*. San Francisco: Chronicle Books.

Leslie, Esther. 2002. *Hollywood Flatlands: Animation, Critical Theory and the Avant-Garde*. London: Verso.

Levi, Antonia, Mark McHarry, and Dru Pagliassotti, eds. 2010. *Boys' Love Manga: Essays on the Sexual Ambiguity and Cross-Cultural Fandom of the Genre*. Jefferson, NC: McFarland.

Levitz, Paul. 2010. *75 Years of DC Comics: The Art of Modern Mythmaking*. Cologne: Taschen.

Levitz, Paul. 2013a. *The Golden Age of DC Comics, 1935–1956*. Cologne: Taschen.

Levitz, Paul. 2013b. *The Silver Age of DC Comics, 1956–1970*. Cologne: Taschen.

Levitz, Paul. 2015. *The Bronze Age of DC Comics, 1970–1984*. Cologne: Taschen.

Lewis, A. David, and Martin Lund, eds. 2017. *Muslim Superheroes: Comics, Islam, and Representation*. Cambridge, MA: Harvard University Press.

Lewis, Lisa A., ed. 1992. *The Adoring Audience: Fan Culture and Popular Media*. Abingdon, Oxon., England: Routledge.

L'Hoeste, Héctor Fernández. 2013. "Superhero for a New Age: Latino Identity in the US Comics Industry." In *Ages of Heroes, Eras of Men: Superheroes and the American Experience*, edited by Julian C. Chambliss, William Svitavsky, and Thomas Donaldson, 196–213. Newcastle upon Tyne: Cambridge Scholars Publishing.

L'Hoeste, Héctor Fernández, and Juan Poblete, eds. 2009. *Redrawing the Nation: National Identity in Latin/o American Comics*. New York: Palgrave Macmillan.

Li, Luyuan, Yongtao Wang, Zhi Tang, and Liangcai Gao. 2014. "Automatic Comic Page Segmentation Based on Polygon Detection." *Multimedia Tools and Applications* 69, no. 1 (March): 171–97.

Licona, Adela C. 2012. *Zines in Third Space: Radical Cooperation and Borderlands Rhetoric*. Albany: State University of New York Press.

Lim, Cheng-Tju. 2018. "Singapore Cartoons in the Anti-Comics Movement of the 1950s and 1960s." In *Comics Studies Here and Now*, edited by Frederick Luis Aldama, 123–30. New York: Routledge.

Liming, Drew. 2012. "Bloggers and Webcomic Artists: Careers in Online Creativity." *Occupational Outlook Quarterly* 56, no. 3 (Fall): 16–21. https://www.bls.gov/careeroutlook/2012/fall/art02.pdf.

Lin, Shu-Fen, Huann-shyang Lin, Ling Lee, and Larry D. Yore. 2015. "Are Science Comics a Good Medium for Science Communication? The Case for Public Learning of Nanotechnology." *International Journal of Science Education, Part B: Communication and Public Engagement* 5, no. 3 (September): 276–94.

Lioi, Anthony. 2016. *Nerd Ecology: Defending the Earth with Unpopular Culture*. London: Bloomsbury.

Little, Ben. 2010. "*2000AD*: Understanding the 'British Invasion' of American Comics." In *Comics as a Nexus of Cultures: Essays on the Interplay of Media, Disciplines and International Perspectives*, edited by Mark Berninger, Jochen Ecke, and Gideon Haberkorn, 140–52. Jefferson, NC: McFarland.

Liu, Chang-de. 2006. "Negative Impact of Digital Technologies on Artists: A Case Study of Taiwanese Cartoonists and Illustrators." *International Journal of Comic Art* 8, no. 1 (Spring): 456–65.

Llorence, Jeremy J. 2011. "Exploring Graphic Literature as a Genre and Its Place in Academic Curricula." *McNair Scholars Journal* 15, no. 1: 31–40. https://scholarworks.gvsu.edu/cgi/viewcontent.cgi?article=1305&context=mcnair.

LoCicero, Don. 2008. *Superheroes and Gods: A Comparative Study from Babylonia to Batman.* Jefferson, NC: McFarland.

Lopes, Paul. 2009. *Demanding Respect: The Evolution of the American Comic Book.* Philadelphia: Temple University Press.

Loubert, Deni, ed. 1997. *How to Get Girls (into Your Store): A Friends of Lulu Retailers Handbook.* San Diego: Friends of Lulu.

Lowe, John. 2017. *Working Methods: Comics Creators Detail Their Storytelling and Artistic Processes.* Raleigh, NC: TwoMorrows Publishing.

Ludewig, Julia. 2019. "The Art of Comic Reportage." *Diegesis, Interdisciplinary E-Journal for Narrative Research / Interdisziplinäres E-Journal für Erzählforschung* 8, no. 1: 1–24. https://www.diegesis.uni-wuppertal.de/index.php/diegesis/article/view/352/558.

Lyons, James. 2013. "'It Rhymes with Lust': The Twisted History of Noir Comics." In *A Companion to Film Noir,* edited by Andrew Spicer and Helen Hanson, 258–66. Chichester, W. Susx., England: Wiley-Blackwell.

MacWilliams, Mark W., ed. 2008. *Japanese Visual Culture: Explorations in the World of Manga and Anime.* Abingdon, Oxon., England: Routledge.

Madison, Nathan Vernon. 2013. *Anti-Foreign Imagery in American Pulps and Comic Books, 1920–1960.* Jefferson, NC: McFarland.

Madrid, Mike. 2009. *The Supergirls: Fashion, Feminism, Fantasy, and the History of Comic Book Heroines.* Minneapolis: Exterminating Angel Press.

Madrid, Mike. 2013. *Divas, Dames and Daredevils: Lost Heroines of Golden Age Comics.* Minneapolis: Exterminating Angel Press.

Madrid, Mike. 2014. *Vixens, Vamps and Vipers: Lost Villainesses of Golden Age Comics.* Minneapolis: Exterminating Angel Press.

Maglio, Mitch. 2017. *Fiction House: From Pulps to Panels, from Jungles to Space.* San Diego: Yoe Books.

Magnussen, Anne. 2004. "Spanish Underground Comics and Society." In *Reading the Popular in Contemporary Spanish Texts,* edited by Shelley Godsland and Nickianne Moody, 100–112. Newark: University of Delaware Press.

Magnussen, Anne. 2014. "Spanish Comics and Politics: From Propaganda and Censorship through Political Activism to Cultural Reflections." In *Comics & Politik / Comics & Politics,* edited by Stephan Packard, 157–78. Berlin: Christian A. Bachmann Verlag.

Magnussen, Anne, and Hans-Christian Christiansen, eds. 2000. *Comics and Culture: Analytical and Theoretical Approaches to Comics.* Copenhagen: Museum Tusculanum Press.

Maguire, Lori. 2012. "Supervillains and Cold War Tensions in the 1950s." In *The Ages of Superman: Essays on the Man of Steel in Changing Times*, edited by Joseph J. Darowski, 16–28. Jefferson, NC: McFarland.

Mahamood, Muliyadi. 2003. "Japanese Style in Malaysian Comics and Cartoons." *International Journal of Comic Art* 5, no. 2 (Fall): 194–204.

Maidment, Brian. 2013. *Comedy, Caricature and the Social Order, 1820–50*. Manchester: Manchester University Press.

Mainardi, Patricia. 2007. "The Invention of Comics." *Nineteenth-Century Art Worldwide* 6, no. 1 (Spring). http://www.19thc-artworldwide.org/spring07/145-the-invention-of-comics.

Malloy, Alex G., ed. 1993. *Comic Book Artists*. Radnor, PA: Wallace-Homestead.

Mamolo, Leo A. 2019. "Development of Digital Interactive Math Comics (DIMaC) for Senior High School Students in General Mathematics." *Cogent Education* 6, no. 1. https://www.tandfonline.com/doi/pdf/10.1080/2331186X.2019.1689639?needAccess=true.

Manchester, Ashley. 2017. "Teaching Critical Looking: Pedagogical Approaches to Using Comics as Queer Theory." *SANE Journal: Sequential Art Narrative in Education* 2, no. 2: 1–23. https://digitalcommons.unl.edu/cgi/viewcontent.cgi?article=1046&context=sane.

Mandaville, Alison, and John Paul Avila. 2009. "It's a Word! It's a Picture! It's Comics! Interdisciplinary Approaches to Teaching Comics." In *Teaching the Graphic Novel*, edited by Stephen E. Tabachnick, 245–53. New York: Modern Language Association of America.

Manfredi, Mirella, Neil Cohn, and Marta Kutas. 2017. "When a Hit Sounds Like a Kiss: An Electrophysiological Exploration of Semantic Processing in Visual Narrative." *Brain and Language* 169 (June): 28–38. https://www.ncbi.nlm.nih.gov/pmc/articles/PMC5465314/.

Mangels, Andy. 1988a. "Out of the Closet and into the Comics: The Creations and the Creators, Part I." *Amazing Heroes*, no. 143 (June): 39–54.

Mangels, Andy. 1988b. "Out of the Closet and into the Comics: The Creations and the Creators, Part II." *Amazing Heroes*, no. 144 (July): 47–67.

Marcoci, Roxana. 2007. *Comic Abstraction: Image-Breaking, Image-Making*. New York: Museum of Modern Art.

Marion, Philippe. 1993. *Trace en cases: Travail graphique, figuration narrative et participation du lecteur; Essai sur la bande dessinée*. Louvain: Université Catholique de Louvain / Academia.

Martin, Côme. 2017. "With, Against or Beyond Print? Digital Comics in Search of a Specific Status." *The Comics Grid: Journal of Comics Scholarship* 7, no. 1: 1–16. https://www.comicsgrid.com/article/id/3555/.

Martin, Gary, with Steve Rude and Leo Vitalis. 2019. *The Art of Comic Book Inking*. Milwaukie, OR: Dark Horse.

Martinbrough, Shawn. 2007. *How to Draw Noir Comics: The Art and Technique of Visual Storytelling*. New York: Watson-Guptill.

Marx, Christy. 2006. *Writing for Animation, Comics, and Games*. Burlington, MA: Focal Press.

Masahiro, Toyoura, Mamoru Kunihiro, and Ziaoyang Mao. 2012. "Film Comic Reflecting Camera-Works." In *Advances in Multimedia Modeling: 18th International Conference, MMM 2012, Proceedings*, edited by Klaus Schoeffmann, Bernard Merialdo, Alexander

G. Hauptmann, Chong-Wah Ngo, Yiannis Andreopoulos, and Christian Breiteneder, 406–17. Berlin: Springer Verlag.

Maslon, Laurence, and Michael Kantor. 2013. *Superheroes! Capes, Cowls, and the Creation of Comic Book Culture.* New York: Crown Archetype.

Mason, Andy. 2002. "Black and White in Ink: Discourses of Resistance in South African Cartooning." *African and Asian Studies* 1, no. 4 (January): 385–406.

Massironi, Manfredo. 2001. *The Psychology of Graphic Images: Seeing, Drawing, Communicating.* Translated by Nicola Bruno. Mahwah, NJ: Lawrence Erlbaum Associates.

Matthiessen, Christian M. I. M. 2007. "The Multimodal Page: A Systematic Functional Exploration." In *New Directions in the Analysis of Multimodal Discourse*, edited by Terry D. Royce and Wendy L. Bowcher, 1–62. Mahwah, NJ: Lawrence Erlbaum Associates.

Mayer, Ruth. 2013. *Serial Fu Manchu: The Chinese Supervillain and the Spread of Yellow Peril Ideology.* Philadelphia: Temple University Press.

Maynard, Patrick. 2001. "The Time It Takes." In *The Graphic Novel*, edited by Jan Baetens, 191–210. Leuven: Leuven University Press.

Mazur, Dan, and Alexander Danner. 2014. *Comics: A Global History, 1968 to the Present.* London: Thames and Hudson.

McAllister Matthew P. 1992. "Comic Books and AIDS." *Journal of Popular Culture* 26, no. 2 (Fall): 1–24.

McAllister, Matthew P., and Stephanie Orme. 2018. "Cinema's Discovery of the Graphic Novel: Mainstream and Independent Adaptation." In *The Cambridge History of the Graphic Novel*, edited by Jan Baetens, Hugo Frey, and Stephen E. Tabachnick, 543–57. Cambridge: Cambridge University Press.

McBride, Patrizia. 2012. "Narrative Resemblance: The Production of Truth in the Modernist Photobook of Weimar Germany." *New German Critique: An Interdisciplinary Journal of German Studies* 39, no. 1 (Winter): 169–97.

McCloud, Scott. 1994. *Understanding Comics: The Invisible Art.* New York: HarperCollins.

McCloud, Scott. 2000. *Reinventing Comics: How Imagination and Technology Are Revolutionizing an Art Form.* New York: HarperCollins.

McCloud, Scott. 2006. *Making Comics: Storytelling Secrets of Comics, Manga, and Graphic Novels.* New York: William Morrow.

McCracken, Ellen. 2001. "Hybridity and Postmodernity in the Argentine Meta-Comic: The Bridge Texts of Julio Cortázar and Ricardo Piglia." In *Latin American Literature and Mass Media*, edited by Edmundo Paz Soldán and Debra A. Castillo, 139–51. New York: Garland Publishing.

McDermott, Jason E., Matthew Partridge, and Yana Bromberg. 2018. "Ten Simple Rules for Drawing Scientific Comics." *PLOS Computational Biology* 14, no. 1 (January): 1–10. https://journals.plos.org/ploscompbiol/article?id=10.1371/journal.pcbi.1005845.

McEniry, Matthew J., Robert Moses Peaslee, and Robert G. Weiner, eds. 2016. *Marvel Comics into Film: Essays on Adaptations since the 1940s.* Jefferson, NC: McFarland.

McGlade, Rhiannon. 2018. "Dissenting Voices? Controlling Children's Comics under Franco." *European Comic Art* 11, no. 1 (Spring): 30–47.

McHale, Brian. 2010. "Narrativity and Segmentivity; or, Poetry in the Gutter." In *Intermediality and Storytelling*, edited by Marina Grishakova and Marie-Laure Ryan, 27–48. Berlin: Walter de Gruyter.

McKean, Dave. 1995. "Storytelling in the Gutter." *History of Photography* 19, no. 4: 193–97.

McLaughlin, Jeff. 2009. "Comic Book Artists and Writers and Philosophers." *International Journal of Comic Art* 11, no. 2 (Fall): 364–71.

McLaughlin, Mark J. 2013. "Rise of the Eco-Comics: The State, Environmental Education and Canadian Comic Books, 1971–1975." *Revue de la Culture Matérielle* 77–78 (Spring–Fall): 9–20. https://journals.lib.unb.ca/index.php/MCR/article/view/22080/25636.

Mellier, Denis. 2017. "World Building and Metafiction in Contemporary Comic Books: Metalepsis and Figurative Process of Graphic Fiction," In *World Building: Transmedia, Fans, Industries*, edited by Marta Boni, 304–18. Amsterdam: Amsterdam University Press.

Mendonça, Penelope. 2016. "Graphic Facilitation, Sketchnoting, Journalism and 'The Doodle Revolution': New Dimensions in Comics Scholarship." *Studies in Comics* 7, no. 1 (July): 127–52.

Menu, Jean-Christophe. 2011. *La Bande dessinée et son double: Langage et marges de la bande dessinée; Perspectives pratiques, théoriques et éditoriales*. Paris: L'Association.

Méon, Jeran-Matthieu. 2018. "Sons and Grandsons of Origins: Narrative Memory in Marvel Superhero Comics." In *Comics Memory: Archives and Styles*, edited by Maaheen Ahmed and Benoît Crucifix, 189–209. Cham, Switzerland: Palgrave Macmillan.

Méon, Jeran-Matthieu. 2019. "Comics in Museums and at Their Periphery: Hierarchical Reaffirmation and Domination Adjustments in French Art Museums." *ImageTexT: Interdisciplinary Comics Studies* 10, no. 3. http://imagetext.english.ufl.edu/archives/v10_3/meon/.

Merino, Ana. 2001. "Women in Comics: A Space for Recognizing Other Voices." *The Comics Journal*, no. 237 (September): 44–48.

Merino, Ana. 2008. "Feminine Territoriality: Reflections on the Impact of the Underground and Post-Underground." *International Journal of Comic Art* 10, no. 2 (Fall): 70–88.

Meskin, Aaron. 2007. "Defining Comics?" *Journal of Aesthetics and Art Criticism* 65, no. 4 (Fall): 369–79.

Meskin, Aaron. 2012. "The Ontology of Comics." In *The Art of Comics: A Philosophical Approach*, edited by Aaron Meskin and Roy T. Cook, 31–46. Chichester, W. Susx., England: Wiley-Blackwell.

Meskin, Aaron, and Roy T. Cook, eds. 2012. *The Art of Comics: A Philosophical Approach*. Chichester, W. Susx., England: Wiley-Blackwell.

Meyer, Christina. 2012. "Patriotic Laughter? World War I in British and American Newspaper and Magazine Comics." In *Heroisches Elend: Der Erste Weltkrieg im intellektuellen, literarischen und bildnerischen Gedächtnis der europäischen Kulturen*, edited by Gislinde Seybert and Thomas Stauder, 1525–52. Frankfurt am Main: Peter Lang.

Mickwitz, Nina. 2016. *Documentary Comics: Graphic Truth-Telling in a Skeptical Age.* Basingstoke, Hants., England: Palgrave Macmillan.

Mickwitz, Nina. 2020. "Introduction: Discursive Contexts, 'Voice,' and Empathy in Graphic Life Narratives of Migration and Exile." *a/b: Auto/Biography Studies* 35, no. 2 (Spring): 459–65.

Miers, John. 2015. "Depiction and Demarcation in Comics: Towards an Account of the Medium as a Drawing Practice." *Studies in Comics* 6, no. 1 (July): 145–56.

Mikkonen, Kai. 2010. "Remediation and the Sense of Time in Graphic Narratives." In *The Rise and Reason of Comics and Graphic Literature: Critical Essays on the Form*, edited by Joyce Goggin and Dan Hassler-Forest, 74–86. Jefferson, NC: McFarland.

Mikkonen, Kai. 2011a. "Graphic Narratives as a Challenge to Transmedial Narratology: The Question of Focalization." *Amerikastudien / American Studies* 56, no. 4: 637–52.

Mikkonen, Kai. 2011b. "The Implicit Narrator in Comics: Transformations of Free Indirect Discourse in Two Graphic Adaptations of *Madame Bovary*." *International Journal of Comic Art* 13, no. 2 (Fall): 473–87.

Mikkonen, Kai. 2013. "Subjectivity and Style in Graphic Narratives." In *From Comic Strips to Graphic Novels: Contributions to the Theory and History of Graphic Narrative*, edited by Daniel Stein and Jan-Noël Thon, 101–23. Berlin: Walter de Gruyter.

Mikkonen, Kai. 2017. *The Narratology of Comic Art.* New York: Routledge.

Miller, Ann. 2007. *Reading Bande Dessinée: Critical Approaches to French-Language Comic Strip.* Bristol: Intellect Books.

Miller, Ann. 2008. "Citizenship and City Spaces: *Bande Dessinée* as Reportage." In *History and Politics in French-Language Comics and Graphic Novels*, edited by Mark McKinney, 97–116. Jackson: University Press of Mississippi.

Miller, Ann. 2011. "Autobiography in *Bande Dessinée*." In *Textual and Visual Selves: Photography, Film, and Comic Art in French Autobiography*, edited by Natalie Edwards, Amy L. Hubbell, and Ann Miller, 235–62. Lincoln: University of Nebraska Press.

Miller, Ann, and Murray Pratt. 2004. "Transgressive Bodies in the Work of Julie Doucet, Fabrice Neaud and Jean-Christophe Menu: Towards a Theory of the 'AutobioBD.'" *Belphégor: Littérature Populaire et Culture Médiatique* 4, no. 1 (November). https://da space.library.dal.ca/bitstream/handle/10222/47696/04_01_Miller_trnsgr_en_cont .pdf?sequence=1&isAllowed=y.

Miller, Brian, and Kristy Miller. 2008. *Hi-Fi Color for Comics: Digital Techniques for Professional Results.* Cincinnati: Impact Books.

Miller, Matthew L., ed. 2015. *Class, Please Open Your Comics: Essays on Teaching with Graphic Narratives.* Jefferson, NC: McFarland.

Miller, Rachel. 2018. "From the Archives: The Queer Zine Archive Project." *Inks: Journal of the Comics Studies Society* 2, no. 3 (Fall): 369–89.

Millidge, Gary Spencer. 2009. *Comic Book Design: The Essential Guide to Creating Great Comics and Graphic Novels.* New York: Watson-Guptill.

Miodrag, Hannah. 2010. "Fragmented Text: The Spatial Arrangement of Words in Comics." *International Journal of Comic Art* 12, no. 2 (Fall): 309–27.

Miodrag, Hannah. 2012. "Narrative, Language, and Comics-as-Literature." *Studies in Comics* 2, no. 2 (January): 263–79.

Miodrag, Hannah. 2013. *Comics and Language: Reimagining Critical Discourse on the Form.* Jackson: University Press of Mississippi.

Misemer, Leah. 2018. "A Historical Approach to Webcomics: Digital Authorship in the Early 2000s." *The Comics Grid: Journal of Comics Scholarship* 9, no. 1: 1–21. https://www.comicsgrid.com/article/id/3588/.

Misemer, Leah, and Margaret Galvan, eds. 2019. "The Counterpublics of Underground Comics." Special issue, *Inks: Journal of the Comics Studies Society* 3, no. 1 (Spring).

Misiroglu, Gina, ed. 2012. *The Superhero Book: The Ultimate Encyclopedia of Comic-Book Icons and Hollywood Heroes.* Canton, MI: Visible Ink Press.

Misiroglu, Gina, and Michael Eury. 2006. *The Supervillain Book: The Evil Side of Comics and Hollywood.* Canton, MI: Visible Ink Press.

Mitaine, Benoît, David Roche, and Isabelle Schmitt-Pitiot, eds. 2018. *Comics and Adaptation.* Translated by Aarnoud Rommens. Jackson: University Press of Mississippi.

Mitchell, Adrielle Anna. 2010. "Distributed Identity: Networking Image Fragments in Graphic Memoirs." *Studies in Comics* 1, no. 2 (November): 257–79.

Mitchell, Adrielle Anna. 2012. "Exposition and Disquisition: Nonfiction Graphic Narratives and Comics Theory in the Literature Classroom." In *Teaching Comics and Graphic Narratives: Essays on Theory, Strategy and Practice*, edited by Lan Dong, 198–209. Jefferson, NC: McFarland.

Mohring, Agatha. 2018. "Therapeutic Journeys in Contemporary Spanish Graphic Novels." *European Comic Art* 11, no. 2 (December): 98–117.

Molotiu, Andrei. 2009. Introduction to *Abstract Comics: The Anthology, 1967–2009*, edited by Andrei Molotiu. Seattle: Fantagraphics Books.

Molotiu, Andrei. 2011. "Abstract Form: Sequential Dynamism and Iconostasis in Abstract Comics and Steve Ditko's Amazing Spider-Man." In *Critical Approaches to Comics: Theories and Methods*, edited by Matthew J. Smith and Randy Duncan, 84–100. New York: Routledge.

Molotiu, Andrei. 2013. "List of Terms for Comics Studies." *Comics Forum*, July 26. https://comicsforum.org/2013/07/26/list-of-terms-for-comics-studies-by-andrei-molotiu/.

Monden, Masafumi. 2014. "Layers of the Ethereal: A Cultural Investigation of Beauty, Girlhood, and Ballet in Japanese Shōjo Manga." *Fashion Theory* 18, no. 3 (June): 251–96.

Monnin, Katie. 2010. *Teaching Graphic Novels: Practical Strategies for the Secondary ELA Classroom.* Mankato, MN: Maupin House.

Mooney, Linda, and Sarah Brabant. 1987. "Two Martinis and a Rested Woman: 'Liberation' in the Sunday Comics." *Sex Roles* 17, no. 7 (October): 409–20.

Moore, Alan, and Jacen Burrows. 2003. *Alan Moore's Writing for Comics.* Rantoul, IL: Avatar Press.

Morgan, Harry. 2009. "Graphic Shorthand: From Caricature to Narratology in Twentieth-Century Bande Dessinée and Comics." *European Comic Art* 2, no. 1 (March): 21–39.

Morris, Jon. 2016. *The Legion of Regrettable Supervillains*. Philadelphia: Quirk Books.

Morrison, Grant. 2011. *Supergods: What Masked Vigilantes, Miraculous Mutants, and a Sun God from Smallville Can Teach Us about Being Human*. New York: Spiegel and Grau.

Morton, Drew. 2015. "The Unfortunates: Towards a History and Definition of the Motion Comic." *Journal of Graphic Novels and Comics* 6, no. 4 (December): 347–66.

Morton, Drew. 2017. *Panel to the Screen: Style, American Film, and Comic Books during the Blockbuster Era*. Jackson: University Press of Mississippi.

Moszkowicz, Julia. 2012. "Time and Narrative: How Philosophical Thinking Can Support the Discipline of Illustration." *VaroomLab* 1, no. 1 (September): 45–58.

Moszkowicz, Julia. 2013. "Time, Narrative and the Gutter: How Philosophical Thinking Can Make Something Out of Nothing." In *Cultural Excavation and Formal Expression in the Graphic Novel*, edited by Jonathan C. Evans and Thomas Giddens, 195–205. Oxford: Oxford University Press.

Moula, Evangelia, and Louiza Christodoulidou. 2018. "Graphic Novels as Self-Conscious Contemplative Metatexts: Redefining Comics and Participating in Theoretical Discourse." *Journal of Literature and Art Studies* 8, no. 2 (February): 181–89. http://www.davidpublisher.com/Public/uploads/Contribute/5a6af695c1f07.pdf.

Muanis, Felipe. 2011. "Between Photography and Drawing: The Documentary Comics as Translation of the City." *International Journal of Comic Art* 13, no. 2 (Fall): 599–613.

Müller, Marion G., and Esra Özcan. 2007. "The Political Iconography of Muhammad Cartoons: Understanding Cultural Conflict and Political Action." *PS: Political Science and Politics* 40, no. 2 (April): 287–91.

Mulligan, Rikk. 2014. "The Reality/Fantasy Narrative and the Graphic Novel." In *The Graphic Novel*, edited by Gary Hoppenstand, 41–54. Ipswich, MA: Salem Press.

Munson, Kim. 2009. "Beyond High and Low: How Comics and Museums Learned to Co-Exist." *International Journal of Comic Art* 11, no. 2 (Fall): 283–98.

Munson, Kim. 2014a. "Hiding the Forbidden Fruit: Comics Censorship in the United States." In *Critical Insights: The American Comic Book*, edited by Joseph Michael Sommers, 20–35. Ipswich, MA: Salem Press.

Munson, Kim. 2014b. "From the Mainstream to the Margins: Independent Comics Find a Voice." In *Critical Insights: The American Comic Book*, edited by Joseph Michael Sommers, 136–52. Ipswich, MA: Salem Press.

Munson, Kim, ed. 2020. *Comic Art in Museums*. Jackson: University Press of Mississippi.

Murphy, AprilJo. 2014. "Homicidal Lesbian Terrorists to Crimson Caped Crusaders: How Folk and Mainstream Lesbian Heroes Queer Cultural Space." In *Heroines of Comic Books and Literature: Portrayals in Popular Culture*, edited by Maja Bajac-Carter, Norma Jones, and Bob Batchelor, 153–68. Lanham, MD: Rowman and Littlefield.

Murray, Chris. 2010. "Signals from Airstrip One: The British Invasion of Mainstream American Comics." In *The Rise of the American Comics Artist: Creators and Contexts*, edited by Paul Williams and James Lyons, 31–45. Jackson: University Press of Mississippi.

Murray, Padmini Ray. 2013. "Behind the Panel: Examining Invisible Labour in the Comics Publishing Industry." *Publishing Research Quarterly* 29, no. 4 (December): 336–43.

Murrell, William. 1935. "Rise and Fall of Cartoon Symbols." *American Scholar* 4, no. 3 (Summer): 306–15.

Myers, Kimberly R., and Michael D. F. Goldenberg. 2018. "Graphic Pathographies and the Ethical Practice of Person-Centered Medicine." *AMA Journal of Ethics* 20, no. 2 (February): 158–66. https://journalofethics.ama-assn.org/article/graphic-pathographies -and-ethical-practice-person-centered-medicine/2018-02.

Nabizadeh, Golnar. 2019. *Representation and Memory in Graphic Novels.* Abingdon, Oxon., England: Routledge.

Nakas, Kassandra, ed. 2004. *Funny Cuts: Cartoons and Comics in Contemporary Art.* Bielefeld, Germany: Kerber Verlag.

Nakazawa, Jun. 2016. "Manga Literacy and Manga Comprehension in Japanese Children." In *The Visual Narrative Reader,* edited by Neil Cohn, 157–84. London: Bloomsbury.

Nama, Adilifu. 2009. "Brave Black Worlds: Black Superheroes as Science Fiction Ciphers." *African Identities* 7, no. 2 (May): 133–44.

Nama, Adilifu. 2011. *Super Black: American Pop Culture and Black Superheroes.* Austin: University of Texas Press.

Nama, Adilifu. 2013. "Staking Out a *Blatino* Borderlands." In *Latinos and Narrative Media: Participation and Portrayal,* edited by Frederick Luis Aldama, 131–41. New York: Palgrave Macmillan.

Napier, Susan J. 1996. *The Fantastic in Modern Japanese Literature: The Subversion of Modernity.* London: Routledge.

Napier, Susan J. 2001. *Anime from Akira to Princess Mononoke: Experiencing Contemporary Japanese Animation.* New York: Palgrave.

Napier, Susan J. 2007. *From Impressionism to Anime: Japan as Fantasy and Fan Cult in the Mind of the West.* New York: Palgrave.

Natoli, Charles. 2009. "The Spirit Passes: The Second Coming of the Comic Strip's Golden Age." *International Journal of Comic Art* 11, no. 2 (Fall): 372–79.

Natsume, Fusanosuke. 1997. *Manga to Sensō.* Tokyo: Kōdansha Gendai Shinsho.

Natsume, Fusanosuke. 2010. "Pictotext and Panels: Commonalities and Differences in Manga, Comics and BD." In *Comics Worlds and the World of Comics: Towards Scholarship on a Global Scale,* edited by Jaqueline Berndt, 40–54. Kyoto: Kyoto Seika University International Manga Research Center.

Nayar, Pramod K. 2015. "Communicable Diseases: Graphic Medicine and the Extreme." *Journal of Creative Communications* 10, no. 2 (July): 161–75.

Ndalianis, Angela, ed. 2009a. *The Contemporary Comic Book Superhero.* New York: Routledge.

Ndalianis, Angela. 2009b. "Enter the Aleph: Superhero Worlds and Hypertime Realities." In *The Contemporary Comic Book Superhero,* edited by Angela Ndalianis, 270–90. New York: Routledge.

Ndalianis, Angela. 2011. "Why Comics Studies?" *Cinema Journal* 50, no. 3 (Spring): 113–17.

Nel, Philip. 2012. "Same Genus, Different Species? Comics and Picture Books." *Children's Literature Association Quarterly* 37, no. 4 (Winter): 445–53.

Nelson, Kyra. 2015. "Women in Refrigerators: The Objectification of Women in Comics." *AWE: A Woman's Experience* 2, no. 2: 73–81. https://scholarsarchive.byu.edu/cgi/view content.cgi?article=1026&context=awe.

Nevins, Jess. 2017. *The Evolution of the Costumed Avenger: The 4,000-Year History of the Superhero.* Santa Barbara, CA: Praeger.

Newall, Michael. 2011. *What Is a Picture? Depiction, Realism, Abstraction.* Basingstoke, Hants., England: Palgrave Macmillan.

Ng, Wai-Ming. 2010. "The Consumption and Perception of Japanese ACG (Animation–Comic–Game) among Young People in Hong Kong." *International Journal of Comic Art* 12, no. 1 (Spring): 460–77.

Nguyen, Nhu-Hoa. 2006. "The Rhetoric of Omission in Comic Art." *International Journal of Comic Art* 8, no. 1 (Spring): 283–300.

Nguyen, Nhu-Van, Christophe Rigaud, and Jean-Christophe Burie. 2018. "Digital Comics Image Indexing Based on Deep Learning." *Journal of Imaging* 4, no. 7 (July): 1–34. https://www.mdpi.com/2313-433X/4/7/89/htm.

Nichols, Jayms Clifford. 2013. "Digital Pages: Reading, Comics and Screens." In *Cultural Excavation and Formal Expression in the Graphic Novel*, edited by Jonathan C. Evans and Thomas Giddens, 303–12. Oxford: Oxford University Press.

Nielsen, Jesper, and Søren Wichmann. 2000. "America's First Comics? Techniques, Contents, and Functions of Sequential Text-Image Pairing in the Classic Maya Period." In *Comics and Culture: Analytical and Theoretical Approaches to Comics*, edited by Anne Magnussen and Hans-Christian Christiansen, 59–77. Copenhagen: Museum Tusculanum Press.

Nijdam, Elizabeth. 2020. "Transnational Girlhood and the Politics of Style in German Manga." *Journal of Graphic Novels and Comics* 11, no. 1 (February): 31–51.

Nikolajeva, Maria, and Carole Scott. 2001. *How Picturebooks Work.* New York: Routledge.

Nodelman, Perry. 1988. *Words about Pictures: The Narrative Art of Children's Picture Books.* Athens: University of Georgia Press.

Nodelman, Perry. 1991. "The Eye and the I: Identification and First-Person Narratives in Picture Books." *Children's Literature* 19: 1–30.

Noh, Sueen. 2008. "Science, Technology, and Women Represented in Korean Sci-Fi Girls' Comics." *International Journal of Comic Art* 10, no. 2 (Spring): 209–34.

Nolan, Michelle. 2008. *Love on the Racks: A History of American Romance Comics.* Jefferson, NC: McFarland.

Noomin, Diane, ed. 1991. *Twisted Sisters: A Collection of Bad Girl Art.* New York: Penguin.

Norcliffe, Glen, and Olivero Rendace. 2003. "New Geographies of Comic Book Production in North America: The New Artisan, Distancing, and the Periodic Social Economy." *Economic Geography* 79, no. 3 (July): 241–63.

Norris, Craig. 2005. "Cyborg Girls and Shape-Shifters: The Discovery of Difference by Anime and Manga Fans in Australia." *Refractory: A Journal of Entertainment Media* 8:

1–10. http://refractory.unimelb.edu.au/2005/10/14/cyborg-girls-and-shape-shifters-the -discovery-of-difference-by-anime-and-manga-fans-in-australia-craig-norris/.

Novak, Ryan J. 2014. *Teaching Graphic Novels: Building Literacy and Comprehension.* Waco, TX: Prufrock Press.

Noys, Benjamin. 2018. "No Future: Punk and the Underground Graphic Novel." In *The Cambridge History of the Graphic Novel,* edited by Jan Baetens, Hugo Frey, and Stephen E. Tabachnick, 235–50. Cambridge: Cambridge University Press.

Nyberg, Amy Kiste. 1998. *Seal of Approval: The History of the Comics Code.* Jackson: University Press of Mississippi.

Nyberg, Amy Kiste. 2006. "Theorizing Comics Journalism." *International Journal of Comic Art* 8, no. 2 (Fall): 98–112.

Oberman, Jeffrey. 2015. "How Hollywood Sold Its Soul to the Comic Book Fanboy." *Inroads,* no. 37 (Summer–Fall): 101–12. https://inroadsjournal.ca/how-hollywood-sold -its-soul-to-the-comic-book-fanboy/.

O'Brien, Richard. 1977. *The Golden Age of Comic Books, 1937–1945.* New York: Ballantine Books.

Odell, Colin, and Michelle Le Blanc. 2013. *Anime.* Harpenden, Herts., England: Kamera Books.

Oehlert, Mark. 2000. "From Captain America to Wolverine: Cyborgs in Comic Books; Alternative Images of Cybernetic Heroes and Villains." In *The Cybercultures Reader,* edited by David Bell and Barbara M. Kennedy, 112–23. London: Routledge.

Ōgi, Fusami. 2001. "Beyond Shoujo, Blending Gender: Subverting the Homogendered World in Shoujo Manga (Japanese Comics for Girls)." *International Journal of Comics* 3, no. 2 (Fall): 151–56.

Ōgi, Fusami. 2003. "Female Subjectivity and *Shoujo* (Girls) *Manga* (Japanese Comics): *Shoujo* in Ladies' Comics and Young Ladies' Comics." *Journal of Popular Culture* 36, no. 4 (May): 780–803.

Ōgi, Fusami. 2011. "Inspiring Women: 40 Years' Transformation of *Shōjo Manga* and Women's Voices." *International Journal of Comic Art* 13, no. 2 (Fall): 32–57.

Ōgi, Fusami, Rebecca Suter, Kazumi Nagaike, and John A. Lent, eds. 2019. *Women's Manga in Asia and Beyond: Uniting Different Cultures and Identities.* Cham, Switzerland: Palgrave Macmillan.

Okamoto, Rei. 2001. "Images of the Enemy in Wartime Manga Magazine, 1941–1945." In *Illustrating Asia: Comics, Humor Magazines and Picture Books,* edited by John A. Lent, 204–20. Honolulu: University of Hawai'i Press.

Olaniyan, Tejumola. 2000. "Cartooning in Nigeria: Paradigmatic Traditions." *Ijele: Art eJournal of the African World* 1, no. 1. https://www.africaknowledgeproject.org/index.php/ ijele/article/view/1289.

Olson, Richard D. 1993. "'Say! Dis Is Grate Stuff': The Yellow Kid and the Birth of the American Comics." *Syracuse University Library Associates Courier* 28, no. 1 (Spring): 19–34. https://surface.syr.edu/cgi/viewcontent.cgi?article=1301&context=libassoc.

Oltean, Tudor. 1993. "Series and Seriality in Media Culture." *European Journal of Communication* 8, no. 1 (March): 5–31.

Op de Beeck, Nathalie. 2012. "On Comics-Style Picture Books and Picture-Bookish Comics." *Children's Literature Association Quarterly* 37, no. 4 (Winter): 468–76.

Oppolzer, Markus. 2020. *Reading Autobiographical Comics: A Framework for Educational Settings.* Berlin: Peter Lang.

Orbaugh, Sharalyn. 2003. "Creativity and Constraint in Amateur *Manga* Production." *U.S.-Japan Women's Journal*, no. 25: 104–24.

Orlov, Pavel, and Ksenia Gorshkova. 2016. "Gaze-Based Interactive Comics." In *NordiCHI '16: Proceedings of the 9th Nordic Conference on Human-Computer Interaction*, 1–16. New York: Association for Computing Machinery.

Orme, Stephanie. 2016. "Femininity and Fandom: The Dual-Stigmatisation of Female Comic Book Fans." *Journal of Graphic Novels and Comics* 7, no. 4 (December): 403–16.

Oropeza, B. J., ed. 2005. *The Gospel According to Superheroes: Religion and Popular Culture.* New York: Peter Lang.

Oxoby, Marc. 2013. "Comics Code Authority." In *St. James Encyclopedia of Popular Culture*, vol. 1, edited by Sara Pendergast and Tom Pendergast, 667–68. Farmington Hills, MI: St. James Press.

Packalen, Leif, and Sharad Sharma. 2007. *Grassroots Comics: A Development Communication Tool.* Helsinki: Ministry of Foreign Affairs, Finland.

Packard, Stephan. 2006. "Reflections of the Cartoon." *International Journal of Comic Art* 8, no. 2 (Fall): 113–25.

Packard, Stephan. 2015. "Closing the Open Signification: Forms of Transmedial Storyworlds and Chronotopoi in Comics." *Storyworlds: A Journal of Narrative Studies* 7, no. 2 (Winter): 55–74.

Packard, Stephan. 2016. "The Drawn-Out Gaze of the Cartoon: A Psychosemiotic Look at Subjectivity in Comic Book Storytelling." In *Subjectivity across Media: Interdisciplinary and Transmedial Perspectives*, edited by Maike Sarah Reinerth and Jan-Noël Thon, 111–24. New York: Routledge.

Packard, Stephan. 2018. "Historical Time in Panel Spaces: Chronotopic Appropriations in Comics." In *Geschichte im Comic: Befunde–Theorien–Erzählweisen*, edited by Bernd Dolle-Weinkauff, 57–74. Berlin: Christian A. Bachmann Verlag.

Padva, Gilad. 2005. "Dreamboys, Meatmen and Werewolves: Visualizing Erotic Identities in All-Male Comic Strips." *Sexualities: Studies in Culture and Society* 8, no. 5 (December): 587–99.

Pagello, Federico. 2017. "The 'Origin Story' Is the Only Story: Seriality and Temporality in Superhero Fiction from Comics to Post-Television." *Quarterly Review of Film and Video* 34, no. 8: 725–45.

Pagliassotti, Dru. 2017. "'People Keep Giving Me Rings, but I Think a Small Death Ray Might Be More Practical': Women and Mad Science in Steampunk Comics." In *Neo-Victorian Humour: Comic Subversions and Unlaughter in Contemporary Historical Re-Visions*, edited by Marie-Luise Kohlke and Christian Gutleben, 213–46. Leiden: Brill Rodopi.

Palmer, Rebecca. 2014. "Combining the Rhythms of Comics and Picturebooks: Thoughts and Experiments." *Journal of Graphic Novels and Comics* 5, no. 3 (September): 297–310.

Palpanadan, Sarala Thulasi, Asliaty Atim, Zulida Abdul Kair, Venosha K. Ravana, and Muhammad Aiman Mohammed. 2019. "Improving Students' Mastery of Vocabulary through Flip Book Approach." *English Literature and Language Review* 5, no. 7 (July): 117–22. https://www.arpgweb.com/pdf-files/ellr5(7)117-122.pdf.

Palumbo, Donald E. 1983. "Modern Fantasy and Marvel Comics." In *Survey of Modern Fantasy Literature*, edited by Frank N. Magill, 2464–80. Englewood Cliffs, NJ: Salem Press.

Palumbo, Donald E. 1999. "Science Fiction in Comics Books: Science Fiction Colonizes a Fantasy Medium." In *Young Adult Science Fiction*, edited by C. W. Sullivan III, 161–82. Westport, CT: Greenwood Press.

Pantaleo, Sylvia. 2013. "Paneling 'Matters' in Elementary Students' Graphic Narratives." *Literacy Research and Instruction* 52, no. 2: 150–71.

Parkinson, Gavin, ed. 2015. *Surrealism, Science Fiction and Comics*. Liverpool: Liverpool University Press.

Parson, Sean, and J. L. Schatz, eds. 2019. *Superheroes and Masculinity: Unmasking the Gender Performance of Heroism*. Lanham, MD: Lexington Books.

Pasfield-Neofitou, Sarah, and Cathy Sell, with Queenie Chan, eds. 2016. *Manga Vision: Cultural and Communicative Perspectives*. Clayton, Vic., Australia: Monash University Publishing.

Patten, Fred. 2004. *Watching Anime, Reading Manga: 25 Years of Essays and Reviews*. Berkeley, CA: Stone Bridge Press.

Pearson, Laura. 2018. "Alternative Canadian Comics / Alternative Graphic Fiction." *Dalhousie Review* 98, no. 2 (Summer): 248–53.

Peaslee, Robert Moses, and Robert G. Weiner, eds. 2020. *The Supervillain Reader*. Jackson: University Press of Mississippi.

Pederson, Kaitlin, and Neil Cohn. 2016. "The Changing Pages of Comics: Page Layouts across Eight Decades of American Superhero Comics." *Studies in Comics* 7, no. 1 (July): 7–28.

Pedler, Martyn. 2007. "Suffering and Seriality: Memory, Continuity and Trauma in Monthly Superhero Adventures." Paper presented at the Creativity, Ownership, and Collaboration in the Digital Age conference, Cambridge, MA, April. http://web.mit.edu/comm-forum/legacy/mit5/papers/Pedler_Suffering_and_Seriality.pdf.

Pedler, Martyn. 2009. "The Fastest Man Alive: Stasis and Speed in Contemporary Superhero Comics." *Animation* 4, no. 3 (November): 249–63.

Pedri, Nancy. 2013. "Graphic Memoir: Neither Fact nor Fiction." In *From Comic Strips to Graphic Novels: Contributions to the Theory and History of Graphic Narrative*, edited by Daniel Stein and Jan-Noël Thon, 127–53. Berlin: Walter de Gruyter.

Pedri, Nancy, ed. 2015a. "The Narrative Functions of Photography in Comics." Special issue, *Image [&] Narrative: Online Magazine of the Visual Narrative* 16, no. 2 (July). http://www imageandnarrative.be/index.php/imagenarrative/issue/view/52.

Pedri, Nancy. 2015b. "What's the Matter of Seeing in Graphic Memoir?" *South Central Review* 32, no. 3 (Fall): 8–29.

Pedri, Nancy, ed. 2017. "Mixing Visual Media in Comics." Special issue, *ImageTexT: Interdisciplinary Comics Studies* 9, no. 2. http://imagetext.english.ufl.edu/archives/v9_2/.

Pedri, Nancy. 2018. "Breaking Into and Out of Panels: Formal Expressions of Subjectivity in Graphic Memoir." *Studies in Comics* 9, no. 2 (December): 297–334.

Pedri, Nancy. 2019. "Telling It Authentically: Documents in Graphic Illness Memoirs." *Diegesis, Interdisciplinary E-Journal for Narrative Research / Interdisziplinäres E-Journal für Erzählforschung* 8, no. 1: 48–66. https://www.diegesis.uni-wuppertal.de/index.php/diegesis/article/view/333/539.

Pedri, Nancy, and Helene Staveley. 2018. "Not Playing Around: Games in Graphic Illness Narratives." *Literature and Medicine* 36, no. 1 (Spring): 230–56.

Peeters, Benoît. 1998. *Case, planche, récit: Lire la bande dessinée*. Paris: Casterman.

Peeters, Benoît. 2007. "Four Conceptions of the Page." Translated by Jesse Cohn. *ImageTexT: Interdisciplinary Comics Studies* 3, no. 3: 41–60. (First published in *Case, planche, récit: Lire la bande dessinée* [Paris: Casterman, 1998], 41–60.) https://imagetextjournal.com/four-conceptions-of-the-page/.

Peeters, Benoît. 2010. "Between Writing and Image: A Scriptwriter's Way of Working." *European Comic Art* 3, no. 1 (March): 105–16.

Peeters, Benoît, and Marie-Françoise Plissart. 1995. "*Roman-photo* Revisited." *History of Photography* 19, no. 4 (Winter): 298–300.

Pellitteri, Marco. 2018. "Kawaii Aesthetics from Japan to Europe: Theory of the Japanese 'Cute' and Transcultural Adoption of Its Styles in Italian and French Comics Production and Commodified Culture Goods." *Arts* 7, no. 3 (July): 1–21. https://www.mdpi.com/2076-0752/7/3/24/htm.

Pellitteri, Marco. 2019a. "The Aural Dimension in Comic Art." In *The Oxford Handbook of Sound and Imagination*, vol. 1, edited by Mark Grimshaw-Aagaard, Mads Walther-Hansen, and Martin Knakkergaard, 511–47. Oxford: Oxford University Press.

Pellitteri, Marco. 2019b. "Lettering in Comics: Giving Sound to a Silent Medium." In *Critical Survey of Graphic Novels: History, Theme, and Technique*, edited by Bart Beaty and Stephen Weiner, 263–65. 2nd ed. Ipswich, MA: Salem Press.

Peltz, Amy. 2013. "A Visual Turn: Comics and Art after the Graphic Novel." *Art in Print* 2, no. 6 (March–April): 8–14. https://artinprint.org/article/a-visual-turn-comics-and-art-after-the-graphic-novel/.

Peñalba García, Mercedes. 2014. "La temporalidad en el cómic / The Construction of Time in Comics." *Signa: Revista de la Asociación Española de Semiótica* 23: 687–713. http://revistas.uned.es/index.php/signa/article/view/11753/11200.

Penney, Matthew. 2007. "'War Fantasy' and Reality: 'War as Entertainment' and Counter-Narratives in Japanese Popular Culture." *Japanese Studies* 27, no. 1: 35–52.

Peppard, Anna F. 2019. "The Power of the Marvel(ous) Image: Reading Excess in the Styles of Todd McFarlane, Jim Lee, and Rob Liefeld." *Journal of Graphic Novels and Comics* 10, no. 3 (June): 320–41.

Peppard, Anna F., ed. 2020. *Supersex: Sexuality, Fantasy, and the Superhero.* Austin: University of Texas Press.

Pérez Laraudogoitia, Jon. 2009. "The Composition and the Structure of the Comic." *Journal of Quantitative Linguistics* 16, no. 4 (November): 327–53.

Perna, Laura. 2008. "(Re)Constructing History: Italy's Post-War Resistance Movement in Contemporary Comics." *SCAN: Journal of Media Arts Culture* 5, no. 2 (September). http://scan.net.au/scan/journal/display.php?journal_id=117.

Perret, Marion D. 2001. "'And Suit the Action to the Word': How a Comics Panel Can Speak Shakespeare." In *The Language of Comics: Word and Image,* edited by Robin Varnum and Christina T. Gibbons, 123–44. Jackson: University Press of Mississippi.

Perron, Bernard. 2016. "Wandering the Panels, Walking through Media: Zombies, Comics, and the Post-Apocalyptic World." *Journal of Graphic Novels and Comics* 7, no. 3 (September): 306–18.

Perron, Bernard. 2017. "Zombie Escape and Survival Plans: Mapping the Transmedial World of the Dead." In *World Building: Transmedia, Fans, Industries,* edited by Marta Boni, 215–30. Amsterdam: Amsterdam University Press.

Petersen, Robert S. 2007. "The Acoustics of Manga: Narrative Erotics and the Visual Presence of Sound." *International Journal of Comic Art* 9, no. 1 (Spring): 578–90.

Petersen, Robert S. 2010. *Comics, Manga, and Graphic Novels: A History of Graphic Narratives.* Santa Barbara, CA: Praeger.

Peterson, James Braxton. 2010. "Graphic Black Nationalism: Visualizing Political Narratives in the Graphic Novel." In *The Rise and Reason of Comics and Graphic Literature: Critical Essays on the Form,* edited by Joyce Goggin and Dan Hassler-Forest, 202–21. Jefferson, NC: McFarland.

Pfalzgraf, Markus. 2012. *Stripped: The Story of Gay Comics.* Berlin: Bruno Gmünder Verlag.

Phillips, Nickie D., and Staci Strobl. 2013. *Comic Book Crime: Truth, Justice, and the American Way.* New York: New York University Press.

Picone, Michael D. 2009. "Teaching Franco-Belgian *Bande Dessinée.*" In *Teaching the Graphic Novel,* edited by Stephen E. Tabachnick, 299–323. New York: Modern Language Association of America.

Picone, Michael D. 2013. "Comic Art in Museums and Museums in Comic Art." *European Comic Art* 6, no. 2 (December): 40–68.

Pieper, Gail W., with Kenneth D. Nordin and Joseph Ursitti, eds. 1997. *Understanding the Funnies: Critical Interpretations of Comic Strips.* Lisle, IL: Procopian Press.

Piepmeier, Alison. 2009. *Girl Zines: Making Media, Doing Feminism.* New York: New York University Press.

Piepoli, Angelo. 2011. "Sequential Art between Language and Textuality." *International Journal of Comic Art* 13, no. 2 (Fall): 458–72.

Pigeon, Gérard G. 1996. "Black Icons of Colonialism: African Characters in French Children's Comic Strip Literature." *Social Identities: Journal for the Study of Race, Nation and Culture* 2, no. 1 (February): 135–59.

Pike, Deidre M. 2012. *Enviro-Toons: Green Themes in Animated Cinema and Television.* Jefferson, NC: McFarland.

Pilcher, Tim, and Gene Kannenberg Jr. 2008. *Erotic Comics: A Graphic History from Tijuana Bibles to Underground Comix.* New York: Harry N. Abrams.

Pillai, Nicolas. 2013. "'What Am I Looking At, Mulder?' Licensed Comics and the Freedoms of Transmedia Storytelling." *Science Fiction Film and Television* 6, no. 1 (Spring): 101–17.

Pitkäsalo, Eliisa, and Laura Kalliomaa-Puha. 2019. "Democratizing Access to Justice: The Comic Contract as Intersemiotic Translation." *Translation Matters* 1, no. 2 (Autumn): 30–42. https://ojs.letras.up.pt/index.php/tm/article/view/6713/6218.

Pizzino, Christopher. 2016. *Arresting Development: Comics at the Boundaries of Literature.* Austin: University of Texas Press.

Pizzino, Christopher. 2018. "When Realism Met Romance: The Negative Zone of Marvel's Silver Age." In *The Cambridge History of the Graphic Novel,* edited by Jan Baetens, Hugo Frey, and Stephen E. Tabachnick, 107–23. Cambridge: Cambridge University Press.

Pizzino, Christopher. 2020. "The Cartoon on the Comics Page: A Phenomenology." In *The Oxford Handbook of Comic Book Studies,* edited by Frederick Luis Aldama, 115–31. Oxford: Oxford University Press.

Pleban, Dafna. 2006. "Investigating the Clear Line Style." *ComicFoundry,* November 7.

Poharec, Lauranne. 2018. "Focalized Split Panels: Bridging the Borders in Comics Form." *Studies in Comics* 9, no. 2 (December): 315–31.

Polak, Kate. 2017. *Empathy in the Gutter: Empathy and Historical Fiction in Comics.* Columbus: Ohio State University Press.

Poletti, Anna. 2008a. "Auto/Assemblage: Reading the Zine." *Biography: An Interdisciplinary Quarterly* 31, no. 1 (Winter): 85–102.

Poletti Anna. 2008b. *Intimate Ephemera: Reading Youth Lives in Australian Zine Culture.* Melbourne: Melbourne University Publishing.

Poletti, Anna. 2008c. "Where the Popular Meets the Mundane: The Use of Lists in Personal Zines." *Canadian Review of American Studies* 38, no. 3 (Winter): 333–49.

Pollmann, Joost. 2001. "Shaping Sounds in Comics." *International Journal of Comic Art* 3, no. 1 (Spring): 9–21.

Pont, Xavier Marcó del. 2012. "Confronting the Whiteness: Blankness, Loss and Visual Disintegration in Graphic Narratives." *Studies in Comics* 3, no. 2 (December): 253–74.

Poore, Benjamin, ed. 2017. *Neo-Victorian Villains: Adaptations and Transformations in Popular Culture.* Leiden: Brill Rodopi.

Postema, Barbara. 2007. "Draw a Thousand Words: Signification and Narration in Comics Images." *International Journal of Comic Art* 9, no. 1 (Spring): 487–501.

Postema, Barbara. 2013. *Narrative Structure in Comics: Making Sense of Fragments.* Rochester, NY: Rochester Institute of Technology Press.

Postema, Barbara. 2014. "Following the Pictures: Wordless Comics for Children." *Journal of Graphic Novels and Comics* 5, no. 3 (September): 311–22.

Postema, Barbara. 2016. "Silent Comics." In *The Routledge Companion to Comics*, edited by Frank Bramlett, Roy T. Cook, and Aaron Meskin, 217–24. New York: Routledge.

Postema, Barbara. 2018. "Long-Length Wordless Books: Frans Masereel, Milt Gross, Lynd Ward, and Beyond." In *The Cambridge History of the Graphic Novel*, edited by Jan Baetens, Hugo Frey, and Stephen E. Tabachnick, 59–74. Cambridge: Cambridge University Press.

Potsch, Elisabeth, and Robert F. Williams. 2012. "Image Schemas and Conceptual Metaphor in Action Comics." In *Linguistics and the Study of Comics*, edited by Frank Bramlett, 13–36. Basingstoke, Hants., England: Palgrave Macmillan.

Pratha, Nimish K., Natalie Avunjian, and Neil Cohn. 2016. "Pow, Punch, Pika, and Chu: The Structure of Sound Effects in Genres of American Comics and Japanese Manga." *Multimodal Communication* 5, no. 2 (October): 93–109.

Pratt, Henry John. 2009a. "Medium Specificity and the Ethics of Narrative in Comics." *Storyworlds: A Journal of Narrative Studies* 1, no. 1: 97–113.

Pratt, Henry John. 2009b. "Narrative in Comics." *Journal of Aesthetics and Art Criticism* 67, no. 1 (Winter): 107–17.

Pratt, Henry John. 2012. "Making Comics into Film." In *The Art of Comics: A Philosophical Approach*, edited by Aaron Meskin and Roy T. Cook, 147–64. Chichester, W. Susx., England: Wiley-Blackwell.

Pratt, Henry John. 2013. "Why Serials Are Killer." *Journal of Aesthetics and Art Criticism* 71, no. 3 (August): 266–70.

Pratt, Henry John. 2017. "Comics and Adaptation." In *The Routledge Companion to Comics*, edited by Frank Bramlett, Roy T. Cook, and Aaron Meskin, 230–38. New York: Routledge.

Proctor, William. 2012a. "Beginning Again: The Reboot Phenomenon in Comic Books and Film." *SCAN: Journal of Media Arts Culture* 9, no. 1 (March). http://scan.net.au/scn/journal/vol9number1/William-Proctor.html.

Proctor, William. 2012b. "Regeneration and Rebirth: Anatomy of the Franchise Reboot." *Scope: An Online Journal of Film and Television Studies*, no. 22 (February). http://www.nottingham.ac.uk/scope/documents/2012/february-2012/proctor.pdf.

Proctor, William. 2013. "Ctl-Alt-Delete: Retcon, Relaunch, or Reboot?" *Sequart Organization Magazine* (February 8). http://sequart.org/magazine/18508/ctl-alt-delete-retcon-re launch-or-reboot/.

Proctor, William. 2017a. "Reboots and Retroactive Continuity." In *The Routledge Companion to Imaginary Worlds*, edited by Mark J. P. Wolf, 224–35. New York: Routledge.

Proctor, William. 2017b. "Schrödinger's Cape: The Quantum Seriality of the Marvel Multiverse." In *Make Ours Marvel: Media Convergence and a Comics Universe*, edited by Matt Yockey, 319–45. Austin: University of Texas Press.

Proctor, William. 2018. "Transmedia Comics: Seriality, Sequentiality, and the Shifting Economies of Franchise Licensing." In *The Routledge Companion to Transmedia Studies*, edited by Matthew Freeman and Renira Rampazzo Gambarato, 52–61. New York: Routledge.

Prough, Jennifer S. 2011. *Straight from the Heart: Gender, Intimacy, and the Cultural Production of Shōjo Manga*. Honolulu: University of Hawai'i Press.

Purse, Lisa. 2019. "The New Dominance: Action-Fantasy Hybrids and the New Superhero in 2000s Action Cinema." In *A Companion to the Action Film*, edited by James Kendrick, 55–73. Hoboken, NJ: Wiley-Blackwell.

Pustz, Matthew J. 1999. *Comic Book Culture: Fanboys and True Believers*. Jackson: University Press of Mississippi.

Pustz, Matthew J. 2007. "'Let's Rap with Cap': Fan Interaction in Comic Book Letters Pages." In *Inside the World of Comic Books*, edited by Jeffery Klaehn, 163–85. Montreal: Black Rose Books.

Quaresima, Leonardo, Laura Ester Sangalli, and Federico Zecca, eds. 2009. *Cinema e fumetto / Cinema and Comics*. Udine, Italy: Forum Editrice Universitaria Udinese.

Quattro, Ken. 2020. *Invisible Men: The Trailblazing Black Artists of Comic Books*. San Diego: Yoe Books.

Quesenberry, Krista. 2017. "Intersectional and Non-Human Self-Representation in Women's Autobiographical Comics." *Journal of Graphic Novels and Comics* 8, no. 5 (October): 417–32.

Rabanal, Daniel. 2005. "Comics Production in Colombia." In *Cartooning in Latin America*, edited by John A. Lent, 177–87. Cresskill, NJ: Hampton Press.

Rabkin, Eric S. 2009. "Reading Time in Graphic Narrative." In *Teaching the Graphic Novel*, edited by Stephen E. Tabachnick, 34–43. New York: Modern Language Association of America.

Radway, Janice. 2011. "Zines, Half-Lives, and Afterlives: On the Temporalities of Social and Political Change." *PMLA* 126, no. 1 (January): 140–50.

Raeburn, Daniel. 2004. "Two Centuries of Underground Comic Books." In *Strips, Toons, and Bluesies: Essays in Comics and Culture*, edited by Douglas Bevan Dowd and Todd M. Hignite, 34–45. New York: Princeton Architectural Press.

Rageul, Anthony. 2018. "On the Pleasure of Coding Interface Narratives." *The Comics Grid: Journal of Comics Scholarship* 8, no. 1: 1–17. https://www.comicsgrid.com/article/id/3563/.

Ratto, Casey M. 2017. "Not Superhero Accessible: The Temporal Stickiness of Disability in Superhero Comics." *Disability Studies Quarterly* 37, no. 2 (Spring). http://dsq-sds.org/article/view/5396.

Rauscher, Andreas, Daniel Stein, and Jan-Nöel Thon, eds. 2020. *Comics and Videogames: From Hybrid Medialities to Transmedia Expansions*. Abingdon, Oxon., England: Routledge.

Reimer, Marvis, Nyala Ali, Deanna England, and Melanie Dennis Unrau, eds. 2014. *Seriality and Texts for Young People: The Compulsion to Repeat*. Basingstoke, Hants., England: Palgrave Macmillan.

Reynolds, Richard. 1994. *Super Heroes: A Modern Mythology*. Jackson: University Press of Mississippi.

Reyns, Bradford W., and Billy Henson. 2010. "Superhero Justice: The Depiction of Crime and Justice in Modern-Age Comic Books and Graphic Novels." *Sociology of Crime, Law and Deviance* 14 (April): 45–66.

Rhoades, Shirrel. 2008a. *Comic Books: How the Industry Works.* New York: Peter Lang.

Rhoades, Shirrel. 2008b. *A Complete History of American Comic Books.* New York: Peter Lang.

Riches, Adam. 2009. *When the Comics Went to War: Comic Book War Heroes.* Edinburgh: Mainstream Publishing.

Rickman, Lance. 2009. "The Appropriated Sequence: Montage on Paper and Film in 1901." In *Cinema e fumetto / Cinema and Comics,* edited by Leonardo Quaresima, Laura Ester Sangalli, and Federico Zecca, 251–61. Udine, Italy: Forum Editrice Universitaria Udinese.

Rifas, Leonard. 1988. "Educational Comics: A Message in a Bubble." *Print* 42, no. 6 (November–December): 145–57.

Rifas, Leonard. 2018. "The Politics of Underground Comix and the Environmental Crisis." *International Journal of Comic Art* 20, no. 2 (Fall–Winter): 128–50.

Rifkind, Candida. 2008. "Drawn from Memory: Comics Artists and Intergenerational Auto/Biography." *Canadian Review of American Studies* 38, no. 3 (October): 399–427.

Rifkind, Candida. 2015. "The Seeing Eye of Scientific Graphic Biography." *Biography: An Interdisciplinary Quarterly* 38, no. 1 (Winter): 1–22.

Rifkind, Candida. 2019. "Research Methods for Studying Graphic Biography." In *Research Methodologies for Auto/biography Studies,* edited by Kate Douglas and Ashley Barnwell, 68–75. New York: Routledge.

Rifkind, Candida, and Linda Warley, eds. 2016. *Canadian Graphic: Picturing Life Narratives.* Waterloo, Ont., Canada: Wilfrid Laurier University Press.

Ripley, Doré. 2012. "Classroom Comics: Children's Medium and the New Literacy." *Interdisciplinary Humanities Journal* 29, no. 1 (Spring): 99–113.

Rippl, Gabriele, and Lukas Etter. 2013. "Intermediality, Transmediality, and Graphic Narrative." In *From Comic Strips to Graphic Novels: Contributions to the Theory and History of Graphic Narrative,* edited by Daniel Stein and Jan-Noël Thon, 191–217. Berlin: Walter de Gruyter.

Risner, Jonathan. 2010. "'Authentic' Latinas/os and Queer Characters in Mainstream and Alternative Comics." In *Multicultural Comics: From "Zap" to "Blue Beetle,"* edited by Frederick Luis Aldama, 39–54. Austin: University of Texas Press.

Robb, Jenny E. 1995. *Before the Yellow Kid: Precursors of the American Newspaper Comic Strip.* Columbus: Ohio State University Libraries.

Robbins, Trina. 2002. "No Man Is My Master: American Romance Comics of the 1970s and the Women's Liberation Movement." *International Journal of Comic Art* 4, no. 1 (Spring): 151–62.

Robbins, Trina. 2013. *Pretty in Ink: American Women Cartoonists, 1896–2013.* Seattle: Fantagraphics Books.

Robertson, Derik. 2015. "Justification of Poetry Comics: A Multimodal Theory of an Improbable Genre." *The Comics Grid: Journal of Comics Scholarship* 5, no. 9. https://www.comicsgrid.com/articles/10.5334/cg.bg/.

Robertson, Wes. 2019. "Scripted Voices: Script's Role in Creating Japanese Manga Dialogue." *Journal of Graphic Novels and Comics* 10, no. 1 (February): 87–105.

Roeder, Katherine. 2011. "Seeing Inside-Out in the Funny Pages." *American Art* 25, no. 1 (Spring): 24–27.

Rogers, Marc C. 2006. "Understanding Production: The Stylistic Impact of Artisan and Industrial Methods." *International Journal of Comic Art* 8, no. 1 (Spring): 509–17.

Romagnoli, Alex S., and Gian S. Pagnucci. 2013. *Enter the Superheroes: American Values, Culture, and the Canon of Superhero Literature.* Lanham, MD: Scarecrow Press.

Romaguera, Gabriel E. 2015. "Waiting for the Next Part: How the Temporal Dimensions of Digital Serialisation Have Changed Author-Reader Dynamics." *Networking Knowledge: Journal of the MeCCSA Postgraduate Network* 8, no. 4 (June). http://ojs.meccsa.org.uk/ index.php/netknow/article/view/388/217.

Romero-Jódar, Andrés. 2013. "Comic Books and Graphic Novels in Their Generic Context: Towards a Definition and Classification of Narrative Iconical Texts." *Atlantis: Journal of the Spanish Association of Anglo-American Studies* 35, no. 1 (June): 117–35.

Rommens, Aarnoud. 2000. "Manga Story-Telling / Showing." *Image [&] Narrative: Online Magazine of the Visual Narrative* 1, no. 1 (January). http://www.imageandnarrative.be/ inarchive/narratology/aarnoudrommens.htm.

Rommens, Aarnoud. 2019. "'Deep' Time in Times of Precarity: Comics and Anthropocene Poetics." *Revue Captures* 4, no. 2 (November). http://www.revuecaptures.org/node/4001.

Rommens, Aarnoud, Crucifix Benoît, Björn-Olav Dozo, Erwin Dejasse, and Pablo Turnes, eds. 2019. *Abstraction and Comics / Bande dessinée et abstraction.* Liège: Presses Universitaires de Liège / La Cinquième Couche.

Root, Tom, and Andrew Kardon. 2004. *Writers on Comics Scriptwriting.* Vol. 2. London: Titan Books.

Rosemont, Franklin. 1979. "Surrealism in the Comics." *Cultural Correspondence,* nos. 10–11 (Fall): 57–72.

Rosen, Elizabeth. 2009. "The Narrative Intersection of Image and Text: Teaching Panel Frames in Comics." In *Teaching the Graphic Novel,* edited by Stephen E. Tabachnick, 58–66. New York: Modern Language Association of America.

Rosenberg, Robin S., with Jennifer Canzoneri, eds. 2008. *The Psychology of Superheroes: An Unauthorized Exploration.* Dallas: BenBella Books.

Rosenkranz, Patrick. 2008. *Rebel Visions: The Underground Comix Revolution, 1963–1975.* Seattle: Fantagraphics Books.

Rossiter, Caroline. 2009. "Early French Caricature (1795–1830) and English Influence." *European Comic Art* 2, no. 1 (June): 41–64.

Rota, Valerio. 2008. "Aspects of Adaptation: The Translation of Comics Formats." In *Comics in Translation,* edited by Federico Zanettin, 79–97. Manchester: St. Jerome.

Rothman, Alexander. 2015. "What Is Comics Poetry?" *Indiana Review* 37, no. 1 (Summer). https://indianareview.org/2015/06/what-is-comics-poetry-by-alexander-rothman/.

Round, Julia. 2007. "Visual Perspective and Narrative Voice in Comics: Redefining Literary Terminology." *International Journal of Comics Art* 9, no. 2 (Fall): 316–29.

Round, Julia. 2008. "London's Calling: Alternate Worlds and the City as Superhero in Contemporary British-American Comics." *International Journal of Comic Art* 10, no. 1 (Spring): 24–31.

Round, Julia. 2013. "Anglo-American Graphic Narrative." In *From Comic Strips to Graphic Novels: Contributions to the Theory and History of Graphic Narrative*, edited by Daniel Stein and Jan-Noël Thon, 325–45. Berlin: Walter de Guyter.

Round, Julia. 2014a. *Gothic in Comics and Graphic Novels: A Critical Approach*. Jefferson, NC: McFarland.

Round, Julia. 2014b. "We Share Our Mothers' Health: Temporality and the Gothic in Comic Book Landscapes." In *Comic Book Geographies*, edited by Jason Dittmer, 127–40. Stuttgart: Franz Steiner Verlag.

Rowe, Christopher. 2016. "Dynamic Drawings and Dilated Time: Framing in Comics and Film." *Journal of Graphic Novels and Comics* 7, no. 4 (December): 348–68.

Roy, Thomas, and Bill Schelly, eds. 2008. *Alter Ego: The Best of the Legendary Comics Fanzine*. Raleigh, NC: TwoMorrows Publishing.

Royal, Derek Parker. 2010. "Native Noir: Genre and the Politics of Indigenous Representation in Recent American Comics." *ImageTexT: Interdisciplinary Comics Studies* 5, no. 3. http://www.english.ufl.edu/imagetext/archives/v5_3/royal/.

Rubenstein, Anne. 1998. *Bad Language, Naked Ladies, and Other Threats to the Nation: A Political History of Comic Books in Mexico*. Durham, NC: Duke University Press.

Runacres, Ian, and Michael K. Mackenzie. 2016. "Classical Allusion in Modern British Political Cartoons." In *Son of Classics and Comics*, edited by George Kovacs and C. W. Marshall, 161–78. Oxford: Oxford University Press.

Ryerson, Rachael. 2019. "Disidentification, Disorientation, and Disruption: Queer Multimodal Rhetoric in Queer Comics." *Journal of Multimodal Rhetorics* 3, no. 1: 49–67.

Sabhaney, Vidyun. 2014. "Panels, Registers and Frames: Creative Engagements with Traditional Visual Narrative Forms." *MARG* 66, no. 2 (December): 26–39.

Sabin, Roger. 1993. *Adult Comics: An Introduction*. New York: Routledge.

Sabin, Roger. 1996. *Comics, Comix and Graphic Novels: A History of Comic Art*. New York: Phaidon Press.

Sabin, Roger, and Teal Triggs, eds. 2001. *Below Critical Radar: Fanzines and Alternative Comics from 1976 to Now*. Brighton and Hove, E. Susx., England: Slab-O-Concrete.

Sadri, Houman. 2018. "Mass Surveillance and the Negation of the Monomyth." *Fafnir: Nordic Journal of Science Fiction and Fantasy Research* 5, no. 1: 21–33. http://journal.finfar.org/articles/mass-surveillance-and-the-negation-of-the-monomyth/.

Saduov, Ruslan P. 2019. "North American Practices of Comics Production and Contemporary Russian Comics Industry." *Studia Litterarum* 4, no. 1: 274–85. https://doaj.org/article/87d226d63ca14f65bf9afe880602oc2a.

Saguisag, Lara. 2013. "The 'Secret Tracts' of the Child's Mind: Theorizing Childhood in Early 20th Century Fantasy Strips." *International Journal of Comic Art* 15, no. 1 (Spring): 35–67.

Saguisag, Lara. 2016. "Comics, Children's Literature, and Childhood Studies." In *The Routledge Companion to Comics*, edited by Frank Bramlett, Roy T. Cook, and Aaron Meskin, 433–42. New York: Routledge.

Saguisag, Lara. 2017. "RAW and Little Lit: Resisting and Redefining Children's Comics." In *Picturing Childhood: Youth in Transnational Comics*, edited by Mark Heimermann and Brittany Tullis, 128–47. Austin: University of Texas Press.

Saint, Lily. 2010. "Not Western: Race, Reading, and the South African Photocomic." *Journal of Southern African Studies* 36, no. 4 (December): 939–58.

Saitō, Tamaki. 2011. *Beautiful Fighting Girl*. Translated by J. Keith Vincent and Dawn Lawson. Minneapolis: University of Minnesota Press.

Salgueiro, Jorge. 2008. "Synthesia and Onomatopoeia in Graphic Literature." *International Journal of Comic Art* 10, no. 2 (Spring): 581–97.

Salinas, Jason. 2015. "More than Storyboards: Maintaining a Space for Graphic Novels in the Face of Film Adaptation." In *Class, Please Open Your Comics: Essays on Teaching with Graphic Narratives*, edited by Matthew L. Miller, 117–30. Jefferson, NC: McFarland.

Salisbury, Mark. 2002. *Writers on Comics Scriptwriting*. Vol. 1. London: Titan Books.

Salkowitz, Rob. 2012. *Comic-Con and the Business of Pop Culture: What the World's Wildest Trade Show Can Tell Us about the Future of Entertainment*. New York: McGraw-Hill.

Salmi, Charlotta. 2019. "Sequential Art in the Age of Postcolonial Production: Comics Collectives in Israel and South Africa." In *Popular Postcolonialisms: Discourses of Empire and Popular Culture*, edited by Nadia Atia and Kate Houlden, 70–86. New York: Routledge.

Sammond, Nicholas. 2018. "Meeting in the Archive: Comix and Collecting as Community." *Feminist Media Histories* 4, no. 3 (Summer): 96–118.

Sanders, Joe Sutliff. 2013. "Chaperoning Words: Meaning-Making in Comics and Picture Books." *Children's Literature* 41, no. 1: 57–90.

Sandifer, Philip. 2008. "Amazing Fantasies: Trauma, Affect, and Superheroes." *English Language Notes* 46, no. 2 (Fall–Autumn): 175–92.

Sante, Luc. 2004. "The Clear Line." In *Give Our Regards to the Atomsmashers! Writers on Comics*, edited by Sean Howe, 24–32. New York: Pantheon Books.

Sante, Luc. 2009. "The Clear Line." In *Kill All Your Darlings: Pieces, 1990–2005*, by Luc Sante, 229–37. Portland, OR: Verse Chorus Press.

Santos, Jorge J., Jr. 2019. *Graphic Memories of the Civil Rights Movement: Reframing History in Comics*. Austin: University of Texas Press.

Saraceni, Mario. 2003. *The Language of Comics*. London: Routledge.

Saraceni, Mario. 2016. "Relatedness: Aspects of Textual Connectivity in Comics." In *The Visual Narrative Reader*, edited by Neil Cohn, 115–29. London: Bloomsbury.

Sasaki, Maana. 2013. "Gender Ambiguity and Liberation of Female Sexual Desire in Fantasy Spaces of *Shojo* Manga and the *Shojo* Subculture." *Critical Theory and Social Justice* 3, no. 1 (Spring). https://scholar.oxy.edu/bitstream/handle/20.500.12711/4277/Sasaki.pdf?sequence=1&isAllowed=y.

Saunders, Ben. 2011. *Do the Gods Wear Capes? Spirituality, Fantasy, and Superheroes.* London: Continuum.

Savage, William W., Jr. 1998. *Commies, Cowboys, and Jungle Queens: Comic Books and America, 1945–1954.* Middletown, CT: Wesleyan University Press.

Schatz, J. L., and Sean Parson, eds. 2018. *Superheroes and Critical Animal Studies: The Heroic Beasts of Total Liberation.* Lanham, MD: Lexington Books.

Schell, John Logan. 2020. "This Is Who I Am: Hybridity and Materiality in Comics Memoir." In *The Oxford Handbook of Comic Book Studies*, edited by Frederick Luis Aldama, 256–67. Oxford: Oxford University Press.

Schelly, Bill. 1999. *The Golden Age of Comics Fandom.* Seattle: Hamster Press.

Schelly, Bill. 2018. *Sense of Wonder: My Life in Comic Fandom—The Whole Story.* Berkeley, CA: North Atlantic Books.

Scherr, Rebecca. 2013. "Teaching 'The Auto-Graphic Novel': Autobiographical Comics and the Ethics of Readership." In *Graphic Novels and Comics in the Classroom: Essays on the Educational Power of Sequential Art*, edited by Carrye Kay Syma and Robert G. Weiner, 134–44. Jefferson, NC: McFarland.

Schiller, Liz. 1997. "Doesn't She Know This Is a Comics Shop? How to Treat the Customer." In *How to Get Girls (into Your Store): A Friends of Lulu Retailers Handbook*, edited by Deni Loubert, 11–15. San Diego: Friends of Lulu.

Schilperoord, Joost. 2013. "Raising the Issue: A Mental-Space Approach to Iwo Jima–Inspired Editorial Cartoons." *Metaphor and Symbol* 28, no. 3 (July–September): 185–212.

Schilperoord, Joost, and Alfons Maes. 2009. "Visual Metaphoric Conceptualization in Editorial Cartoons." In *Multimodal Metaphor*, edited by Charles J. Forceville and Eduardo Urios-Aparisi, 213–40. Berlin: Mouton de Gruyter.

Schlichting, Laura. 2016. "Interactive Graphic Journalism." *VIEW: Journal of European Television History and Culture* 5, no. 10: 22–39. https://www.viewjournal.eu/articles/10.18146/2213-0969.2016.jethc110/.

Schmid, Johannes C. P. 2019. "Documentary Webcomics: Mediality and Context." In *Perspectives on Digital Comics: Theoretical, Critical and Pedagogical Essays*, edited by Jeffrey S. J. Kirchoff and Mike P. Cook, 63–88. Jefferson, NC: McFarland.

Schmidt, Andy. 2018. *Comics Experience Guide to Writing Comics: Scripting Your Story Ideas from Start to Finish.* Cincinnati: Impact Books.

Schmitz-Emans, Monika. 2011. "The Languages of Music in Comics, Bandes Dessinées and Fumetti." In *Translation & Multilingual Literature / Traduction & littérature multilingue*, edited by K. Alfons Knauth, 195–213. Münster, Germany: LIT Verlag.

Schneider, Christian W. 2013. "The Cognitive Grammar of 'I': Viewing Arrangements in Graphic Autobiographies." *Studies in Comics* 4, no. 2 (October): 307–32.

Schneider, Greice. 2010. "Comics and Everyday Life: From Ennui to Contemplation." *European Comic Art* 3, no. 1 (March): 37–63.

Schneider, Greice. 2011. "The Joy and the Burden of the Comics Artist: The Role of Boredom in the Production of Comics." *Comics Forum*, August 8. http://comicsforum

.org/2011/08/08/the-joy-and-the-burden-of-the-comics-artist-the-role-of-boredom-in -the-production-of-comics-by-greice-schneider/.

Schneider, Greice. 2016. *What Happens When Nothing Happens: Boredom and Everyday Life in Contemporary Comics.* Leuven: Leuven University Press.

Schodt, Frederik L. 1986. *Manga! Manga! The World of Japanese Comics.* Tokyo: Kodansha International.

Schodt, Frederik L. 1996. *Dreamland Japan: Writings on Modern Manga.* Berkeley, CA: Stone Bridge Press.

Schoell, William. 2010. *The Silver Age of Comics.* Albany, GA: BearManor Media.

Schoell, William. 2014. *The Horror Comics: Fiends, Freaks and Fantastic Creatures, 1940s–1980s.* Jefferson, NC: McFarland.

Schott, Gareth. 2010. "From Fan Appropriation to Industry Re-Appropriation: The Sexual Identity of Comic Superheroes." *Journal of Graphic Novels and Comics* 1, no. 1 (January): 17–29.

Schroff, Simone. 2019. "An Alternative Universe? Authors as Copyright Owners: The Case of the Japanese Manga Industry." *Creative Industries Journal* 12, no. 1 (March): 125–50. https://www.tandfonline.com/doi/full/10.1080/17510694.2018.1563420?scroll=top& needAccess=true.

Schultz, Henry E. 1949. "Censorship and Self Regulation?" *Journal of Educational Sociology* 23, no. 4 (December): 215–24.

Schumer, Arlen. 2012. "The Auteur Theory of Comics." *International Journal of Comic Art* 14, no. 1 (Spring): 474–84.

Schumer, Arlen. 2014. *The Silver Age of Comic Book Art.* Bloomington, IN: Archway Publishing.

Schwarcz, Joseph H. 1982. *Ways of the Illustrator: Visual Communication in Children's Literature.* Chicago: American Library Association.

Schwartz, Adam, and Eliane Rubinstein-Ávila. 2006. "Understanding the Manga Hype: Uncovering the Multimodality of Comic-Book Literacies." *Journal of Adolescent and Adult Literacy* 50, no. 1 (September): 40–49.

Schwartz, Ben, ed. 2010. *The Best American Comics Criticism.* Seattle: Fantagraphics Books.

Schwenger, Peter. 2011. "Abstract Comics and the Decomposition of Horror." *Horror Studies* 2, no. 2 (October): 265–80.

Scolari, Carlos, Paolo Bertetti, and Matthew Freeman. 2014. *Transmedia Archaeology: Storytelling in the Borderlines of Science Fiction, Comics and Pulp Magazines.* Basingstoke, Hants., England: Palgrave Macmillan.

Scott, Cord. 2008. "The Return of the War Comic: A Revival of Military Themes and Characters in Comic Books." *International Journal of Comic Art* 10, no. 2 (Spring): 649–59.

Scott, Jeffery. 2016. *The Posthuman Body in Superhero Comics: Human, Superhuman, Transhuman, Post/Human.* New York: Palgrave Macmillan.

Scott, Suzanne. 2013. "Fangirls in Refrigerators: The Politics of (In)visibility in Comic Book Culture." *Transformative Works and Cultures,* no. 13 (June). https://journal.transforma tiveworks.org/index.php/twc/article/view/460/384.

Scott, Suzanne. 2019. *Fake Geek Girls: Fandom, Gender, and the Convergence Culture Industry*. New York: New York University Press.

Screech, Matthew. 2005. *Masters of the Ninth Art: Bandes Dessinées and Franco-Belgian Identity*. Liverpool: Liverpool University Press.

Screech, Matthew. 2016. "Continuing Clear Line 1983–2013." In *The Comics of Hergé: When the Lines Are Not So Clear*, edited by Joe Sutliff Sanders, 79–97. Jackson: University Press of Mississippi.

Scully, Richard, and Marian Quartly, eds. 2009. *Drawing the Line: Using Cartoons as Historical Evidence*. Clayton, Vic., Australia: Monash University ePress.

Sealy-Morris, Gabriel. 2015. "The Rhetoric of the Paneled Page: Comics and Composition Pedagogy." *Composition Studies* 43, no. 1 (Spring): 31–50.

Sennitt, Stephen. 1999. *Ghastly Terror! The Horrible Story of the Horror Comics*. Manchester: Critical Vision.

Sereni, Eleonora. 2020. "'When I'm Bad, I'm Better': From Early Villainesses to Contemporary Antiheroines in Superhero Comics." *Helden, Heroes, Héros: E-Journal zu Kulturen des Heroischen* 8, no. 1: 31–41. https://doi.org/10.6094/helden.heroes.heros./2020/01/04.

Serrano, Nhora Lucía. 2020. "Columbia and the Editorial Cartoon." In *The Oxford Handbook of Comic Book Studies*, edited by Frederick Luis Aldama, 190–202. Oxford: Oxford University Press.

Servitje, Lorenzo, and Sherryl Vint, eds. 2016. *The Walking Med: Zombies and the Medical Image*. University Park: Pennsylvania State University Press.

Sewell, Edward H., Jr. 2001. "Queer Characters in Comic Strips." In *Comics and Ideology*, edited by Matthew P. McAllister, Edward H. Sewell Jr., and Ian Gordon, 251–74. New York: Peter Lang.

Shamoon, Deborah. 2008. "Situating the *Shōjo* in *Shōjo Manga*: Teenage Girls, Romance Comics, and Contemporary Japanese Culture." In *Japanese Visual Culture: Explorations in the World of Manga and Anime*, edited by Mark W. MacWilliams, 137–54. Abingdon, Oxon., England: Routledge.

Sheikh, Faiz. 2014. "The Zombie Apocalypse: A Fictional State of Nature?" In *Comics as History, Comics as Literature: Roles of the Comic Book in Scholarship, Society, and Entertainment*, edited by Annessa Ann Babic, 195–208. Madison, NJ: Fairleigh Dickinson University Press.

Shen, Kuiyi. 1997. "Comics, Picture Books, and Cartoonists in Republican China." *Inks: Cartoon and Comic Arts Studies* 4, no. 2 (Summer): 2–15.

Shepherd, Kameshia. 2011. "The Superhero Genre: Exhibitions Which Explore the Identities, Costumes, and Missions of the Superheroes in Contemporary Times." *Kritische Berichte* 39, no. 1: 114–23. https://journals.ub.uni-heidelberg.de/index.php/kb/article/view/77786/71714.

Sheppard, Alice. 1994. *Cartooning for Suffrage*. Albuquerque: University of New Mexico Press.

Sheyahshe, Michael A., ed. 2008. *Native Americans in Comics Books: A Critical Study*. Jefferson, NC: McFarland.

Shigematsu, Setsu. 1999. "Dimensions of Desire, Sex, Fantasy, and Fetish in Japanese Comics." In *Themes and Issues in Asian Cartooning: Cute, Cheap, Mad, and Sexy*, edited by John A. Lent, 127–63. Bowling Green, OH: Bowling Green State University Popular Press.

Shinohara, Kazuko, and Yoshihiro Matsunaka. 2009. "Pictorial Metaphors of Emotion in Japanese Comics." In *Multimodal Metaphor*, edited by Charles J. Forceville and Eduardo Urios-Aparisi, 265–93. Berlin: Mouton de Gruyter.

Shivener, Rich. 2019. "Re-Theorizing the Infinite Canvas: A Space for Comics and Rhetorical Theories." In *Perspectives on Digital Comics: Theoretical, Critical and Pedagogical Essays*, edited by Jeffrey S. J. Kirchoff and Mike P. Cook, 46–62. Jefferson, NC: McFarland.

Shores, Corry. 2016. "'Ragged Time' in Intra-Panel Comics Rhythms." *The Comics Grid: Journal of Comics Scholarship* 6, no. 1: 1–15.

Shwed, Ally. 2020. "Efficacy of Social Commentary through Cartooning." In *The Oxford Handbook of Comic Book Studies*, edited by Frederick Luis Aldama, 203–15. Oxford: Oxford University Press.

Shyminsky, Neil. 2011. "'Gay' Sidekicks: Queer Anxiety and the Narrative Straightening of the Superhero." *Men and Masculinities* 14, no. 3 (August): 288–308.

Sigall, Martha. 2005. *Living Life inside the Lines: Tales from the Golden Age of Animation*. Jackson: University Press of Mississippi.

Simone, Gail. 2012. "Women in Refrigerators." Women in Refrigerators, January 11. http://web.archive.org/web/20120111060731/http://www.unheardtaunts.com/wir/.

Singer, Marc. 1999. "Invisible Order: Comics, Time and Narrative." *International Journal of Comic Art* 1, no. 2 (Fall): 29–40.

Singer, Marc. 2019. *Breaking the Frames: Populism and Prestige in Comics Studies*. Austin: University of Texas Press.

Singsen, Doug. 2014. "An Alternative by Any Other Name: Genre-Splicing and Mainstream Genres in Alternative Comics." *Journal of Graphic Novels and Comics* 5, no. 2 (April): 170–91.

Singsen, Doug. 2017. "Critical Perspectives on Mainstream, Groundlevel, and Alternative Comics in *The Comics Journal*, 1977 to 1996." *Journal of Graphic Novels and Comics* 8, no. 2 (April): 156–72.

Skidmore, Max J., and Joey Skidmore. 1983. "More than Mere Fantasy: Political Themes in Contemporary Comic Books." *Journal of Popular Culture* 17, no. 1 (Summer): 83–92.

Skinn, Dez. 2004. *Comix: The Underground Revolution*. London: Collins and Brown.

Sklar, Howard. 2012. "Narrative Empowerment through Comics Storytelling: Facilitating the Life Stories of the Intellectually Disabled." *Storyworlds: A Journal of Narrative Studies* 4: 123–49.

Slipp, Nicole. 2017. "*Ménage à 3*: Webcomics, Creative Freedom, and Sexual Diversity." *Journal of Comics and Culture* 2 (Fall): 29–46.

Smith, Craig. 2012. "Motion Comics: Modes of Adaptation and the Issue of Authenticity." *Animation Practice, Process and Production* 1, no. 2 (June): 357–78.

Smith, Craig. 2015. "Motion Comics: The Emergence of a Hybrid Medium." *Writing Visual Culture* 7, no. 1. https://www.herts.ac.uk/__data/assets/pdf_file/0018/100791/wvc-dc7 -smith.pdf.

Smith, Greg M. 2011. "It Ain't Easy Studying Comics." *Cinema Journal* 50, no. 3 (Spring): 110–12.

Smith, Greg M. 2013. "Comics in the Intersecting Histories of the Window, the Frame, and the Panel." In *From Comic Strips to Graphic Novels: Contributions to the Theory and History of Graphic Narrative*, edited by Daniel Stein and Jan-Noël Thon, 219–37. Berlin: Walter de Gruyter.

Smith, Greg M., Thomas Andrae, Scott Bukatman, and Thomas LaMarre. 2011. "Surveying the World of Contemporary Comics Scholarship: A Conversation." *Cinema Journal* 50, no. 3 (Spring): 135–47.

Smith, Matthew J. 2014. "Silver Age Playbook: Minting the Modern Superhero." In *Critical Insights: The American Comic Book*, edited by Joseph Michael Sommers, 104–18. Ipswich, MA: Salem Press.

Smith, Matthew J., and Randy Duncan, eds. 2011. *Critical Approaches to Comics: Theories and Methods*. New York: Routledge.

Smith, Matthew J., and Randy Duncan, eds. 2017. *The Secret Origins of Comics Studies*. New York: Routledge.

Smith, Philip. 2014. "From the Page to the Tablet: Digital Media and the Comic Book." In *Critical Insights: The American Comic Book*, edited by Joseph Michael Sommers, 153–69. Ipswich, MA: Salem Press.

Smith, Philip, and Michael Goodrum. 2017. "'Corpses . . . Coast to Coast!' Trauma, Gender, and Race in 1950s Horror Comics." *Literature Compass* 14, no. 9 (September): 1–15.

Smith, Scott T., and José Alaniz, eds. 2020. *Uncanny Bodies: Superhero Comics and Disability*. University Park: Pennsylvania State University Press.

Smith, Sidonie. 2011. "Human Rights and Comics: Autobiographical Avatars, Crisis Witnessing, and Transnational Rescue Networks." In *Graphic Subjects: Critical Essays on Autobiography and Graphic Novels*, edited by Michael A. Chaney, 61–72. Madison: University of Wisconsin Press.

Smolderen, Thierry. 2014a. *The Origins of Comics: From William Hogarth to Winsor McCay*. Translated by Bart Beaty and Nick Nguyen. Jackson: University Press of Mississippi.

Smolderen, Thierry. 2014b. "Graphic Hybridization, the Crucible of Comics." In *The French Comics Theory Reader*, edited by Ann Miller and Bart Beaty, 47–61. Leuven: Leuven University Press.

Sofalvi, Alan J., and Judy C. Drolet. 1986. "Health-Related Content of Selected Sunday Comic Strips." *Journal of School Health* 56, no. 5 (May): 53–67.

Sommers, Joseph Michael. 2014. "Negotiating Popular Genres in Comic Books: An Impossible Mission. Against All Odds. Yet, Somehow, the Chapter Is Saved!" In *Critical Insights: The American Comic Book*, edited by Joseph Michael Sommers, 73–89. Ipswich, MA: Salem Press.

Soper, Kerry D. 2001. "Gentrifying the Alternatives or Alternifying the Mainstream? Consolidation, Incorporation, and the State of Comic Strip Satire in Alternative Weeklies, 1985–2000." *International Journal of Comic Art* 3, no. 2 (Fall): 189–201.

Sousanis, Nick. 2012. "The Shape of Our Thoughts: A Meditation on and in Comics." *Visual Arts Research* 38, no. 1 (Summer): 1–10.

Sousanis, Nick. 2015. *Unflattening*. Cambridge, MA: Harvard University Press.

Sousanis, Nick. 2017. "Beyond Illustration." In *Science Meets Comics: Proceedings of the Symposium on Communicating and Designing the Future of Food in the Anthropocene*, edited by Reinhold Leinfelder, Alexandra Hamann, Jens Kirstein, and Marc Schleunitz, 13–17. Berlin: Christian A. Bachmann Verlag.

Spandler, Helen. 2020. "Crafting Psychiatric Contention through Single-Panel Cartoons." In *PathoGraphics: Narrative, Aesthetics, Contention, Community*, edited by Susan Merrill Squier and Irmela Marei Krüger-Fürhoff, 115–34. University Park: Pennsylvania State University Press.

Spaulding, Amy. 1984. "A Study of the Picture Book as Storyboard." *Top of the News* 40, no. 4 (Summer): 443–44.

Spaulding, Amy. 1995. *The Page as a Stage Set: Storyboard Picture Books*. Lanham, MD: Scarecrow Press.

Speckman, Karon Reinboth. 2004. "The Bush-Blair Duo before 2003 Iraqi War: Cartoons from London Newspapers." *International Journal of Comic Art* 6, no. 2 (Fall): 118–37.

Spector, Nicole Audrey. 2016. "The Subversive Superheroes of Indie Comics." *Publishers Weekly* 263, no. 34 (August 22). https://www.publishersweekly.com/pw/by-topic/authors/pw-select/article/71228-the-subversive-superheros-of-indie-comics.html.

Spencer, David R. 2007. "The Press and the Spanish American War: Political Cartoons of the Yellow Journalism Age." *International Journal of Comic Art* 9, no. 1 (Spring): 262–80.

Spiegelman, Art. 1988. "Commix: An Idiosyncratic Historical and Aesthetic Overview." *Print* 42, no. 6: 61–73, 195–96.

Spiggle, Susan. 1986. "Measuring Social Values: A Content Analysis of Sunday Comics and Underground Comix." *Journal of Consumer Research* 13, no. 1 (June): 100–113.

Spitz, Ellen Handler. 2000. *Inside Picture Books*. New Haven, CT: Yale University Press.

Spivey, Michael, and Steven Knowlton. 2008. "Anti-Heroism in the Continuum of Good and Evil." In *The Psychology of Superheroes: An Unauthorized Exploration*, edited by Robin S. Rosenberg and Jennifer Canzoneri, 201–12. Dallas: BenBella Books.

Spurgeon, Tom. 2005. "Mini-Comics: Comics' Secret Lifeblood." In *The Education of a Comics Artist: Visual Narrative in Cartoons, Graphic Novels, and Beyond*, edited by Michael Dooley and Steven Heller, 133–37. New York: Allworth Press.

Squier, Susan Merrill. 2007. "Beyond Nescience: The Intersectional Insights of Health Humanities." *Perspectives in Biology and Medicine* 50, no. 3 (Summer): 334–47.

Squier, Susan Merrill. 2008. "So Long as They Grow Out of It: Comics, the Discourse of Developmental Normalcy, and Disability." *Journal of Medical Humanities* 29, no. 2 (June): 71–88.

Squier, Susan Merrill, and Irmela Marei Krüger-Fürhoff, eds. 2020. *PathoGraphics: Narrative, Aesthetics, Contention, Community*. University Park: Pennsylvania State University Press.

Staats, Hans. 2016. "Mastering Nature: War Gothic and the Monstrous Anthropocene." In *War Gothic in Literature and Culture*, edited by Agnieszka Soltysik Monnet and Steffen Hantke, 80–97. New York: Routledge.

Stainbrook, Eric. 2016. "A Little Cohesion between Friends; or, We're Just Exploring Our Textuality: Reconciling Cohesion in Written Language and Visual Language." In *The Visual Narrative Reader*, edited by Neil Cohn, 129–54. London: Bloomsbury.

Starkings, Richard, and John Roshell. 2003. *Comic Book Lettering: The Comicraft Way*. Los Angeles: Active Images.

Steiff, Josef, and Tristan D. Tamplin, eds. 2010. *Anime and Philosophy: Wide Eyed Wonder*. Chicago: Open Court.

Steiling, David. 2012. "Reading from Within the Panel." *ImageTexT: Interdisciplinary Comics Studies* 6, no. 2. http://www.english.ufl.edu/imagetext/archives/v6_2/steiling/.

Stein, Daniel. 2013. "Superhero Comics and the Authorizing Functions of the Comic Book Paratext." In *From Comic Strips to Graphic Novels: Contributions to the Theory and History of Graphic Narrative*, edited by Daniel Stein and Jan-Noël Thon, 155–89. Berlin: Walter de Gruyter.

Stein, Daniel. 2016. "'Mummified Objects': Superhero Comics in the Digital Age." *Journal of Graphic Novels and Comics* 7, no. 3 (September): 283–92.

Stein, Daniel. 2018. "Bodies in Transition: Queering the Comic Book Superhero." *Navigationen: Zeitschrift für Medien- und Kulturwissenschaften* 18, no. 1: 15–38. https://media rep.org/bitstream/handle/doc/1822/Navigationen_18_1_15-38_Stein_Bodies_in_tran sition_.pdf?sequence=7&isAllowed=y.

Stein, Daniel, and Lukas Etter. 2018. "Long-Length Serials in the Golden Age of Comic Strips: Production and Reception." In *The Cambridge History of the Graphic Novel*, edited by Jan Baetens, Hugo Frey, and Stephen E. Tabachnick, 39–58. Cambridge: Cambridge University Press.

Stevens, J. Richard, and Christopher Edward Bell. 2013. "Do Fans Own Digital Comic Books? Examining the Copyright and Intellectual Property Attitudes of Comic Book Fans." In *Piracy Cultures: How a Growing Portion of the Global Population Is Building Media Relationships through Alternate Channels of Obtaining Content*, edited by Manuel Castells and Gustavo Cardoso, 59–77. Los Angeles: USC Annenberg Press.

Stevens, John. 1976. "Reflections in a Dark Mirror: Comic Strips in Black Newspapers." *Journal of Popular Culture* 10, no. 1 (Summer): 239–44.

Stoll, Jeremy. 2010. "A Domestic Schizophrenia: Gender and Political Cartoons in the Middle East." *International Journal of Comic Art* 12, no. 1 (Spring): 302–22.

Stoll, Jeremy. 2016. "Between Art and the Underground: From Corporate to Collaborative Comics in India." In *Cultures of Comics Work*, edited by Casey Brienza and Paddy Johnston, 35–50. New York: Palgrave Macmillan.

Streb, Markus. 2016. "Early Representations of Concentration Camps in Golden Age Comic Books: Graphic Narratives, American Society, and the Holocaust." *Scandinavian Journal of Comic Art* 3, no. 1 (Fall): 28–63. http://www.sjoca.com/wp-content/uploads/2017/02/SJoCA-3-1-03-Streb.pdf.

Strickler, Dave. 1995. *Syndicated Comic Strips and Artists, 1924–1995: The Complete Index.* Cambria, CA: Comics Access.

Strömberg, Fredrik. 2012. *Black Images in the Comics: A Visual History.* Seattle: Fantagraphics Books.

Suárez, Fernando, and Enrique Uribe-Jongbloed. 2016. "Making Comics as Artisans: Comic Book Production in Colombia." In *Cultures of Comics Work,* edited by Casey Brienza and Paddy Johnston, 51–64. New York: Palgrave Macmillan.

Sulmicki, Maciej. 2011. "The Author as the Antiquarian: Selling Victorian Culture to Readers of Neo-Victorian Novels and Steampunk Comics." *Otherness: Essays and Studies* 2, no. 1 (August). http://www.otherness.dk/fileadmin/www.othernessandthearts.org/Publications/Journal_Otherness/Otherness__Essays_and_Studies_2.1/6.MaciejSulmicki.pdf.

Sundberg, Martin. 2017. "The Collapse of the Word-Image Dichotomy: Towards an Iconic Approach to Graphic Novels and Artists' Books." *Konsthistorisk Tidskrift / Journal of Art History* 86, no. 1: 31–44.

Surbhi, and Sarita Anand. 2017. "Addressing the Health and Information Needs of the Adolescent Rural Girl: Promoting Menstrual Health Practices through Grassroots Comics." *Social Sciences International Research Journal* 3: 122–27.

Surbhi, and Sarita Anand. 2019. "Notes from the Field: Using Grassroots Comics to Break the Silence on Menstruation." *Indian Journal of Gender Studies* 26, nos. 1–2 (February–June): 171–82. https://journals.sagepub.com/doi/10.1177/0971521518811175.

Surdiacourt, Steven. 2012a. "Can You Hear Me Drawing? 'Voice' and the Graphic Novel." In *Travelling Concepts, Metaphors, and Narratives: Literary and Cultural Studies in an Age of Interdisciplinary Research,* edited by Sibylle Baumbach, Beatrice Michaelis, and Ansgar Nünning, 165–78. Trier, Germany: Wissenschaftlicher Verlag Trier.

Surdiacourt, Steven. 2012b. "*Image [&] Narrative #5*: Graphic Poetry; An (Im)possible Form?" Comics Forum, June 21. https://comicsforum.org/2012/06/21/image-narrative-5-graphic-poetry-an-impossible-form-by-steven-surdiacourt/.

Surdiacourt, Steven. 2012c. "*Image [&] Narrative #8*: Tying Ends Together; Surface and Storyworld in Comics." Comics Forum, December 27. https://comicsforum.org/2012/12/27/image-narrative-8-tying-ends-together-surface-and-storyworld-in-comics-by-steven-surdiacourt/.

Suzuki, Shige. 2010. "Manga/Comics Studies from the Perspective of Science Fiction Research: Genre, Transmedia, and Transnationalism." In *Comics Worlds and the World of Comics: Towards Scholarship on a Global Scale,* edited by Jaqueline Berndt, 68–84. Kyoto: Kyoto Seika University International Manga Research Center.

Swafford, Brian. 2012. "Critical Ethnography: The Comics Shop as Cultural Clubhouse." In *Critical Approaches to Comics: Theories and Methods*, edited by Matthew J. Smith and Randy Duncan, 291–302. New York: Routledge.

Syma, Carrye Kay, and Robert G. Weiner, eds. 2013. *Graphic Novels and Comics in the Classroom: Essays on the Educational Power of Sequential Art*. Jefferson, NC: McFarland.

Szasz, Ferenc Morton. 2012. *Atomic Comics: Cartoonists Confront the Nuclear World*. Reno: University of Nevada Press.

Szawerna, Michał. 2014. "Metaphorical Underpinnings of Panels in Comics." *Academic Journal of Modern Philology* 3: 89–106. http://cejsh.icm.edu.pl/cejsh/element/bwmeta1 .element.desklight-30d117a6-e4c6-4927-8464-a0ff546ac937.

Szawerna, Michał. 2017. *Metaphoricity of Conventionalized Diegetic Images in Comics: A Study in Multimodal Cognitive Linguistics*. Frankfurt am Main: Peter Lang.

Szép, Eszter. 2020. *Comics and the Body: Drawing, Reading, and Vulnerability*. Columbus: Ohio State University Press.

Tabachnick, Stephen E., ed. 2009. *Teaching the Graphic Novel*. New York: Modern Language Association of America.

Tabachnick, Stephen E., and Esther Bendit Saltzman, eds. 2015. *Drawn from the Classics: Essays on Graphic Adaptations of Literary Works*. Jefferson, NC: McFarland.

Tabulo, Kym. 2014. "Abstract Sequential Art." *Journal of Graphic Novels and Comics* 5, no. 1 (February): 29–41.

Talon, Durwin S. 2002. *Panel Discussions: Design in Sequential Art Storytelling*. Raleigh, NC: TwoMorrows Publishing.

Talon, Durwin S. 2004. *Comics above Ground: How Sequential Art Affects Mainstream Media*. Raleigh, NC: TwoMorrows Publishing.

Talon, Durwin S. 2007. "The Technology and Storytelling of Color in the Sequential Narrative: Using Color to Tell Stories." *International Journal of the Book* 4, no. 4 (September): 123–32.

Talon, Durwin S., and Guin Thompson. 2010. "Using Panels to Shape Visual Storytelling: Organizing Flow in the Graphic Narrative." *International Journal of the Book* 7, no. 4 (September): 21–36.

Tan, Ed S. 2001. "The Telling Face in Comic Strip and Graphic Novel." In *The Graphic Novel*, edited by Jan Baetens, 31–46. Leuven: Leuven University Press.

Tan, Xiyuan. 2019. "*Guoxue* Comics: Visualising Philosophical Concepts and Cultural Values through Sequential Narratives." *The Comics Grid: Journal of Comics Scholarship* 9, no. 1: 1–18. https://www.comicsgrid.com/article/id/3589/#!.

Tankel, Jonathan David, and Keith Murphy. 1998. "Collecting Comic Books: A Study of the Fan and Curatorial Consumption." In *Theorizing Fandom: Fans, Subculture and Identity*, edited by Cheryl Harris and Alison Alexander, 55–68. Cresskill, NJ: Hampton Press.

Tarbox, Gwen Athene. 2020. *Children's and Young Adult Comics*. London: Bloomsbury.

Tatalovic, Mico. 2009. "Science Comics as Tools for Science Education and Communication: A Brief, Exploratory Study." *Journal of Science Communication* 8, no. 4 (December).

http://jcom.sissa.it/archive/08/04/Jcom0804%282009%29A02/Jcom0804%282009
%29A02.pdf.

Taylor, Kevin J. 2007. *KA-BOOM! A Dictionary of Comic Book Words, Symbols & Onomatopoeia, and Including . . . BZZURKK! The Thesaurus of Champions*. Morrisville, NC: Lulu Press.

Taylor, Laurie N. 2004. "Compromised Divisions: Thresholds in Comic Books and Video Games. *ImageTexT: Interdisciplinary Comics Studies* 1, no. 1. http://www.english.ufl.edu/imagetext/archives/v1_1/taylor/.

Teampău, Gelu Athene. 2014. "The Comic Books between Fantasy, Science-Fiction and Politics." *Caietele Echinox* 26 (June): 370–87.

Tensuan, Theresa. 2011. "Up from Surgery: The Politics of Self-Representation in Women's Graphic Memoirs of Illness." In *Graphic Subjects: Critical Essays on Autobiography and Graphic Novels*, edited by Michael A. Chaney, 180–94. Madison: University of Wisconsin Press.

Thomas, Cathy. 2018. "'Black' Comics as a Cultural Archive of Black Life in America." *Feminist Media Histories* 4, no. 3 (Summer): 49–95.

Thomas, Evan. 2015. "A Renaissance for Comics Studies: Early English Prints and the Comics Canon." *Partial Answers: Journal of Literature and the History of Ideas* 13, no. 2 (June): 255–66.

Thomas, Lynne M., and Sigrid Ellis, eds. 2014. *Chicks Dig Comics: A Celebration of Comic Books by the Women Who Love Them*. Des Moines, IA: Mad Norwegian Press.

Thomas, P. L. 2010. *Challenging Genres: Comics and Graphic Novels*. Rotterdam: Sense Publishers.

Thomas, P. L. 2011. "Adventures in Genre! Rethinking Genre through Comics/Graphic Novels." *Journal of Graphic Novels and Comics* 2, no. 2 (November): 187–201.

Thomas, Susan E. 2009. "Value and Validity of Art Zines as an Art Form." *Art Documentation* 28, no. 2 (Fall): 27–38.

Thompson, Jason. 2007. *Manga: The Complete Guide*. New York: Del Rey Books.

Thompson, Katrina D. 2006. "The Stereotype in Tanzania Comics: Swahili and the Ethnic Other." *International Journal of Comic Art* 8, no. 2 (Fall): 228–47.

Thon, Jan-Noël. 2013. "Who's Telling the Tale? Authors and Narrators in Graphic Narrative." In *From Comic Strips to Graphic Novels: Contributions to the Theory and History of Graphic Narrative*, edited by Daniel Stein and Jan-Noël Thon, 67–99. Berlin: Walter de Gruyter.

Thon, Jan-Noël. 2014a. "Subjectivity across Media: On Transmedial Strategies of Subjective Representation in Contemporary Feature Films, Graphic Novels, and Computer Games." In *Storyworlds across Media: Toward a Media-Conscious Narratology*, edited by Marie-Laure Ryan and Jan-Noël Thon, 67–102. Lincoln: University of Nebraska Press.

Thon, Jan-Noël. 2014b. "Toward a Transmedial Narratology: On Narrators in Contemporary Graphic Novels, Feature Films, and Computer Games." In *Beyond Classical Narration: Transmedial and Unnatural Challenges*, edited by Jan Alber and Per Krogh Hansen, 25–56. Berlin: Walter de Gruyter.

Thon, Jan-Noël. 2016. *Transmedial Narratology and Contemporary Media Culture*. Lincoln: University of Nebraska Press.

Thon, Jan-Noël. 2017. "Transmedial Narratology Revisited: On the Intersubjective Construction of Storyworlds and the Problem of Representational Correspondence in Films, Comics, and Video Games." *Narrative* 25, no. 3 (October): 286–320.

Thon, Jan-Noël, and Lukas R. A. Wilde. 2016. "Mediality and Materiality of Contemporary Comics." *Journal of Graphic Novels and Comics* 7, no. 3 (September): 233–41.

Thorne, Frank. 2000. *Drawing Sexy Women: Autobiographical Sketches*. Seattle: Fantagraphics Books.

Thoss, Jeff. 2011. "'This Strip Doesn't Have a Fourth Wall': Webcomics and the Metareferential Turn." In *The Metareferential Turn in Contemporary Arts and Media: Forms, Functions, Attempts at Explanation*, edited by Werner Wolf, 551–68. Leiden: Brill Rodopi.

Thoss, Jeff. 2015. *When Storyworlds Collide: Metalepsis in Popular Fiction, Film and Comics*. Leiden: Brill Rodopi.

Tilleuil, Jean-Louis. 2001. "A Story Can Hide Another One: Narrative Specularity and Sociocritical Stakes in the Contemporary French-Speaking Comic Strip Production." In *The Graphic Novel*, edited by Jan Baetens, 145–55. Leuven: Leuven University Press.

Tilley, Carol L. 2012. "Seducing the Innocent: Fredric Wertham and the Falsifications that Helped Condemn Comics." *Information and Culture* 47, no. 4: 383–413.

Tilley, Carol L. 2015. "Children and the Comics: Young Readers Take On the Critics." In *Protest on the Page: Essays on Print and the Culture of Dissent since 1865*, edited by James L. Baughman, Jennifer Ratner-Rosenhagen, and James P. Danky, 161–79. Madison: University of Wisconsin Press.

Tilley, Carol L. 2017. "Superheroes and Identity: The Role of Nostalgia in Comic Book Culture." In *Reinventing Childhood Nostalgia: Books, Toys, and Contemporary Media Culture*, edited by Elisabeth Wesseling, 51–65. Abingdon, Oxon., England: Routledge.

Tilley, Carol L. 2018. "A Regressive Formula of Perversity: Wertham and the Women of Comics." *Journal of Lesbian Studies* 22, no. 4 (January–March): 354–72.

Tilley, Carol L., and Sara Bahnmaier. 2018. "The Secret Life of Comics: Socializing and Seriality." *Serials Librarian* 74, nos. 1–4 (January–June): 54–64. https://www.tandfonline.com/doi/full/10.1080/0361526X.2018.1428456.

Tinker, Emma. 2007. "Manuscript in Print: The Materiality of Alternative Comics." *Literature Compass* 4, no. 4 (July): 1169–82.

Tju, Lim Cheng. 2014. "Current Trends in Singapore Comics: When Autobiography Is Mainstream." *Kyoto Review of Southeast Asia*, no. 16. http://kyotoreview.org/issue-16/current-trends-in-singapore-comics-when-autobiography-is-mainstream/.

Todd, Mark, and Esther Pearl Watson. 2006. *Whatcha Mean, What's a Zine? The Art of Making Zines and Minicomics*. Boston: Houghton Mifflin.

Toku, Masami, ed. 2005. *Shojo Manga! Girl Power! Girls' Comics from Japan*. Chico, CA: Flume Press.

Toku, Masami. 2007. "Shojo Manga! Girls' Comics! A Mirror of Girls' Dreams." *Mechademia: Second Arc* 2, no. 1 (Fall): 19–32.

Tolmie, Jane, ed. 2013. *Drawing from Life: Memory and Subjectivity in Comic Art.* Jackson: University Press of Mississippi.

Töpffer, Rodolphe. 1965. "Essay on Physiognomy." In *Enter: The Comics, Rodolphe Töpffer's Essay on Physiognomy and the True Story of Monsieur Crépin,* edited by Ellen Wiese, 1–36. Lincoln: University of Nebraska Press.

Torres Pastor, Claudia. 2019. "Fantasy Manga as a Reading Motivational Tool for Primary Education." In *In a Stranger Field: Studies of Art, Audiovisuals and New Technologies in Fantasy, SciFi and Horror Genres,* edited by Mario-Paul Martínez Fabre and Fran Mateu, 66–96. Elche, Spain: Fantaelx.

Trabado, José Manuel. 2015. "The Convergence of Graphic-Narrative Discourses: The Picture Book and the Graphic Novel." In *On the Edge of the Panel: Essays on Comics Criticism,* edited by Julio Cañero and Esther Claudio, 44–68. Newcastle upon Tyne: Cambridge Scholars Publishing.

Trebbi, Jean-Charles. 2017. *The Art of Pop-Up: The Magical World of Three-Dimensional Books.* Translated by Thomas Corkett. Barcelona: Promopress.

Trifonova, Temenuga. 2012. "Nouvelle Manga and Cinema." *Studies in Comics* 3, no. 1 (August): 47–62.

Tsai, Yi-Shan. 2018. "Close-Ups: An Emotive Language in Manga." *Journal of Graphic Novels and Comics* 9, no. 5 (October): 473–89.

Tsao, Pamela, and Catherine H. Yu. 2016. "'There's No Billing Code for Empathy': Animated Comics Remind Medical Students of Empathy; A Qualitative Study." *BMC Medical Education* 16, no. 1 (August): 204–12. https://bmcmededuc.biomedcentral.com/articles/10.1186/s12909-016-0724-z.

Tsaousis, Spiros. 1999. "Postmodern Spatiality and the Narrative Structure of Comics." *International Journal of Comic Art* 1, no. 1 (Spring–Summer): 205–18.

Tseng, Chiao-I, Jochen Laubrock, and Jana Pflaeging. 2018. "Character Developments in Comics and Graphic Novels: A Systematic Analytical Scheme." In *Empirical Comics Research: Digital, Multimodal, and Cognitive Methods,* edited by Alexander Dunst, Jochen Laubrock, and Janina Wildfeuer, 154–75. New York: Routledge.

Tu, Ming Hung Alex. 2011. "'Silent Music': Desiring-Machine and Femininity in Some Music-Themed Comics." *International Journal of Comic Art* 13, no. 2 (Fall): 75–86.

Uchmanowicz, Pauline. 2009. "Graphic Novel Decoded: Towards a Poetics of Comics." *International Journal of Comic Art* 11, no. 1 (Spring): 363–85.

Ueno, Junko. 2006. "*Shojo* and Adult Women: A Linguistic Analysis of Gender Identity in *Manga* (Japanese Comics)." *Women and Language* 29, no. 1 (Spring): 16–25. https://linggwistiks.files.wordpress.com/2009/03/g8-linguistic-analysis-of-gender-in-manga.pdf.

Ueno, Toshiya. 2002. "Japanimation: Techno-Orientalism, Media Tribes and Rave Culture." In *Aliens R Us: The Other in Science Fiction Cinema,* edited by Ziauddin Sardar and Sean Cubitt, 94–110. London: Pluto Press.

Uidhir, Christy Mag. 2012. "Comics and Collective Authorship." In *The Art of Comics: A Philosophical Approach*, edited by Aaron Meskin and Roy T. Cook, 47–67. Chichester, W. Susx., England: Wiley-Blackwell.

Uidhir, Christy Mag. 2013. "How to Frame Serial Art." *Journal of Aesthetics and Art Criticism* 71, no. 3 (Summer): 261–65.

Uidhir, Christy Mag. 2017. "Comics and Seriality." In *The Routledge Companion to Comics*, edited by Frank Bramlett, Roy T. Cook, and Aaron Meskin, 248–56. New York: Routledge.

Unser-Schutz, Giancarla. 2010. "Exploring the Role of Language in Manga: Text Types, Their Usages, and Their Distributions." *International Journal of Comic Art* 12, no. 2 (Fall): 25–43.

Unser-Schutz, Giancarla. 2011. "Language as the Visual: Exploring the Intersection of Linguistic and Visual Language in Manga." *Image [&] Narrative: Online Magazine of the Visual Narrative* 12, no. 1 (March): 1–22. http://www.imageandnarrative.be/index.php/imagenarrative/article/view/131/102.

Unser-Schutz, Giancarla. 2015. "What Text Can Tell Us about Male and Female Characters in Shōjo- and Shōnen-manga." *East Asian Journal of Popular Culture* 1, no. 1 (April): 133–53.

Vaccarella, Maria. 2013. "Exploring Graphic Pathographies in the Medical Humanities." *Medical Humanities* 39, no. 1 (June): 70–71.

Vacchelli, Carlotta. 2020. "The Sex of the Angels: Hybridization of Judeo-Christian Motifs in American and Italian Mainstream Comics." *Simultanea: A Journal of Italian Media and Pop Culture* 1, no. 1. http://italianpopculture.org/the-sex-of-the-angels-hybridization-of-judeo-christian-motifs-in-american-and-italian-mainstream-comics/.

Van As, Trevor. 2013. "Glossary of Comic Book Terms." How to Love Comics. https://www.howtolovecomics.com/comic-book-glossary-of-terms/.

Vandenburg, Mary Claire. 2012. "Underground and Independent Comics, Comix, and Graphic Novels." *The Charleston Advisor* 13, no. 4 (April): 51–54.

Vanderbeke, Dirk. 2010. "It Was the Best of Two Worlds, It Was the Worst of Two Worlds: The Adaptation of Novels in Comics and Graphic Novels." In *The Rise and Reason of Comics and Graphic Literature: Critical Essays on the Form*, edited by Joyce Goggin and Dan Hassler-Forest, 104–18. Jefferson, NC: McFarland.

Van Hook, John. 2008. "On the Difficulty of Characterizing What Educational Comics Are About." *ImageTexT: Interdisciplinary Comics Studies* 4, no. 2. http://www.english.ufl.edu/imagetext/archives/v4_2/van_hook/.

Van Lente, Fred, and Ryan Dunlavey. 2012. *The Comic Book History of Comics*. San Diego: IDW Publishing.

Varis, Essi. 2016. "Something Borrowed: Interfigural Characterisation in Anglo-American Fantasy Comics." In *Framescapes: Graphic Narrative Intertexts*, edited by Mikhail Peppas and Sanabelle Ebrahim, 113–22. Oxford: Inter-Disciplinary Press.

Varnum, Robin, and Christina T. Gibbons, eds. 2001. *The Language of Comics: Word and Image*. Jackson: University Press of Mississippi.

Venkatesan, Sathyaraj, and Anu Mary Peter. 2019. "Towards a Theory of Graphic Medicine." *Rupkatha Journal on Interdisciplinary Studies in Humanities* 11, no. 2 (July–September): 1–10. https://rupkatha.com/V11/n2/v11n208.pdf.

Venkatesan, Sathyaraj, and Sweetha Saji. 2016. "Rhetorics of the Visual: Graphic Medicine, Comics and Its Affordances." *Rupkatha Journal on Interdisciplinary Studies in Humanities* 8, no. 3: 221–31. https://rupkatha.com/V8/n3/23_Visual_Rhetorics.pdf.

Venkatesan, Sathyaraj, and Sweetha Saji. 2018a. "Graphic Medicine and the Limits of Biostatistics." *AMA Journal of Ethics* 20, no. 9 (September): 897–901. https://journalof ethics.ama-assn.org/article/graphic-medicine-and-limits-biostatistics/2018-09.

Venkatesan, Sathyaraj, and Sweetha Saji. 2018b. "(Un)bridgeable Chasms? Doctor-Patient Interactions in Select Graphic Medical Narratives." *Journal of Medical Humanities* 40, no. 4 (December): 591–605.

Verano, Frank. 2006. "Spectacular Consumption: Visuality, Production, and Consumption of the Comics Page." *International Journal of Comic Art* 8, no. 1 (Spring): 378–87.

Vergueiro, Waldomiro C. S., and Lucimar Ribeiro Mutarelli. 2002. "Forging a Sustainable Comics Industry: A Case Study on Graphic Novels as a Viable Format for Developing Countries, Based on the Work of a Brazilian Artist." *International Journal of Comic Art* 4, no. 2 (Fall): 157–67.

Versaci, Rocco. 2007. *This Book Contains Graphic Language: Comics as Literature.* London: Bloomsbury.

Vieira, Scott, and Caitlin McGurk. 2018. "Alternative and Underground Comics: Interview with Caitlin McGurk." *Serials Review* 44, no. 1 (February): 57–63.

Voelker-Morris, Robert, and Julie Voelker-Morris. 2014. "Stuck in Tights: Mainstream Superhero Comics' Habitual Limitations on Social Constructions of Male Superheroes." *Journal of Graphic Novels and Comics* 5, no. 1 (February): 101–17.

Voger, Mark. 2006. *The Dark Age: Grim, Great and Gimmicky Post-Modern Comics.* Raleigh, NC: TwoMorrows Publishing.

Vold, Veronica. 2015. "The Aesthetics of Environmental Equity in American Newspaper Strips." In *Ecomedia: Key Issues*, edited by Stephen Rust, Salma Monani, and Sean Cubitt, 66–84. Abingdon, Oxon., England: Routledge.

Wadsworth, Dick. 2019. *Dirty Little Comics: A Pictorial History of Tijuana Bibles and Underground Adult Comics of the 1920s–1950s.* Independently published.

Walker, Mort. (1980) 2000. *The Lexicon of Comicana.* Port Arthur, NY: Museum of Cartoon Art. Reprint, Bloomington, IN: iUniverse.

Wallner, Lars. 2016. "Speak of the Bubble: Constructing Comic Book Bubbles as Literary Devices in a Primary School Classroom." *Journal of Graphic Novels and Comics* 8, no. 2 (April): 173–92.

Wallner, Lars. 2019. "Gutter Talk: Co-Constructing Narratives Using Comics in the Classroom." *Scandinavian Journal of Educational Research* 63, no. 6 (September): 819–38. https://www.tandfonline.com/doi/full/10.1080/00313831.2018.1452290?scroll=top& needAccess=true.

Walton, Michael. 2019. *The Horror Comic Never Dies: A Grisly History.* Jefferson, NC: McFarland.

Wandtke, Terrence R., ed. 2007. *The Amazing Transforming Superhero! Essays on the Revision of Characters in Comics Books, Film and Television.* Jefferson, NC: McFarland.

Wandtke, Terrence R. 2012. *The Meaning of Superhero Comic Books.* Jefferson, NC: McFarland.

Wanzo, Rebecca. 2020. *The Content of Our Caricature: African American Comic Art and Political Belonging.* New York: New York University Press.

Warner, Marina. 2008. "*Phew! Whaam! Aargh! Boo!* Sense, Sensation, and Picturing Sound." *The Soundtrack* 1, no. 2 (August): 107–25.

Wartenberg, Thomas E. 2012. "Wordy Pictures: Theorizing the Relationship between Image and Text in Comics." In *The Art of Comics: A Philosophical Approach,* edited by Aaron Meskin and Roy T. Cook, 87–104. Chichester, W. Susx., England: Wiley-Blackwell.

Wasielewski, Marek. 2009. "Golden Age Comics." In *The Routledge Companion to Science Fiction,* edited by Mark Bould, Andrew M. Butler, Adam Roberts, and Sherryl Vint, 62–70. Abingdon, Oxon., England: Routledge.

Wasko, Janet. 2001. *Understanding Disney: The Manufacture of Fantasy.* Cambridge: Polity Press.

Waugh, Coulton. (1947) 1991. *The Comics.* Jackson: University Press of Mississippi.

Weaver, Tyler. 2013. *Comics for Film, Games, and Animation: Using Comics to Construct Your Transmedia Storyworld.* Burlington, MA: Focal Press.

Weber, Wibke, and Hans-Martin Rall. 2017. "Authenticity in Comics Journalism: Visual Strategies for Reporting Facts." *Journal of Graphic Novels and Comics* 8, no. 4 (August): 376–97.

Weiner, Robert G., ed. 2010. *Graphic Novels and Comics in Libraries and Archives: Essays on Readers, Research, History and Cataloging.* Jefferson, NC: McFarland.

Weiner, Stephen. 2003. *Faster than a Speeding Bullet: The Rise of the Graphic Novel.* New York: Nantier Beall Minoustchine Publishing.

Weinstein, Simcha. 2006. *Up, Up, and Oy Vey! How Jewish History, Culture, and Values Shaped the Comic Book Superhero.* Fort Lee, NJ: Barricade Books.

Welker, James. 2006. "Beautiful, Borrowed, and Bent: 'Boys' Love' as Girls' Love in *Shōjo Manga*." *Signs: Journal of Women in Culture and Society* 31, no. 3 (Spring): 841–70.

Wells, Paul. 1998. *Understanding Animation.* London: Routledge.

Weng, Zinwei, Jun Hu, Bart Hengeveld, and Matthias Rauterberg. 2019. "Expressing Segmentation in D-Comics." In *HCI International 2019, Posters: 21st International Conference, Proceedings, Part 1,* edited by Constantine Stephanidis, 402–9. Berlin: Springer Verlag.

Wershler, Darren. 2011. "Digital Comics, Circulation, and the Importance of Being Eric Sluis." *Cinema Journal* 50, no. 3 (Spring): 127–34.

Wertham, Fredric. 1954. "The Curse of the Comic Books: The Value Patterns and Effects of Comic Books." *Religious Education* 49, no. 6: 394–406.

Wertham, Fredric. 1973. *The World of Fanzines: A Special Form of Communication.* Carbondale: Southern Illinois University Press.

Whaley, Deborah Elizabeth. 2015. *Black Women in Sequence: Re-Inking Comics, Graphic Novels, and Anime.* Seattle: University of Washington Press.

White, William J. 2017. "Optical Solutions: Reception of an NSF-Funded Science Comic Book on the Biology of the Eye." *Technical Communication Quarterly* 26, no. 2 (April–June): 101–15.

Whitlark, James. 1988. *Illuminated Fantasy: From Blake's Visions to Recent Graphic Fiction.* Madison, NJ: Fairleigh Dickinson University Press.

Whitlock, Gillian. 2006. "Autographics: The Seeing 'I' of Comics." *Modern Fiction Studies* 52, no. 4 (Winter): 965–79.

Whitt, David. 2013. "'I Can Get College Credit for Reading *Batman?* That's a Joke, Right?' Confessions of a Fanboy Professor Teaching Comic Books." In *Graphic Novels and Comics in the Classroom: Essays on the Educational Power of Sequential Art*, edited by Carrye Kay Syma and Robert G. Weiner, 50–57. Jefferson, NC: McFarland.

Whitted, Qiana. 2014. "'And the Negro Thinks in Hieroglyphics': Comics, Visual Metonymy, and the Spectacle of Blackness." *Journal of Graphic Novels and Comics* 5, no. 1 (February): 79–100.

Whitted, Qiana. 2019. *EC Comics: Race, Shock, and Social Protest.* New Brunswick, NJ: Rutgers University Press.

Wiater, Stanley, and Stephen R. Bissette. 1993. *Comic Book Rebels: Conversations with the Creators of the New Comics.* New York: D. I. Fine.

Wierszewski, Emily A. 2014. "Creating Graphic Nonfiction in the Postsecondary English Classroom to Develop Multimodal Literacies." *ImageTexT: Interdisciplinary Comics Studies* 7, no. 3. http://www.english.ufl.edu/imagetext/archives/v7_3/wierszewski/.

Wiese, Doro. 2016. "Tinting the Senses, Adjusting the Gaze: Colouring versus Close-Up as a Means to Draw Viewers into Visual Works." *Journal of Graphic Novels and Comics* 7, no. 4 (December): 369–80.

Wilde, Lukas R. A. 2015. "Distinguishing Mediality: The Problem of Identifying Forms and Features of Digital Comics." *Networking Knowledge: Journal of the MeCCSA Postgraduate Network* 8, no. 4 (June): 1–14. https://ojs.meccsa.org.uk/index.php/netknow/article/view/386/215.

Williams, Eric R. 2018. *Screen Adaptation: Beyond the Basics; Techniques for Adapting Books, Comics, and Real-Life Stories into Screenplays.* New York: Routledge.

Williams, Freddie E., II. 2013. *The DC Comics Guide to Digitally Drawing Comics.* New York: Watson-Guptill, 2013.

Williams, Ian. 2011. "Autography as Auto-Therapy: Psychic Pain and the Graphic Memoir." *Journal of Medical Humanities* 32, no. 4 (December): 353–66.

Williams, Ian. 2012. "Graphic Medicine: Comics as Medical Narrative." *Medical Humanities* 38, no. 1 (June): 21–27.

Williams, Jeff. 2000. "The Evolving Novel: The Comic-Book Medium as the Next Stage." *International Journal of Comic Art* 2, no. 2 (Fall): 178–90.

Williams, Paul. 2020. *Dreaming the Graphic Novel: The Novelization of Comics.* New Brunswick, NJ: Rutgers University Press.

Williams, Paul, and James Lyons, eds. 2010. *The Rise of the American Comics Artist: Creators and Contexts.* Jackson: University Press of Mississippi.

Willmott, Glenn. 2012. *Modern Animalism: Habitats of Scarcity and Wealth in Comics and Literature*. Toronto: University of Toronto Press.

Winge, Therèsa M. 2018. *Costuming Cosplay: Dressing the Imagination*. London: Bloomsbury.

Witek, Joseph. 1989. *Comic Books as History: The Narrative Art of Jack Jackson, Art Spiegelman, and Harvey Pekar*. Jackson: University Press of Mississippi.

Witek, Joseph. 2008. "From the Margins of the Margin: Seeing Educational Comics." *ImageTexT: Interdisciplinary Comics Studies* 4, no. 2. http://www.english.ufl.edu/imagetext/archives/v4_2/witek/.

Witek, Joseph. 2009. "The Arrow and the Grid." In *A Comics Studies Reader*, edited by Jeet Heer and Kent Worcester, 149–56. Jackson: University Press of Mississippi.

Withrow, Steven, and Alexander Danner. 2007. *Character Design for Graphic Novels*. Burlington, MA Focal Press.

Wolk, Douglas. 2007. *Reading Comics: How Graphic Novels Work and What They Mean*. Boston: Da Capo Press.

Wong, Wendy Siuyi. 2002. "Manhua: The Evolution of Hong Kong Cartoons and Comics." *Journal of Popular Culture* 35, no. 4 (Spring): 25–47.

Woo, Benjamin. 2011. "The Android's Dungeon: Comic-Bookstores, Cultural Spaces, and the Social Practices of Audiences." *Journal of Graphic Novels and Comics* 2, no. 2 (November): 125–36.

Woo, Benjamin. 2012. "Understanding Understandings of Comics: Reading and Collecting as Media-Oriented Practices." *Participations: Journal of Audience and Reception Studies* 9, no. 2 (November): 180–99.

Woo, Benjamin. 2016. "To the Studio! *Comic Book Artists: The Next Generation* and the Occupational Imaginary of Comics Work." In *Cultures of Comics Work*, edited by Casey Brienza and Paddy Johnston, 189–202. New York: Palgrave Macmillan.

Woo, Benjamin. 2020. "What Kind of Studies Is Comic Studies?" In *The Oxford Handbook of Comic Book Studies*, edited by Frederick Luis Aldama, 3–15. Oxford: Oxford University Press.

Wood, Andrea. 2006. "'Straight' Women, Queer Texts: Body-Love Manga and the Rise of a Global Counterpublic." *Women's Studies Quarterly* 34, nos. 1–2 (Spring–Summer): 394–414.

Wood, Andrea. 2013. "Boys' Love Anime and Queer Desires in Convergence Culture: Transnational Fandom, Censorship and Resistance." *Journal of Graphic Novels and Comics* 4, no. 1 (March): 44–63.

Wood, Andrea. 2015. "Making the Invisible Visible: Lesbian Romance Comics for Women." *Feminist Studies* 41, no. 2: 293–334.

Wood, Christopher. 2020. *Heroes Masked and Mythic: Echoes of Ancient Archetypes in Comic Book Characters*. Jefferson, NC: McFarland.

Wood, Susan. 1989. *The Poison Maiden and the Great Bitch: Female Stereotypes in Marvel Superhero Comics*. San Bernardino, CA: Borgo Press.

Woodis, Woody. 2007. "Caricature in French Political Cartoons." *International Journal of Comic Art* 9, no. 2 (Fall): 275–87.

Worden, Daniel. 2015. "The Politics of Comics: Popular Modernism, Abstraction, and Experimentation." *Literature Compass* 12, no. 2 (February): 59–71.

Worisch, Niklas. 2015. "Movement and Expression: Metamorphosis of Motion into Lines." Issuu, February 25. https://issuu.com/niklasworisch/docs/booklet_loti_inside_inside_whole.

Wright, Bradford W. 2003. *Comic Book Nation: The Transformation of Youth Culture in America*. Baltimore: Johns Hopkins University Press.

Wucher, Joshua. 2019. "Translating the Panel: Remediating a Comics Aesthetic in Contemporary Action Cinema." In *A Companion to the Action Film*, edited by James Kendrick, 187–206. Hoboken, NJ: Wiley-Blackwell.

Wüllner, Daniel. 2010. "Suspended in Mid-Month: Serialized Storytelling in Comics." In *The Rise and Reason of Comics and Graphic Literature: Critical Essays on the Form*, edited by Joyce Goggin and Dan Hassler-Forest, 42–54. Jefferson, NC: McFarland.

Xiao, Tie. 2013. "Masereel, Lu, and the Development of the Woodcut Picture Book in China." *Comparative Literature and Culture* 15, no. 2. https://doi.org/10.7771/1481-4374.2230.

Yezbick, Daniel F. 2015. "'No Sweat!': EC Comics, Cold War Censorship, and the Troublesome Colors of 'Judgment Day!'" In *The Blacker the Ink: Constructions of Black Identity in Comics and Sequential Art*, edited by Frances Gateward and John Jennings, 19–44. New Brunswick, NJ: Rutgers University Press.

Yezbick, Daniel F., and Jonathan Alexandratos. 2020. "Paper or Plastic? Mapping the Transmedial Intersections of Comics and Action Figures." In *The Oxford Handbook of Comic Book Studies*, edited by Frederick Luis Aldama, 510–33. Oxford: Oxford University Press.

York, Chris, and Rafiel York, eds. 2012. *Comic Books and the Cold War, 1946–1962: Essays on Graphic Treatment of Communism, the Code and Social Concerns*. Jefferson, NC: McFarland.

Yu, Han. 2015. *The Other Kind of Funnies: Comics in Technical Communication*. Amityville, NY: Baywood Publishing.

Yu, Megan. 2018. "Roles of Graphic Pathologies in Clinical Training." *AMA Journal of Ethics* 20, no. 2 (February): 115–21. https://journalofethics.ama-assn.org/article/roles-graphic-pathographies-clinical-training/2018-02.

Yus, Francisco. 2009. "Visual Metaphor versus Verbal Metaphor: A Unified Account." In *Multimodal Metaphor*, edited by Charles J. Forceville and Eduardo Urios-Aparisi, 147–72. Berlin: Mouton de Gruyter.

Żaglewski, Tomasz. 2020. "The Unwrapped Editions: Searching for the 'Ultimate' Format of Graphic Novels and Its Limitations." *ImageTexT: Interdisciplinary Comics Studies* 11, no. 3. http://imagetext.english.ufl.edu/archives/v11_3/zaglewski/.

Zanettin, Federico. 2018. "Translation, Censorship and the Development of European Comics Cultures." *Perspectives* 26, nos. 5–6 (October–December): 868–84.

Zanfei, Anna. 2008. "Defining Webcomics and Graphic Novels." *International Journal of Comic Art* 10, no. 1 (Spring): 55–61.

Zbaracki, Matthew D., and Jennifer Geringer. 2014. "Blurred Vision: The Divergence and Intersection of Illustrations in Children's Books." *Journal of Graphic Novels and Comics* 5, no. 3 (September): 284–96.

Ziang, Xiao, Ho Po-Shiun, Xinran Wang, Karrie Karahalios, and Hari Sundaram. 2019. "Should We Use an Abstract Comic Form to Persuade? Experiments with Online Charitable Donation." *Proceedings of the ACM on Human-Computer Interaction* 3 (November): 1–28.

Zupan, Zdravko. 2000. "The Golden Age of Serbian Comics: Belgrade Comic Art, 1935–1941." *International Journal of Comic Art* 2, no. 1 (Spring): 90–101.

Zurier, Rebecca. 2006. *Picturing the City: Urban Vision and the Ashcan School*. Berkeley: University of California Press.

INDEX OF THEMATIC GROUPINGS

COMICS FORM

COMICS GENRES

DRAWING TERMS

PUBLISHING TERMS

VISUAL ELEMENTS

ABOUT THE AUTHOR

Nancy Pedri is a professor of English at Memorial University of Newfoundland, Canada, where she has been teaching since 2006. Her major fields of research include comics studies, word and image studies, and photography in literature. She has edited several volumes and has published numerous articles in her field. Her coauthored article "Focalization in Graphic Narrative" won the 2012 James Phelan Award. A coauthored book that examines the focalization concept in a broad range of comics is soon to be published with Ohio State University Press.

She can be contacted at npedri@mun.ca, and you can see what she's been up to at https://www.mun.ca/faculty/npedri/.

ABOUT THE ILLUSTRATOR

Chuck Howitt is a proofreader, assistant editor, and illustrator with a certificate in comics studies from Portland State University. He loves cartooning and would draw a lot more if he didn't have joints made of paper plates. He has also written hundreds of thousands of words, though he's never been published.

He has no Instagram, Twitter, or any other way of finding him on the internet, but he can be contacted at chuckhowitt@gmail.com, where you can ask him for PDFs of 1930s-style pulp stories.

Printed in the United States
by Baker & Taylor Publisher Services